# WITHOUT A TEAR

# WITHOUT A TEAR

## Our Tragic Relationship with Animals

MARK H. BERNSTEIN

UNIVERSITY OF ILLINOIS PRESS

Urbana and Chicago

Library of Congress Cataloging-in-Publication Data

Bernstein, Mark H., 1948–
Without a tear : our tragic relationship with animals /
Mark H. Bernstein.
    p.   cm.
Includes bibliographical references and index.
ISBN 0-252-02911-9 (cloth : alk. paper)
ISBN 0-252-07198-0 (pbk. : alk. paper)
    1. Animal welfare. 2. Animal welfare—Moral and
ethical aspects. I. Title.
HV4708.B47    2004
179′.3—dc22    2003022826

For Rebecca

# CONTENTS

# PREFACE

This work is not a labor of love; it is a labor of need. There is no joy in reading countless accounts of what transpires in factory farms, slaughterhouses, animal laboratories, and hunting fields. It is depressing to watch film after film about these events and worse still to see some of these activities firsthand. Demonstrating by simple philosophical argument that we are morally obligated to make large changes was relatively easy. This should strike no one as surprising. In my twenty years of speaking to tens of thousands of people, educating them as to the facts of our relationships with animals, virtually no person has reacted indifferently. Almost all are shocked and almost all agree that some changes need to be made. I hope you concur.

I hope too that my father, Louis, would have been proud of this book had he been alive to see it. I do not need to speculate about my mother, Matilda. Whether it means anything to animals—and this is all that ultimately matters—is no longer in my hands but in yours.

\* \* \*

I owe great debts to persons both human and nonhuman. With respect to the former, I thank Roxanne Cuevas for technical assistance and Steven Bernstein (no familial relation) for research help. Allysun DeLeon saved me from from many grammatical blunders. Mike Almeida especially aided in the construction of chapter 1. Stew Cohen offered helpful comments. Bruce Bethell's editorial assistance was miraculous. Priscilla Cohn carefully read the entire manuscript and offered needed suggestions throughout. I owe the title of the book to her. My greatest debt extends to the Reverend Andrew Linzey, whose patience, encouragement, and criticism were essential to whatever worth the book may have and to whatever good the book may do.

With respect to the latter, who both taught and enriched me, I thank Boomer, Bud, Woody, Mazel, TR, Blaze, Punim, Pretty Face, Baby Kitty, Lox, Bagel, Nosh, Lars, Trevor, Ivy, Tangerine, and of course Knish, whom I miss inexpressibly.

WITHOUT A TEAR

# INTRODUCTION

A phenomenon's very pervasiveness can obscure our vision of it. Facing everyday events, we take no notice of them. Their ubiquity absorbs any impetus to explain them, or stand in awe of them, or perhaps to be outraged by them.

Part of Isaac Newton's genius resided in his ability to question the obvious—to recognize that we could and should try to explain why unimpeded objects fall downward. No event could seem more natural or normal. We can safely presume that no one had ever released an object and seen it float upward, skip sideways, or zigzag through space. Always, without exception, objects fall to the surface of the earth. But surely this is a remarkable fact. If the direction were a matter of chance, this uniformity would defy the laws of probability. There must be some reason, some fundamental truth about the workings of the world, that explains this most pedestrian and yet startling event. Obviously Newton had no idea of the twists and turns that his discovery of gravity would take over the ensuing three centuries, but however sophisticated later theories became, his scientific reputation was forever secured. In the ordinary, he noticed the salient.

Most of us have a bit of this Newtonian quality. We have seen thousands of sunsets. We have viewed them while running on a beach, daydreaming in an office, or driving home in our automobiles. Occasionally the scene strikes us differently. We quite consciously take note of what usually passes for background. We realize how spectacular and beautiful this part of nature really is. The ordinary is extraordinary, and much to our benefit and delight, we are capable of recognizing this.

My goal in this book is to provoke a Newtonian experience. I want to encourage the readers to notice some of the common happenings that make up our world. Unlike viewing beautiful sunsets, however, the consequences will not be pleasant. This new appreciation of everyday events will fill you with neither satisfaction nor awe. You will not feel contentment, let alone happiness, when you discover the exceptional in this segment of the mundane. Quite the contrary. You are apt to experience outrage, revulsion, and disgust. But these feelings are mere intermediaries to what I hope ultimately happens. I hope, and would like to believe, that these feelings will spur fundamental changes in the way you live your life. You will alter your recreational activities. The type of clothing you wear will change. Perhaps most dramatically, the sorts of foods you eat will be greatly modified. And, if my case is particularly telling, you will actively try to change the lives of others.

I am not ingenuous. People will not fundamentally alter the way they live their lives unless they confront a persuasive narrative. After all, most of you are probably fairly satisfied with the ways your lives are progressing. Few would reject offers of a more exciting and fulfilling job with increased salary, a bigger house at a lower mortgage payment, and more paid vacation, but these benefits do not seem to demand changing any basic aspects of your life. Simultaneously, it is not transparent that changing the material in the suits you buy or the kinds of food you eat will better enable you to get what you want for your family and yourself. Why would people change enjoyable lives unless the change would better their own lives and those of their loved ones? Regardless of the cogency of my case, why would people be moved to act if the changes I suggest offer them no benefit?

It's a fair question. A sketch of an answer has two prongs. On the one hand, I try to meet the challenge directly by showing how a person's life is dramatically improved if he or she adopts the recommended changes. Egoists, those driven to action solely in virtue of perceived personal gains, should be moved by these arguments. On the other hand, and more important, I suggest that those who are motivated by compelling universal moral precepts should find incentive to alter their lives. Most of us conceive morality as having a far broader scope than just our personal self-interests. Most of us, that is, take morality *seriously*, as restricting our permissible behaviors toward others. We believe that the interests of others, and not merely our own interests, morally matter. It is for these readers that this work is primarily intended.

We are in the midst of a holocaust. Literally tens of billions of innocent, defenseless lives are being intentionally and unjustifiably destroyed each year. (In the United States alone the figure is in the neighborhood of 10 billion.) Pain, suffering, and terror accompany nearly all these deaths. Virtually every single one of us is party to this mayhem and murder. Most of us do not directly participate. Few of us cut the throat, pull the trigger, or inject the toxin, but we patronize and endorse the individuals and institutions that do. In fact, we are the lifeblood of these practices. Our excuse—and it is not without merit—is our ignorance; almost all of us are unwitting accomplices. Reading this book will eliminate this excuse and may, in some ways, make your life more trying. Still, as is frequently the case, knowledge is liberating, and once the situation is recognized for what it is, your life and the lives of billions of others will be incalculably improved.

The victims of this holocaust are not human, but they are victims nonetheless. The atrocities perpetrated against them should not to be discounted, let alone dismissed. The victims are nonhuman animals. They are the chickens, cows, pigs, and fish we slaughter and devour. They are the minks, chinchillas, and foxes whose skins we rip off and wear. They are the rabbits, ferrets, hamsters, and mice into whose eyes we inject poisons to test cosmetics. They are the doves, squirrels, and deer we shoot with guns and arrows. They are not human, but in the ways that matter most, they are we.

My title has a double meaning. Most—but not all—animals do not cry when they are terrorized and made to suffer; most—but not all—humans do not cry when they see or hear about factory farms, animal laboratories, or hunting fields. My supposition is that if animals cried, so would we. A difference in the way our tear ducts function should not make a difference in the affective, cognitive, and practical ways in which we interact with animals. My goal is not human tears, however, but human action; nevertheless, as is the case with so many substantive changes in our behavior, the former may be a necessary means to the latter.

I will show that altering our relationships with nonhuman animals may offer us perhaps the most significant way to enhance the lives of unfortunate humans. Thus, anyone who believes that our efforts should be directed solely toward the betterment of humankind should vehemently defend a new relationship with animals. In the end, reasonable persons may differ with the details of my proposals. Nevertheless, any of those whose concerns are for the human species should reach conclusions much like my own.

My argument for a radical change in our attitudes and actions toward nonhuman animals revolves about one simple claim, the "Principle of Gratuitous Suffering." This precept tells us that it is wrong to intentionally inflict gratuitous suffering on other, innocent individuals. I believe that this precept has great immediate appeal and that most of us will agree that it encapsulates a fundamental moral view. This principle is deceptively powerful, however, for it requires us to make dramatic changes in the way we currently live. I cannot, therefore, merely submit it as an inarguable truth. My task in chapter 1 is to clearly articulate and defend this principle.

Chapter 2 is an extended argument for the radical idea that nonhuman and human animals share the same kind of *value*. Traditionally humans have been conceived as creatures with a unique kind of value. The worth of human beings does not derive from the service that they provide for others but rather from some special qualities specific to human nature. Simultaneously, the value of animals is thought to be exhausted by what they can do for us. To use quasi-technical language, while humans are thought to have inherent value, animals are seen as having only instrumental value.

This distinction traces its secular ancestry to Aristotle, but religious scripture has undoubtedly played the pivotal role in initiating this dichotomy. Still, although Judeo-Christian texts can certainly be read to justify this difference in value, I cite plausible interpretations of scripture that can warrant our thinking of both humans and animals as possessing inherent value. This suggestion, if accepted, would go a long way toward effecting enormous changes in the way we relate to animals, for once we abdicate our belief that animals have value merely insofar as they are useful commodities to us, we are far less likely to discount their suffering. If we view animals not as mere resources for humans but as the possessors of a value that transcends their instrumental worth, we will be far less inclined to characterize the harm we do to them as unfortunate but necessary. This change in our assessment of animals would force us to reconfigure our personal interactions and our institutionalized practices in ways that would far better harmonize with the fundamental moral belief expressed in the Principle of Gratuitous Suffering.

To change behavior and attitudes, it is essential to recognize the nature of our present dealings with animals. Chapter 3 begins this task by discussing our relationship with literally billions of animals in the factory farming industry. This is not a discussion for the squeamish, but an unsanitized account of what transpires on factory farms is a requirement for large-scale societal change. Chronicling abuse in the transportation, raising, and slaughtering of cows, chickens, and pigs makes for uncomfortable reading, yet this very uneasiness may spur change in the institution that perhaps creates more pain and suffering than any other.

Chapters 4 and 5 address, respectively, the issues of hunting and animal experimentation. More specifically, they address the commonly held beliefs that hunting is required to manage animal populations humanely and that experimentation on animals is needed to develop treatments and cures for maladies such as heart disease and cancer. These alleged truisms are intended to show that, since hunting and vivisection have legitimate justification, the Principle of Gratuitous Suffering is not violated. Putatively all is in moral order. Much of my effort is directed toward demonstrating that these alleged truths are no more than propaganda from powerful interest groups. These segments of supposed common sense are myths. And myths, if they result in atrocities, need to be debunked.

One might think that our legal system ameliorates some of the horrors that animals suffer. Many believe, almost as an article of faith, that our laws circumscribe legally, if not morally, permissible behaviors in any institution that essentially involves animals. Unfortunately the legal system provides animals virtually no relief from suffering. Despite state and federal laws peppered with high-sounding phrases such as "humane treatment" and "no unnecessary cruelty," animals have the legal status of inanimate property. From a legal point of view, the value of a dog is akin to the value of a living room couch; their values are purely instrumental. The sixth chapter largely consists of dissecting cases that validate this judgment about animals. My hope is that astonishment will provide impetus for change.

There are striking and instructive analogies between the way men have traditionally treated women and the way people have traditionally treated animals. Reflection on these analogies motivates the seventh chapter, in which I try to show that recent feminist moral philosophy provides a foundation for a more humane ethic toward animals than do the dominant masculinist conceptions of morality. Feminist ethics has sufficiently rich resources to justify a sea change in our relationships with animals so that, once again, our moral behavior will better fit with the Principle of Gratuitous Suffering. There is some ironic justice in the idea that philosophies introduced primarily by women may help one of the few groups that have suffered even more systematic oppression than they have. Adoption of feminist moral theory is by no means necessary to effect the changes that morality requires, but it can prove useful as a theoretical adjunct to further justify the modifications that we need to make.

\* \* \*

I will not discuss every form of animal exploitation. For example, I will not consider the fur industry or the use of animals for recreation. I do this partly to save space, but more important, many people have already abandoned these practices. The problems associated with the fur and recreation industries have seeped into the American consciousness with severe negative results for both industries. At any rate, if I have a mistaken optimism regarding the end of these institutions, it is easy enough to extrapolate my earlier ideas to these other areas.

I am a professional philosopher. It should not be surprising, therefore, that this book is not merely descriptive. I wish to do far more than just describe the situation. I believe that any person who applies right thinking to the facts at hand will see that our responsibilities to animals are far more significant and stringent than most people believe. I have *arguments* for this position, and so this monograph should not be understood as the mere recordings of someone's idiosyncratic beliefs. If this book were merely a compilation of autobiographical musings, there would be no particular reason to accept my conclusions rather than the opposing conclusions of someone else. I ask only that you give me a fair shake, listening with an open, unprejudicial, reflective mind. A great deal is at stake.

Most animals suffer and die without tears; most of us stand by without weeping. Physiology explains the animals' behavior; ignorance explains ours. The animals need—and deserve—a change in our minds and hearts. Only then will we change our actions.

# CHAPTER ONE

# THE PRINCIPLE OF GRATUITOUS SUFFERING

## A Cornerstone of Morality

My primary aim in this chapter is to introduce, articulate, and defend a fundamental moral principle that I dub the "Principle of Gratuitous Suffering" (PGS). On first hearing, the principle's truth appears virtually self-evident. Perhaps less immediately obvious is that acceptance of this principle has far-reaching effects on the extent of our moral obligations to nonhuman animals. If in the institutions of factory farming, hunting, vivisection, and other animal-related practices we intentionally inflict (or allow) gratuitous pain and suffering, the PGS tells us that we are acting immorally. From a moral point of view, we will be required to dramatically change much in our daily lives.

> (PGS) It is morally wrong to intentionally inflict (or allow the infliction of) gratuitous pain or suffering on another, innocent individual.

Morality being a branch of philosophy, and philosophy promising more than a compendium of common sense, it is incumbent on me to do more than rely on the allegedly evident truth of the PGS for its general acceptance. Science, for example, is replete with examples of putatively obvious truths that turned out to be not only not obvious but also not true. We need only to remind ourselves of the Copernican revolution, which demonstrated the falsity of the "obvious" belief that the earth is the center of the solar system. It would therefore be disingenuous to think that I can leave the viability of the PGS to so-called common sense. I need to explicate the PGS and try to rebut accusations that it is false. Philosophers have denied the existence of the entire external world, thought that we have no knowledge of the existence of minds other than our own, and believed that we never act freely. It should come as something less than a shock that some thinkers may balk at accepting PGS. Moreover, responding to possible criticisms should have a salutary effect even on those who need no convincing. Just as theists may intellectually benefit from being shown that the arguments for atheism are less compelling than they might initially appear, those who intuitively accept the PGS may have their belief strengthened when the disbelievers' objections are deflected.

## The Nature of the PGS

Thought experiments are fictional narratives that prime intuitions to elicit general conclusions. The events described in the narrative may never happen. In fact, both the storyteller and the audience may be quite certain that the events will never occur. All that is required is that the story be intelligible, that we know what the world would be like were these circumstances ever to come into play. To pass muster, a thought experiment need only be logically consistent, or *possibly* true.

Imagine finding yourself at a remote corner of our galaxy. For my purposes, it makes no difference how you arrived. Perhaps you are the lone survivor of a rocket that crashed after traveling far off course. Perhaps God simply willed you to be there. After walking a short distance, you happen on an object unlike anything you have previously seen. It looks a bit like a human and somewhat like a tree and bears some resemblance to a granite boulder. Suppose that you have only the following information (again, perhaps by the grace of God). First, you know that this thing has the capacity to suffer. Like you, it can feel pain, get frustrated, become depressed, and undergo the myriad psychological and physical travails that diminish the quality of a person's life. Second, you know what can cause this object to suffer, how to cause it to suffer, and how to prevent its suffering from sources other than yourself. Last, you know that this thing has neither harmed nor will harm anyone. This odd-looking creature is a complete innocent.

The first question is this: would it be morally wrong of you to intentionally cause pain or suffering to this object? I submit that we do and should answer this question affirmatively. We believe that any pain or suffering brought to this creature would be unwarranted, pointless, unjustified, or as I will typically characterize it, gratuitous. Therefore, reflection on this narrative elicits the moral principle that it is wrong to intentionally inflict gratuitous pain and suffering on an innocent creature. The second question is this: would it be morally wrong of you to intentionally (knowingly and purposefully) allow this innocent creature to suffer gratuitous harm? Again, the answer seems clearly yes. Suppose that you happened on a stranger who intended to bring harm to this alien for no reason. Assume further that you could, with minimal effort and personal risk, deter the stranger from accomplishing his plan. Surely these conditions make it obvious (or as obvious as ethics allows) that it would be wrong of you to allow the alien to suffer. Although I will not press the point, since it is tangential to my concerns, I submit that we also have an obligation to prevent gratuitous suffering even if no persons were involved in bringing about the suffering. If we notice that this creature is traversing a course that will cause it (gratuitous) harm, we have an obligation to notify it. For example, we ought to make the creature aware that if it continues walking in its current direction, it will presently fall off a cliff. In all these cases it would surely be wrong to stand by and not perform the minimal acts necessary to allow the creature to circumvent pain and suffering.

The basic idea is that the world would be a better place if it contained less gratuitous harm and that we all have an obligation to try to make the world better by doing what we reasonably can to reduce such harm. Most directly we can minimize gratuitous suffering by not inflicting it. This, of course, is quite easy. It takes neither great effort nor ingenuity *not* to shoot a deer or push an electric prod into a hog's anus. In all but the most bizarre circumstances, we have control over our actions, especially those that would directly produce gratuitous harm. To fulfill this obligation, we need only do nothing. We also have moral obligations to prevent innocents from enduring gratuitous suffering. Within reasonable, albeit vague limits, we ought not allow innocents to suffer. While freeing an innocent creature from an ominous environment may be comparatively easy, attempting to stop another from gratuitously harming it may be difficult and dangerous. All else being equal, the obligations to prevent harmful behavior gain stringency as the means to stop the gratuitous harm become easier and less risky. We do not believe that someone violates a duty by failing to prevent a relatively minor harm if the intervention requires placing the agent's life in serious peril.

The principle that most simply, directly, and plausibly accounts for these intuitive moral judgments is the PGS. Indeed, the moral assessments that we share regarding the innocent alien are *embodied* in the PGS. Alternatively put, the best candidate for a moral principle that implicitly informs our moral judgments is the PGS. At the end of the day, there is no more potent reason for accepting any moral prescription.

Some may object to the viability of thought experiments in general, and this one specifically, by protesting that they subtly beg the question. In the case at hand, the charge would be that only those who already accept the PGS will consider the alien scenario to imply it. That is, only someone who antecedently believes that it is wrong to intentionally inflict gratuitous pain and suffering on an innocent individual will view the proposed treatment of the alien as morally wrong. The thought experiment is alleged to be impotent to convert skeptics; it is an exercise in preaching to the choir.

This objection would be devastating if it were correct, for a significant number of philosophical disputes rely on the viability of thought experiments structurally similar to the one I propose. From the problem of reconciling free will with a deterministic universe, to the puzzle of giving an adequate account of knowledge, to the conundrum of providing a satisfying functionalist account of the nature of the mind, philosophers have perennially relied on imaginary scenarios either to bolster their cause or to attack the positions of others. Fortunately, the objection is meretricious. Recall that we use thought experiments primarily to elicit or unearth principles. In particular, my thought experiment is intended to elicit the principle that best explains why you agree (and you do, don't you?) that in the circumstances adumbrated, it would be morally wrong to harm the alien or allow it to be harmed when this requires minimal effort and risk. That is, I ask you to use your moral intuitions (and not some moral theory or moral precept) to make a moral judgment and then to seek the moral principle that best explains this judgment. The PGS is the obvious choice. Indeed, one is hard-pressed to conceive of any other plausible candidate.

Thus, there is no prior appeal to the PGS or, for that matter, to any other moral principle. In fact, I urge readers to abandon any principle or theory they may have prior to making a moral assessment in the alien case. This avoids any question begging or subtle cheating. In fact, the claim that only those who accept the PGS will agree that it is morally wrong to harm the innocent actually *confirms* the efficacy of the thought experiment, for this effectively means that PGS is the best explanation available for the judgment. As long as one does not *use* the PGS to elicit the judgment—and one cannot, if moral intuition is the means employed—the cogency of the imaginary excursion remains untainted.

Although lacking the purity of the thought experiment, the real-life tragedy of Kitty Genovese exemplifies the PGS. In 1964 a man mercilessly stabbed Genovese to death in the New York borough of Queens. Surely we all believe that what this man did was horribly wrong; he ought not to have caused an innocent woman great pain and suffering, let alone her death. Unbelievably, none of the apartment dwellers who viewed this spectacle took any action. While most would agree that these spectators had no obligation to intervene directly in the attack, they surely did have the duty to try to get help—say, by calling the police. Remarkably, even this minimum moral requirement went unsatisfied. These onlookers had an obligation to help Kitty Genovese; they were duty bound to do what they reasonably could do to prevent her gratuitous suffering. Because they flouted this duty—and thus violated the PGS's "allowance" clause—we justifiably think of them as having done something wrong.

Admittedly, countenancing obligations to prevent the gratuitous suffering of innocents muddies the PGS's pristine clarity. We now need to determine what count as "reasonable" obligations to impose on persons in any particular situation. Nevertheless, these nuances have little effect on animal issues: could any but the most self-serving believe that it is *unreasonable* to forgo some gustatory pleasure so that the factory farming of animals can be terminated? Indeed, a relevant disanalogy between the passive residents and meat-eaters disadvantages the latter. Although most of us are not factory farmers and so are not directly inflicting pain and suffering on animals, our consumption of flesh products means that we do not just allow great harm to happen but actively contribute to the existence of the harmful institution. Repugnant as the passivity of the onlookers was, their inaction did not cause Genovese's assailant to act as he did, but the relationship between flesh consumer and flesh producer is more intimate than that between onlooker and assailant. Our not boycotting meat products is the very lifeblood of the industry. If the inactive viewers had intervened actively, the practice of murder would probably not have ended. If we stop consuming cows, hogs, and chickens, however, the practice of factory farming will terminate. If we were not to allow the gratuitous pain and suffering inherent in factory farming, we would obviate the institution. Having no patrons, the practice would be economically pointless. We can do so much by doing so little.

One may have qualms regarding the relevance of the PGS to the Genovese case. Perhaps the assailant's act was immoral not because it subjected Genovese to great pain and suffering but because it violated her rights. Since the PGS makes no reference to rights, it provides little if any principled explanation of what makes the killer's attack morally wrong.

Although the PGS does not explicitly invoke rights, there is no real problem in couching the principle in these terms. As I use the terms, if it is morally wrong to act a certain way toward a person, then that person has a right not to be acted on in that particular manner. (I briefly discuss other stylistic variants of the PGS later in this chapter.) Thus, if it is morally wrong to intentionally inflict gratuitous pain and suffering on an innocent, then that innocent has a right not to have pain and suffering inflicted on it. I take this as nothing more than exemplifying ordinary usage.

Perhaps the objection is not that the PGS cannot be understood in terms of rights but rather that the wrong done to Genovese was not merely (or even most significantly) the violation of her right not to be gratuitously harmed. Perhaps the suggestion is that the assailant violated other rights as well. For example, the attacker surely prevented Genovese from reaching her door, and so it might be argued that part of the immorality of the assailant derived from his interference with her "right of mobility."

I am willing, for the sake of discussion, to grant that Genovese had a right to move where she desired and that the assailant violated this right. But surely his interference with this right is not the source of our moral outrage. To see this, subtract the stabbings, the pain, and the suffering that Genovese endured. I suspect that your repulsion and horror have diminished enormously. Conversely, imagine—difficult as this is—that her mobility had not been affected despite the stabbings. Now I suspect that your outrage has not subsided at all. Clearly the horrible gratuitous pain and suffering that Genovese experienced is the source of our moral condemnation.

I am also willing to grant that Genovese had a "right to life," and I agree that we would be morally outraged if the assailant had "merely" killed Genovese without causing her great pain and suffering. Still, most of us believe that the real case is worse than this hypothetical one—that the assailant acted morally worse by causing her to suffer before she died. Torturing an innocent to death is more morally repellent than painlessly ending her life. Thus the Genovese case does support the PGS.

I do not, however, claim the PGS to be exhaustive. The PGS does not subsume every case of moral wrongness; we can act immorally without causing gratuitous pain and suffering to an innocent. Still, in the Genovese case, whatever other moral wrongs attach to her attacker and even the passive viewers, the assailant acted immorally by inflicting pain on an undeserving victim, and the onlookers acted immorally by passively allowing it to continue.

The intentional infliction of pain and suffering on an innocent individual demands reasoned explanation. By asking the agent why he or she inflicted pain and suffering, we manifest this demand. A shrug of the shoulders, silence, or a response of "I just wanted to inflict pain" does not justify this behavior to any extent. To say that the infliction of pain and suffering is *gratuitous,* then, is tantamount to saying that there is no justification for it. If one purposively inflicts pain and suffering on an innocent creature but has no good reasons doing so, it is difficult to see how this behavior can be anything but wrong. The PGS is a somewhat formal expression of this insight.

Attending to the so-called argument from evil can help further clarify the notion of a gratuitous act. Many atheists have pointed to the occurrence of evil as a justification for denying the existence of a deity like that in the

Judeo-Christian tradition. God's omniscience guarantees that he knows of all the evil in the world. His omnipotence ensures that he has the power to rid the world of all evil. His perfect benevolence ensures that he wants to rid the world of evil. The theist must thus explain how to reconcile the existence of such an entity with an evil-plagued world.

There is a striking similarity between the plausibility of the PGS and the plausibility of the argument from evil.[1] Theists typically admit that there is evil but add that it has a purpose. Some claim that without evil in the world, it would be impossible for us to recognize goodness and act morally. Some use the "vale of soul-making" explanation. On this account, evil is necessary for improving our characters by affording us the opportunity to fight through adversity. Some utilize the free-will defense: any world comprising creatures with free will inevitably includes evil. On this view, God could have created a world without evil only at the cost of eliminating free-willed humans from it. In all these cases, a world with evil is morally preferable to one without it.

Both the attacks on and the defenses of God's existence agree that an omnipotent, omniscient, perfectly benevolent deity would neither create nor allow gratuitous, extraneous, pointless evil. Showing that this sort of evil infects the world would establish God's nonexistence. The PGS makes a similar point. It challenges the idea that one can intentionally inflict gratuitous harm and suffering on an innocent and not do something wrong. Indeed, answers to these problems are inextricably linked. If the existence of evil can be reconciled with an all-powerful, all-knowing, all-good God, then we would have at least the beginnings of an answer to the implicit challenge offered in the PGS. Conversely, any adequate account that justifies intentionally inflicting gratuitous pain and suffering on innocents would constitute a large step toward resolving the problem of evil.

I use the term *intentional* with broad and vague scope. Normally intentional acts are performed purposively, freely, voluntarily, and knowledgeably. Opposing intentional action is reflexive, accidental, or inadvertent behavior. The word *intentional* is a term of ordinary language rather than some philosopher's neologism, and its ordinary use is quite different from the far more narrow and technical use that often occupies philosophers. In fact, using the term in some technical or stipulative manner would undermine the force of the PGS.

The PGS is morally noncommittal about intentionally and gratuitously bringing about pain or suffering on oneself. Here, I think, intuitions differ. Some believe that persons are the sole owners of their bodies, so that there are no moral proscriptions circumscribing their behaviors in this regard. Your body is as much your property as is a lamp that you purchase, so that from a moral point of view, anything you want to do with it is permissible. Others disagree. Some may dissent in virtue of religious convictions, claiming our bodies belong to God and not to ourselves. To destroy this gift from God is an act of disrespect or even blasphemy; there is a moral imperative that you do nothing offensive to your benevolent creator. Some may say that it is wrong to create needless pain and suffering no matter in whom this pain and suffering resides. This much-discussed topic is interesting in its own right; it is just not one that engages my discussion of the PGS.

The semantic status of the PGS is an important issue. Some may agree that the PGS is true—indeed, even obviously true—but characterize it as an empty truth, not a substantive moral principle. They will charge that the PGS buys its truth with vacuity; that is, since it owes its truth solely to the meanings of the terms it employs, the PGS is really no more than an implicit definition. In philosophical jargon, the PGS is analytically true.

By way of illustration, consider the statement "All bachelors are unmarried." This statement is obviously true. It owes its truth solely to the meanings of the terms involved. The word *bachelor* simply means "unmarried adult male," and so the statement is true by definition. There is nothing inherently onerous about this. A problem emerges when someone believes that "All bachelors are unmarried" provides us with substantive information about the world or that the source of the truth of "All bachelors are unmarried" is a fact about our empirical world. Anyone who believes this has a mistaken idea about the nature of the statement; they mistakenly believe that "All bachelors are unmarried" adds to their stock of truths about the world we perceive. These people erroneously believe that someone who learns that all bachelors are unmarried is learning something about the world in the same way as does someone who learns that Sacramento is the capital of California. In fact, they are learning only the relationship we hold among certain words in our language. Unlike "Sacramento is the capital of California," whose truth is a product of various legislative and other historical facts, "All bachelors are unmarried" owes its truth to synonymy of terms. So when we discover that bachelors are unmarried, we do not discover anything about bachelors; we discover something about the word *bachelors*. We learn that the terms *bachelor* and *unmarried* are definitionally related.

If the PGS is an analytic truth, a claim owing its truth merely to the meanings of the terms involved, it cannot serve as a fundamental moral principle. Just as "All bachelors are unmarried" illuminates nothing about unmarried people, the PGS would shine no light on moral ways of behaving. As a claim that owes its truth to definitions, yielding no information about the "real" world, it would be vacuously true and so could not have the substantive power that I attribute to it.

If correct, this would be a powerful criticism of the PGS. It would destroy any hope for using it to perform moral work. Fortunately, the principle is not true merely in virtue of the definitions of its terms. The intended analogy between the PGS and "all bachelors are unmarried" is illicit.

That the comparison fails is easily shown. All we need do is look up the relevant words in our dictionary and notice that there are no definitional equivalences among the terms. For example, the definitions of *gratuitous, suffering,* and *pain* make no reference to wrong. Thus, unlike "All bachelors are unmarried," where the term *bachelor* is defined as "unmarried adult male," making the statement a mere tautology, the PGS is not true by definition. Therefore, it is an error to think that the PGS cannot function as a substantive moral principle because it expresses an empty linguistic truth. Although mistaken, the objection has the beneficial effect of clarifying the substantive moral status of the PGS. Just as "Sacramento is the capital of California" really provides us substantive legislative information, the PGS really does tell us something about the nature of morality.

## Global Objections to PGS

The most sweeping objection to the PGS comes from the moral nihilist, who denies that there is any such thing as morality, that there are either morally good or morally bad ways of behaving. According to nihilists, there is no moral right or wrong. Nihilists, then, would reject the PGS since it implies that at least one thing is morally wrong—namely, the intentional infliction of gratuitous pain or suffering on innocents.

I will not try to argue that nihilism is false. I do not need to, since no one truly practices nihilism. No one, I claim, believes that none of the acts of Hitler, Stalin, or Pol Pot were morally wrong. Nor, to bring the point closer to home, would anyone fail to consider the rape of his or her mother a morally wrong act. A committed nihilist may accept these empirical claims as facts but respond that they show only that we act *as if* morality exists and act *as if* some behaviors are right and some wrong. Nihilists may go so far as to say that, as a matter of psychological or even biological fact, we must act as if there is moral behavior. Nonetheless, they maintain that an accurate inventory of the facts describing our world would include no moral claims.

We must not underestimate how radical nihilism is. There are thinkers who believe that morality is relative, that what is right or wrong is a function of the culture, society, or era in which the act is performed. There are those who believe that morality is all "in the head," that moral facts are a subset of psychological facts in the minds of persons. In this view, as in others, morality is conceived as a human contrivance, not something that exists independently of the way we think. A frequent addendum to these views incorporates the idea that we "project" morality onto the world, and so morality is inevitably an anthropocentric invention shaped by our idiosyncratic ways of conceiving of, and interacting with, the world. However extreme these views, all stand at odds with nihilism. These views all agree that morality exists and that some actions are either morally right or morally wrong. They offer us an account or an interpretation of these moral facts. Nihilists offer no account of morality, since they believe that there is nothing to explain.

It is ironic that Nietzsche, who is typically heralded as the founder of contemporary nihilism, was anything but a nihilist. True, he did satirize the notions that moral values should be based on our Judeo-Christian heritage and that the traditional schism between good and bad accurately separates the moral wheat from chaff, but Nietzsche nevertheless held that some ways of acting are morally superior to others. Rather than deny the existence of moral values, Nietzsche reassessed them. According to Nietzsche, the Christian values eviscerate humans. The ideas that all people are essentially created equal and are deserving of equal moral attention and concern or that we ought to "turn the other cheek" when threatened and attacked should appear laughable to the best of humans. Nietzsche claimed that we act our best when we exercise our power over others. In one of his primary contributions to moral philosophy, Nietzsche questioned the moral status quo and suggested that a reevaluation of values was in order. Such a position would be clearly inconsistent with the nihilist denial of the existence of any moral values whatsoever.

A more serious threat to the acceptance of the PGS comes from moral relativists. Unlike nihilists, moral relativists believe that there is morality; they accept the ordinary belief that some ways of acting are morally better than others. Their unique contribution to the debate about the nature of morality is the idea that the rightness or wrongness of acts is relative to the particular era, culture, or society in which the act is performed. So, for example, a relativist may hold that the institution of slavery was right (or at least morally permissible) in the early nineteenth century in the United States, whereas that institution is wrong today. Relativists are opposed to moral absolutists, who believe that moral acts are right or wrong independently of the times, culture, or society in which they occur. Absolutists insist slavery is wrong (assuming, as they undoubtedly would claim, that slavery *is* wrong) throughout all times, cultures, and societies.

Although relativism is clearly not as radical an idea as nihilism, we should be careful not to confuse it with a far more benign notion. Few would deny that different cultures, societies, or eras have harbored different opinions about which actions are right and which are wrong. No doubt the majority of early nineteenth-century Americans viewed slavery as a morally permissible institution. Currently the overwhelming majority of people believe that slavery is an immoral, horrid practice. Significantly, however, this difference of *belief* in distinct societies is compatible with slavery's actually being an immoral (or moral, for that matter) institution in both societies. Differences in beliefs do not suffice to make relativism true. Relativists adopt the stronger position that some acts are right (or at least permissible) in some societies while the same acts are wrong in others.

A relativist rendering of the PGS would make the intentional, gratuitous infliction of pain or suffering wrong only relative to particular times, cultures, or societies. A relativist regarding the PGS would at least hold out the possibility that in certain eras, cultures, or societies such infliction of pain or suffering is morally permissible and perhaps even the right thing to do.

Moral relativism has been with us at least since Greek antiquity, when Protagoras announced that "man is the measure of all things." The ensuing centuries have seen modifications, nuances, and subtleties that make any serious and detailed discussion difficult. This is surely not the place for it. Instead, let me make just two brief points. First, even if we consider the PGS to be a relativized truth, this gives no reason to think that it is false in our current situation in the world. Moreover, we have powerful intuitive or commonsense reasons for thinking that it is true. Thus, unless the relativist can demonstrate that we are now in one of those cultures, societies, or eras in which the PGS is false, we should now—and in the foreseeable future—act in accordance with it. If the PGS is true now, in our culture and in our society, the relativity of its truth in no way diminishes its power as a fundamental moral precept *for us*.

Second, I challenge anyone who believes the PGS's truth to be merely relative either to recall an actual culture, society, or era in which the principle was false or to intelligibly describe some culture, society, or era in which the PGS would be false. The task is more difficult than imagining isolated cases that putatively violate the PGS (I will soon look at some of these), for the challenge requires it to be *generally* false, or false throughout the society. The task passes from the difficult to the unimaginable if we adhere to our original intuitions regarding the innocent alien of our thought experiment.

The PGS informs us of sufficient grounds for judging an action to be morally wrong. It tells us that if one intentionally inflicts gratuitous pain or suffering on an innocent, then the agent of this action has done something wrong. It does not claim that the intentional infliction of gratuitous pain or suffering is a necessary condition for doing wrong. In other words, it may well be that someone can do wrong without this sort of intentional behavior. As a possible example of this latter case, consider the case—perhaps bastardized—of Mr. Spock, a character in the *Star Trek* series. Assume for the sake of discussion that Spock has no emotions or feelings. (I don't think that this was actually the case, but it doesn't matter; Data, of the *Next Generation* series, may be a better, though less famous example of the type of character I am envisioning.) No one can cause him pain or suffering. Still, it may be that you can wrong Spock by illegitimately interfering with his autonomy. Despite his incapacity to experience pain or to suffer, Spock still has desires and regulates his own behavior in accordance with them. If we violate his autonomy, if we eradicate or diminish his self-control, it is reasonable to think that we wrong him although he does not feel any discomfort from this interruption of his self-governance.

This example is probably more complicated than it first appears, but even if it should be accepted at face value, it is no threat to the PGS. It does nothing to show that the intentional infliction of gratuitous pain and suffering on another is not wrong. At most it demonstrates that this intentional act is not necessary for doing wrong to another. An advocate of the PGS can accept this with equanimity.

## Local Objections to PGS

Local objections to the PGS can be clothed in thought experiments of their own. I call the first "Mugger."

> Two prospective muggers, Max and Milton, intend to pounce on and rob Valerie. Max and Milton are brave when together but quite cowardly individually. Valerie knows this and therefore knows that were she to strike either Max or Milton, the other would-be mugger would run away. As it happens, Valerie strikes Max, and consequently Milton briskly leaves the scene. Valerie continues her walk unscathed.

According to this objection, Valerie's intentional infliction of pain on Max is gratuitous, for she could have escaped by striking Milton instead of Max. Since Valerie acts purposefully, the case provides an example of intentionally inflicting gratuitous pain and suffering. The PGS informs us that Valerie does something wrong, however, even though we clearly intuit that Valerie does nothing wrong. Certainly her striking Max is morally permissible.

This example will have force against the PGS only if we cast Max and Milton as innocent. One might argue that since they never actually do anything to Valerie—recall that neither lays a hand on her—they are innocent at the moment when Valerie strikes Max. One may respond to this by extending the idea of innocence to exclude even the possibility or potential of evil; since both Max and Milton were potentially evil, neither should be considered innocent. This suggestion should be resisted. Since the possibility of evil lurks in virtually any situation, this approach would trivialize the notion of innocence. A more compelling reply is to suggest that their evil intentions undermine any claim to innocence; moral evil, unlike legal evil, can reside in the heart as well as the body.

However one reacts to these suggestions, we have more to learn from Mugger. Bracketing the question of innocence, both apologists for and dissenters to the PGS acknowledge that Valerie performs an intentional act that causes pain to Max and that this specific act is not necessary since she could accomplish the same purpose (i.e., her safety) by doing something else—namely, striking Milton.

But this has force against the PGS only if Valerie's unnecessary act is gratuitous. In cases of overdetermination such as this one, we ought not identify gratuitous acts with unnecessary ones. In effect, something justifiably needs to be done (either attacking Max or Milton), so that performing either of the alternatives is not pointless.

It is important to note that Mugger is mute about the relative suffering Valerie inflicts on Max or Milton. I suggest that Valerie's act is gratuitous only if she creates *more* pain and suffering than she would have caused had she performed any other act sufficient to accomplish her justifiable goal of self-protection. Bringing about this additional pain *is* pointless; it does nothing to help Valerie. The residual belief that Valerie would be (morally) permitted to hit Max even if this were to bring about more pain than her striking Milton results from assuming both that Valerie has no knowledge of the relative suffering that she will bring about and that she is justified in this ignorance. Undoubtedly real-life situations conform to these assumptions, and so actual situations cannot meet the criteria set out in the PGS as a sufficient condition of immoral action. Thus, if you ever find yourself in Valerie's unenviable position, your likely response will probably not be morally inhibited by the PGS.

This response to Mugger harmonizes well with legal principles. The law generally limits the use of force to the least amount necessary to accomplish the legally permissible end. If an attack by a mugger is imminent and one can stop the attack equally well by screaming or by shooting, the law requires that one scream. Of course, real-life victims rarely know that the methods work equally well and are typically (but not always) shielded from murder or manslaughter charges. Still, the theoretical legal point persists. Defense of the PGS is in line with our law.

Giving Mugger a twist, we have "Pistol."

> Max and Milton have guns and intend to kill Valerie. Valerie has a pistol but has time to kill only Max or Milton. Their deaths would be equally painful. Unfortunately for Valerie, then, she will die regardless of which option she takes—shoot Max, shoot Milton, or shoot neither. Valerie knows all these contingencies, and yet she shoots Milton.

Valerie is charged with intentionally inflicting gratuitous suffering on Milton. She would have been equally guilty of wrongdoing if she had shot Max. After all, it does her no good to shoot just one of her assailants, since the other will succeed in his dastardly deed. But surely Valerie does nothing wrong in shooting either Max or Milton. Therefore, the PGS, which tells us that Valerie does wrong in this situation, must be in error.

Unlike Mugger, where Valerie accomplishes her goal regardless of whom she attacks, Pistol pictures a scenario where Valerie's aim of survival is thwarted no matter what she does. In Mugger Valerie can meet her goal by performing either of two possible actions. In Pistol none of her options will help her to reach her goal, and so the killing is hailed as pointless or gratuitous. The PGS is alleged to entail the counterintuitive conclusion that Valerie is morally required to shoot neither Max nor Milton, because killing either assailant does not help satisfy her desire to survive and so lacks justification.

We should insist that Max and Milton are not innocent. This is confirmed by the fact that if Valerie kills either Max or Milton, we would say that he "got what he deserved." While it is true that Valerie loses her life whatever she chooses, and so any possible act of hers is pointless relative to her continued life, the evil intent of her prospective murderers immunizes the PGS against a threat from Pistol.

The third thought experiment, "Dentist," has relevance to biomedical experimentation on nonhuman animals.

> Don, a dentist, is testing a new plaque removal technique on his patient. The technique may be superior to the orthodox treatment. It is not necessary for Don to test it on Jim, however; he has other

patients who are equally good candidates for this procedure. This new procedure causes slightly more pain to its subject than does the orthodox means of removing plaque. Don explains the situation to Jim and then receives his fully informed consent.

The complaint is that Don acts gratuitously twice over. Don could have tested on someone other than Jim, and he brings about more suffering than is necessary to accomplish his laudable goal since he could have used the more traditional plaque-removal procedure. The PGS seems to make Don's actions wrong, a verdict conflicting with our moral intuitions that Don does nothing ethically askew.

That Don could have collected the same result with a means other than the one he used parallels the overdetermining circumstances that face Valerie in Mugger, so that the response to this part of the thought experiment has already been given. Mugger shows that just because a purpose could have been satisfied in a different way does not make the chosen course of action gratuitous. The novel objection suggested by Dentist is that the PGS overstates its case. Inflicting gratuitous pain and suffering on another may not always be wrong. If the subject of the pain gives his fully informed consent, the agent of the suffering does nothing wrong.

The PGS can account for this objection. Either the subject who gives his informed, willing consent has a reason for consenting or he does not. If he does, and if the reason is sufficiently strong, the infliction of the suffering is not gratuitous. If the reason fails to be of sufficient quality or if the subject has no reason at all, the intentional infliction of this suffering is gratuitous (despite the subject's wanting to be subjected to it), and so the agent is acting wrongly.

Admittedly the notion of "sufficient quality" is vague. This is a virtue, however, not a vice. Any attempt to provide a specific amount of "reasonableness" that a reason must have to render the intentional infliction of pain not gratuitous would certainly be ad hoc. The idea of "sufficient quality" is also relative. A community best determines what constitutes sufficient quality at a particular time. Place the intentional infliction of suffering in a different community or at a different time and the assessment of the reason may well differ. This sort of relativism is not ominous. It makes good sense to think that knowledge of the historical context of a reason is essential for determining its quality.

The other half of the reply may appear counterintuitive. If the reason fails to meet the community's standard of sufficient quality or the agent desires to be subjected to the suffering for no reason at all (this can be seen as the limiting point of lack of sufficient quality), does it really seem correct to characterize the infliction of suffering as gratuitous? The attraction of answering no resides in the fact that, whatever the failure of reason on the subject's behalf, he or she still wants to be subjected to the suffering. How can an agent be acting gratuitously—and thus wrongly by the lights of the PGS—when acting in accordance to the subject's desires? In fact, an argument can be made that, all else being equal, to discount the subject's desires in this way is wrong because it violates the subject's autonomy.

But it is not unusual for us to act contrary to a person's desires when the person's reasons for being subjected to pain and suffering are of insufficient quality. These paternalistic actions are not always viewed as wrong. A mentally deranged individual who repeatedly asks to be tortured should not be. Anyone who succumbs to the mentally ill person's desires would be causing gratuitous suffering, and we would properly evaluate the act as evil.

Not all reasons for wanting additional suffering fail the quality requirement. Consider St. Francis, who begged God to increase his suffering so that he could be a better person. St. Francis thought that increased suffering would help him better empathize with a large segment of the population, which would in turn help him better care for the disadvantaged. If you find this act to be heroic, as many do, you must find St. Francis's request intelligible and reasonable. Further evidence for this assessment derives from the presumption that the church would not classify a mentally deranged person as a saint.

Perhaps even more significant than the formal rebuttals of these attempts to refute the PGS is the realization that these complaints are rather technical in nature and can scarcely be applied to the way it affects our moral relationships with animals. The notions of overdetermination (in Mugger), inevitability (in Pistol), and informed consent (in Dentist) are not issues that arise in the areas of factory farming, hunting, vivisection, and the like. Thus, even if these issues reflected real problems with the principle's general applicability (and I insist they do not), its viability concerning human-animal relationships would continue.

## Additional Articulations of the PGS

There are other ways of expressing the PGS. Perhaps some may discern morally significant differences among these formulations in the sense that they can envision situations in which one of the formulations is true and another false. In addition, one can no doubt make arcane distinctions among the different terms that the interpretations employ so that the equivalence that I claim for these formulations disappears. So be it. Although I believe that most readers will naturally see these characterizations as "materially equivalent," as amounting to the same thing, those who demur can just take them as stipulated identities.

To facilitate the discussion, I repeat the Principle of Gratuitous Suffering:

(PGS) It is morally wrong to intentionally inflict (or allow the infliction of) gratuitous pain or suffering on another, innocent individual.

To say that an agent is morally wrong in performing some action is to say that the agent (morally) ought not have performed that act. Therefore we have, as equivalent to the PGS,

(PGSO) One morally ought not to intentionally inflict (or allow the infliction of) gratuitous pain or suffering on another, innocent individual.

And although some thinkers may see or invent a distinction, I understand the PGSO as just another way of saying the next version:

(PGSL) One has a moral obligation not to intentionally inflict (or allow the infliction of) gratuitous pain or suffering on another, innocent individual.

Nowhere is the importance of understanding intentional action as knowledgeable action more pronounced than in the following:

(PGSB) A person is morally blameworthy if he or she intentionally inflicts (or allows the infliction of) gratuitous pain or suffering on another, innocent individual.

If we think that intentional action can exist without the agent's knowledge, and perhaps even without the agent's belief that he or she is inflicting suffering, attaching blame to the agent may not be warranted. The justification offered for the harmful act may have various sources. One may have good reason to believe that the relevant behavior is not causing any pain or suffering. One may have good reason to believe that the infliction of the pain and suffering is not gratuitous. One may have good reason to think that the recipient of the behavior is wicked and not innocent. There is clearly a gap between what one may legitimately believe about an action and the nature of that action. Blameworthiness must take into account the agent's state of mind, and so blame cannot be legitimately attributed to someone solely because the act has certain characteristics. This moral attitude is common. Justifications are simply explanations that attempt to clear an agent of wrongdoing in particular circumstances. If I violate the speed limit but explain to the police officer that my passenger has a severe head wound that may prove fatal without quick treatment, the officer will probably not issue a ticket. Most of us would think that I acted perfectly properly and would be appalled if the officer insisted on issuing a summons.

On the other hand, the PGS should not be understood as implying the following principle:

> (PGSP) One who intentionally inflicts (or allows the infliction of) gratuitous pain and suffering on an innocent deserves (warrants, ought to receive) punishment.

Theories of punishment take widely different forms. Some theorists hold, for example, that punishment as a retributive act is never justified. They would prefer that wrongdoers materially compensate the victim or the victim's family. Utilitarians—those who justify punishment on the basis of its consequences for society—may even differ among themselves about the warrant for punishment. They may have different predictions of the consequences of punishing someone who intentionally inflicts gratuitous pain. The nature of punishment is simply too hotly contested to allow inferences to it from such a fundamental moral principle as the PGS.

The different formulations of the PGS capture the idea that the terms *wrong, ought not,* and *obligation not to* compose a tight-knit family of concepts. This is reflected in our ordinary speech and behavior. It is a rare person who would contend that an action may be morally wrong yet still morally permissible or that we ought not to perform an action even though it is the right one to perform in the circumstances. Making these connections explicit has heuristic and explanatory value. Some of us find that one expression of the moral principle is more easily understood, more intuitive, or a more natural characterization than another. Overtly acknowledging the interchangeability of different statements of the same fundamental moral principle leaves us free to use whichever formulation we find most helpful. In addition, the various articulations of the same principle may help clarify the principle itself. For example, once the PGS is explicitly acknowledged as equivalent to the PGSO, some may find themselves with a better understanding of the principle basic to all these incarnations. And this in turn may trigger the descriptions of obviousness or intuitiveness that I have claimed for the principle. From a psychological perspective, forwarding different though equivalent formulations of one idea is far from a trivial or vacuous exercise. In cases such as this, where the moral principle stated in the PGS and its equivalent descriptions is of fundamental significance to the task at hand, we should always welcome complementary characterizations.

## The PGS and Peter Singer's Principle

The Australian philosopher Peter Singer has introduced a moral principle that is quite similar in spirit to the PGS.[2] His principle, which I will call "the Principle of Moral Importance" (PMI), runs as follows:

> If it is in our power to prevent something bad from happening, without thereby sacrificing anything of comparable moral importance, we ought, morally, to do it.

Singer tells us that "without sacrificing anything of comparable moral importance" means "without causing anything equally bad to occur, or doing something that is intrinsically wrong, or failing to promote some moral good, comparable in importance to the bad that can be prevented."[3]

The PMI yields the same result as the PGS in the thought experiment involving the space alien. Feeling pain and suffering are bad things. We can spare the creature from having this experience simply by not striking it. Furthermore, our forbearance costs us nothing of comparable moral significance; indeed, we sacrifice at most some perverse, momentary pleasure. Therefore, we ought not to strike the creature; were we to hit it, we would be doing something morally wrong. In fact, the PMI sanctions the PGS. Pain and suffering are in and of themselves always bad things, and the fact that the infliction of pain and suffering is gratuitous guarantees that nothing of comparable moral significance would be sacrificed were we to prevent the pain and suffering. Thus, we ought not to intentionally bring about the pain and suffering; equivalently, were we to intentionally cause the pain and suffering, we would be acting immorally. Therefore, if the PMI is true, so is the PGS.

Without additional assumptions, however, the truth of the PGS does not guarantee the truth of the PMI. The PGS addresses only the moral propriety of inflicting gratuitous pain and suffering, whereas the PMI speaks to bad things in general. The latter collection is larger than the former; that is, badness or evil can result from things other than the infliction of gratuitous pain and suffering. Furthermore, the PGS never mentions the idea of "comparable moral significance." Finally, although calling the pain and suffering gratuitous entails that nothing of comparable moral significance has been gained, the fact that nothing of comparable moral significance has been sacrificed does not entail that infliction of gratuitous pain and suffering has occurred. The PGS is therefore a narrower and so a safer principle to espouse. We should, if anything, have more confidence in the truth of the PGS than in the PMI.

The narrower scope of the PGS shields it from certain criticisms that can be leveled at the PMI. In fact, these criticism may fail even for the PMI, but they certainly fail for the PGS. I'll consider the PMI first. It may be argued that the acceptance of the PMI destroys the viable distinction between acts of charity and acts of obligation or, similarly, between supererogatory acts (acts above and beyond the call of duty) and acts of obligation. We typically think of a moderately affluent American who gives $1,000 to Cancer Care as acting charitably or beyond what duty or obligation requires. The PMI suggests otherwise. Assuming that this $1,000 provides significant help for a family that has a member suffering from cancer and that the sacrifice of $1,000 means virtually nothing to this moderately affluent American, the PMI tells us that the latter has an obligation to give the $1,000. The potential donor has the power to prevent something bad from happening without sacrificing anything of comparable moral significance and so ought to give the $1,000 to the cancer charity. According to this principle, the plaudits frequently given those who extend these charitable contributions are misplaced. These people are just doing what they ought to do.

The significance of this objection depends on the depth of one's commitment to the traditional distinction between charitable and obligatory acts. I take little theoretical issue with redefining the boundary between obligation and supererogation. There is something unctuous about the very rich receiving encomia for parting with a relatively tiny percentage of their resources. Still, practical issues suggest keeping the distinction. Perhaps without the attention and honors from others, such donors would reduce their "charitable" contributions, and the poor, ill, and needy would be the worse for it. As any Las Vegas casino owner will attest, the best way to keep people betting is to reward the behavior intermittently. Just as the occasional payoff keeps the slot machines profitable, the occasional dinner party and pat on the back may well keep the contributions coming.

A second criticism points to the PMI's potential to destroy the notion of property rights. After all, our money is ours, and thus we have the right to do with it pretty much as we please. Although there might be some limits to the way we dispense the money—perhaps we morally ought not use it to support racist groups—we should certainly not be coerced into giving any of it to charity. To impose an *obligation* to give away some of our money is to grant others a right to it. But the money is our property, which means that no one else has a right to it. The PMI, therefore, poses a grave threat to one of the central tenets of our way of life.

The force of this objection depends on one's commitment to a strong individualistic conception of property rights. Communitarians, for example, may find the locus of property ownership in the community rather than the individual, making it illegitimate to speak in terms of money or any other resource as being at the disposal of a single individual. Some may argue that the fault in thinking of individual property rights is that it assumes an atomistic picture of society, where the fortune and welfare of each member is largely independent of others in the society. This assumption can be challenged by pointing out that any individual's lot in life is inextricably interwoven with other lives, and so thinking that the resource belongs to just one person is hopelessly idealistic. The owner of a grocery store depends on customers; it is essentially a reciprocal arrangement. To place the sole decision-making power about the distribution of income in the hands of one person is to misunderstand the nature of the production of wealth.

Another argument against private ownership comes from biology. It might be argued that the money and resources one accumulates is never a matter of unalloyed desert. The characteristics necessary to the production of wealth, such as intelligence and perseverance, themselves result from a genetic lottery that no one deserves to win. The person who inherits these characteristics is lucky. The argument concludes that the only fair alternative is to divide the property and resources among a group of people. Such an argument need not lead to egalitarianism, where all goods and burdens are divided equally among all, but it will entail that the notion of an individual having complete discretion over the disbursement of resources is morally misguided.

A satisfactory answer to this question would require delving into the vexing "nature vs. nurture" debate as well as thorny philosophical issues regarding free will. Bracketing these investigations, we can note the consequences of accepting the idea that luck in the genetic lottery dictates our entire future behavior. If we consistently adopt the idea that our actions are based on events over which we have no control, it becomes difficult to see how we can ever ascribe moral responsibility to anyone. There would be no self for which we would be responsible. Moreover, we probably cannot adopt such an attitude for any length of time. We may be psychologically incapable of forswearing our attitudes of praise and blame even when faced with compelling biological and philosophical reasons for doing so. Our incapacity to rescind both our pervasive moral attitudes and our self-concept as free initiators of action may be a sufficient reason for thinking that such arguments are flawed even if we cannot pinpoint the error.

A fourth objection suggests that the PMI is self-defeating. If we prevent some bad things from happening, we may ensure that even more bad things will happen in the future. Reflect on what would happen if we were to prevent the starvation and death of many people in the poorer nations in the world. More people would live, which would further strain resources, causing more people to starve later on. The solution, as gruesome as it may immediately appear, may be to do nothing to help these people, for any temporary help will inevitably be followed by additional poverty and starvation.

A defender of the PMI may admit that although this abject consequence *can* result from our well-intentioned application of the principle, it certainly need not. This objection shows only that we must exercise care in preventing bad things. Presumably it would be better to show these poorer nations how best to utilize their lands than to give them large quantities of food without further assistance. Education about sex and reproduction would probably be useful, too, as would establishing a program of incentives that would better motivate behavior based on foresight. Certainly many programs have failed to reach laudable goals, but such failure should not be seen as reason to abdicate the PMI; rather, it should serve as a reason to be more creative about ways of implementing the moral principle.

Last, one may object to the PMI on the grounds that adherence to it is unrealistic. The PMI sets too high a standard for ordinary humans.

It is probably true that few can continuously live by such a high standard. Still, this in itself is not a flaw. After all, it is better for us to set our sights too high than too low. In addition, many useful notions outstrip human capacity, but that does not force us to abandon them. No one can ever draw a perfect circle, but we do not therefore modify our concept of circularity or believe that the concept serves no purpose; similarly, the fact that we will not regularly act saintly is no reason to think that such an unattainable goal should be changed or that it has no value. Setting high goals and earnestly trying to reach them will likely produce the greatest diminution of evil in the world. As long as we see the journey as producing incremental gains rather than overcoming large obstacles, good intentions should maintain operable levels.

Since I do not wish to give the impression that the PMI faces insuperable objections, I have supplied its defenders with what I think are plausible responses. Undoubtedly different individuals will evaluate these responses differently. The PGS, being a more circumscribed principle, remains free of these objections. It does not redraw the line between obligatory and supererogatory acts, undermine individual property rights, face any threat from charges of self-defeat, or set an especially high standard.

The PMI and the PGS yield the same practical conclusions concerning our moral obligations toward nonhuman animals. Since my concern is with our care and treatment of animals, it better and more directly suits my purposes to rely on the intuitive PGS. I believe that the PMI is true and that all objections to it can be satisfactorily deflected. Still, we should not fight unnecessary battles, especially when the lives and welfare of billions of animals are at stake.

## PGS and Painless Death

Some engaged in animal-related practices may see the PGS as offering them a moral reprieve since it remains silent about the moral legitimacy of bringing about the painless deaths of animals. Although the PGS does not encourage or endorse the painless killing of animals, neither does it condemn such a practice. Thus, at least insofar as the PGS is concerned, institutions that essentially cause animals to die do nothing morally untoward as long as the animals experience no pain or suffering.

This observation should bring little solace to virtually any animal-related industry, let alone the three that I will explicitly address. Factory farming and vivisection inflict pain and suffering to virtually every animal in their hegemonies. It might be thought that hunting escapes censure from the PGS, since hunters kill animals instantaneously with either a bullet or an arrow. The popular idea that deer, for example, do not suffer a lingering death in virtue of the great marksmanship of hunters is a myth of mammoth proportions. In fact, although I will not dwell on it here, some 50 percent of hunted game animals die from wounds, and a much higher percentage do not die immediately from being shot.

At any rate, the PGS can be slightly amended to include the painless deaths of animals.

> (PGSD) It is morally wrong to intentionally inflict (or allow) gratuitous pain and suffering on another, innocent individual, and it is morally wrong to intentionally and gratuitously kill (or allow another to kill) another, innocent individual.

Why do I offer the PGS as my cornerstone moral principle rather than the more inclusive PGSD? After all, offering the PGSD instead of the PGS would automatically foreclose the moral acceptability of painlessly killing animals.

There are several pragmatic reasons for choosing the PGS rather than the PGSD as my basic moral precept. First, some may find the PGSD far too broad. We kill or cause the death of tomato plants, but neither I nor probably anyone else would characterize this killer as acting immorally. If we restrict the moral principle to pain and suffering, we circumscribe the discussion to things with consciousness and minds. Tomato plants, nonhuman animals, and humans all live and eventually die; only those in the latter two groups have the capacity to feel pain and suffer. The PGS is thus tidier than the PGSD.

Second, while it is all but universally acknowledged, even among philosophers, that suffering and pain are intrinsically bad to the subject who experiences them, the same consensus cannot be found regarding death. There is a large philosophical literature, beginning with the ancient philosopher Epicurus, that challenges the commonsense idea that death is bad for the person who dies. The guiding idea is that death has no subject. An individual who still lives has not been touched by death, and after death the individual no longer exists to be affected. Since the person must be either alive or dead, no one can ever directly experience death, and so it is a mistake to think of death as something bad that happens to an individual. Although I believe that this challenge can be met, the discussion would be recondite and tortuous. Promoting the PGS instead of the PGSD makes this Epicurean debate peripheral.

The final reason to choose the PGS is that it marginalizes the importance of yet another hotly contested question. Some philosophers believe that death can be bad only for an individual who has self-consciousness and that virtually—if not veritably—all nonhuman animals lack self-consciousness. For these thinkers, death free from pain or suffering is not a bad thing or a harm to nonhuman animals. In this case, the grounding idea is that only self-conscious creatures have the concept of themselves enduring through time (the concept of one's self). It is further claimed that the possession of this concept is necessary to having plans, hopes, and expectations, and so it is only concerning these individuals that it even makes sense to speak of the thwarting of these psychological states. If we accept the idea that the harm of death is constituted by the irrevocable frustration of these states, we reach the conclusion that death (again, absent any pain and suffering) is not a bad thing for the animal.

This is a confused argument. Death is a bad thing to my cat and dog even if the highly questionable assumption that these animals lack self-consciousness is true. The primary harm that death brings to the individual who dies is that it irreversibly deprives the individual of any further good and pleasant experiences.[4] Such deprivation requires only a conscious (and not self-conscious) creature.

Admittedly, this is just a skeleton of an argument within a vigorously debated issue. The PGS nullifies the necessity for engaging in this debate. Virtually all animals in institutions that use them for some purpose or other experience pain and suffering. Even if death did not carry an additional harm to these animals, the gratuitous pain and suffering suffice to render these practices immoral. Thus, it serves me well not to amend the PGS.

## PGS and the Doctrine of Double Effect

The Doctrine of Double Effect (DDE) was formulated in the late Middle Ages to justify actions contrary to what was known as "natural law"—laws that ought to hold in any state.[5] Since such laws were conceived as expressions of God's will, violations of natural law were considered to be serious offenses. Nevertheless, some occasions seem to call for courses of action that breach natural law.

Fundamentally the DDE distinguishes the foreseen consequences of a voluntary act from the agent's intentions, placing the moral weight on the latter. Consider two examples. In the first case a pregnant woman has a diseased uterus that will kill her unless removed. The DDE permits killing the fetus if the doctors *intend* only to remove the uterus rather than kill the fetus, since the fetus's death is a foreseen but unintended consequence.

For another example, consider the case of a pilot in wartime. His mission is to bomb enemy territory to facilitate his country's victory. Nevertheless, he knows that the bombs he drops will end many innocent lives. The DDE can be used to justify the pilot's mission by claiming that the pilot intends only to facilitate his country's victory. He does not intend, even as a means to accomplishing his goal, that innocent lives be lost. The deaths of these innocents are unintended albeit foreseen consequences of his intended action. The DDE gives the pilot moral cover. It tells us that we are justified in bringing about events that, were they intended, would be morally impermissible.

It serves us well to formulate the DDE with greater specificity. The doctrine informs us that acts with both good and bad effects are morally permissible if and only if (1) the bad effects are *unavoidable* if we are to obtain the good; (2) the bad effects, although foreseen, are unintended; and (3) the good effects outweigh the bad effects.

Those arguing for the moral propriety of saving the mother's life in a troubled pregnancy may invoke the DDE. Suppose that saving the mother unavoidably entails killing the fetus, that the death of the fetus is foreseen but unintended, and that the good of the mother's continued life outweighs the badness of the death of the fetus; the DDE justifies performing the operation. Nevertheless, the DDE will not sanction intentionally smashing the fetus's head as a means to save the mother's life, since requirement 2 would be violated.

A similar strategy serves to justify the pilot's mission. If the loss of innocent lives is necessary to his country's victory and foreseen but not intended, and the victory for the pilot's country contains more good than the evil of the innocent lives lost, the DDE permits the bombing. Nevertheless, the DDE will not permit intending to kill the foreign innocents to facilitate victory, since that would flout condition 2.

My purpose here is not to defend the DDE. Rather, I want to investigate whether this doctrine can abet intensive farming or vivisection. First, the factory-farming advocate may claim that the industry's intended goal is to feed many people and that even though the means to this goal—including transportation, confined rearing, and slaughter—inflict great pain and suffering, this misery is an unintended but foreseen consequence. This appeal to the DDE clearly fails, however. The pain and suffering caused to innocent animals is not necessary to accomplish this laudable goal. Hundreds of millions of vegetarians prove that people can eat and survive quite well without factory farming. Second, it is highly questionable whether condition 3 is satisfied. The goodness in our consumption of meat products no doubt pales compared to the badness inherent to the suffering of billions of animals. By any reasonable accounting, such a defense tilts the scales of good and evil against the welfare of cows, hogs, and chickens.

Similarly, a researcher may try to justify sacrificing millions of animals by claiming that the intended goal is to save many lives from the ravages of heart disease and cancer; the killing of the animals—foreseen but not intended—is a necessary means to this good end. As I will show more clearly later, however, nonhuman animal testing is not necessary to accomplish this good end. Indeed, I will argue that animal experimentation is frequently detrimental to the laudable goal of ridding our world of disease. Also relevant is the less clear issue as to whether condition 3 is satisfied. Circumscribing the constitution of good and bad to the degree of pleasure and pain produced by a particular act, it is far from obvious that eliminating some of our most horrible diseases would provide more good than the bad that results from experimenting on animals.

Although these appeals to the DDE fail to justify factory farming or vivisection, it is interesting to note that they rest on a tacit acceptance of the PGS. Recall that the DDE is used to justify a prima facie evil, which is precisely what the PGS says these practices are. It would be odd to try to justify them by appealing to the DDE if neither the farmer nor the researcher believed, all else being equal, that they *would* be doing wrong were their infliction of pain and suffering on animals intended.

## Agents and Patients

A moral agent is an individual capable of deliberating and acting morally. The domain of moral agents is not identical to the set of human beings. For example, some humans are incapable of moral deliberation and action. Extremely young infants have not reached the cognitive and emotional maturity to act morally. So-called marginal human beings—those who suffer from serious brain damage, advanced Alzheimer's disease, retardation, or senility—lack the ability to act morally. Since such people lack the capacity to think and act in moral terms, it would be foolish to hold them morally responsible for their behavior. Infants and the marginalized are *causally* responsible for their behavior, but as common sense suggests, this responsibility does not transfer to the moral realm. Only moral agents, then, can have moral responsibilities or moral obligations. Only moral agents can be legitimately held worthy of either praise or blame for their behavior. There is no moral *ought* that applies to anyone who is not a moral agent.

Conversely, perhaps not all moral agents are human beings. First, cosmologists propose the existence of extraterrestrial life, some of which may surpass human life in every imaginable way. These creatures would be capable of moral deliberation and action and so be moral agents, just as most humans are. Second, some terrestrial nonhumans may be moral agents. No one seriously considers all nonhuman animals to be moral agents, but whether some are remains an open question. Chimpanzees, orangutans, dolphins, and even dogs and cats are just a few of the possible candidates. There is much anecdotal and ethological evidence that speaks in favor of granting these animals moral agency. We have all heard stories of dolphins saving drowning humans and dogs dragging children from fires. Admittedly these tales are hardly decisive, but it is prudent to keep an open mind as to whether any terrestrial nonhumans can think in moral terms.

More important for my purposes is using the notion of moral agency to clarify the idea of a moral patient. Whereas moral agents are capable of moral behavior, moral patients have the capacity to be treated morally. This entails that they have the capacity to be made (prudentially) better and worse off. Moral patients have welfare or well-being.

Although the domains of moral agents and moral patients overlap considerably, they are not identical. All normal adult human beings are both moral agents and moral patients, but I have already shown that not all humans are moral agents. Most significantly, some moral patients are not human, and here we need not enter the speculative world of creatures from outer space. We find many nonhuman moral patients on our own planet in the form of (nonhuman) animals.

Almost all of us find the idea of animals as moral patients thoroughly unquestionable. Even though some animals probably cannot feel pain and suffer—the primary way in which a moral patient can be made worse off—virtually none of us denies the seemingly transparent fact that dogs, cats, chimps, cows, goats, pigs, and countless other animals have the capacity to undergo unpleasant experiences. It is admittedly difficult to draw the line between those who are moral patients and those who are not. Do termites have the capacity to suffer? What of roaches, snails, shrimp, or mosquitoes? Nevertheless, even if we cannot draw a sharp line between the two groups, we can still pick out some animals that definitely do have the capacity to feel pain and suffer.

There are two explanations for our difficulty in sharply distinguishing creatures that have the capacity to feel pain and suffer from those that do not. The first explanation applies when we assume that the relevant capacity is a binary affair: something either has it or doesn't have it. This means that there is always a fact of the matter, so that our inability to sharply distinguish the groups is a function of our ignorance. If so, scientific advances could presumably help us make the distinction in the future.

The second explanation for our inability to differentiate sharply between moral and nonmoral patients applies when we assume the relevant capacity to reflect the vagueness or indeterminacy that infects the world. That is, the distinction is not an either/or affair of sharp divisions; rather, there are only gradations. We cannot draw any sharp line between the two categories because there is no sharp distinction between the two categories to be drawn.

To see how this can be so, consider baldness, a property far more familiar than that of being a moral patient. There is no sharp line between bald and nonbald men. Is a man with 50 hairs on his head bald? What of 150, or 400? It seems arbitrary to think that some specific number of hairs entails nonbaldness, such that a man who has one hair fewer is therefore bald. If moral patienthood functions as does baldness, it would be arbitrary to insist on a precise line of separation between moral and nonmoral patients.

Neither of these explanations precludes us from being certain that some particular individuals are or are not moral patients. Despite the fact that we may need to await future research to discover whether mosquitoes and roaches have the capacity to feel pain and suffer, we can now say with complete confidence that typical adult human beings and dogs have this capacity, while rocks and pencils do not. If *moral patient* resembles *bald* in being an inherently vague term, then just as we can now say that some men are bald (e.g., those with no hairs on their head) and some are not (those with 100,000 hairs on their head), there is no logical impediment to claiming that humans and dogs have the capacity to feel pain and suffer whereas rocks and pencils do not.

Philosophers, however, differ markedly from nonphilosophers in certain respects. Some have proffered arguments that, incredibly, banish terrestrial nonhuman animals from the realm of moral patients. As most famously articulated by the seventeenth-century French philosopher René Descartes, such a position denies that chimps, dogs, cats, and so forth possess consciousness and thus the capacity to feel pain and suffer.

The argument begins with Descartes's belief that the world is composed of two basic substances: mind (or soul; he used the two terms interchangeably) and matter. Mind is immaterial and imperceptible; it cannot be seen, smelled, touched, tasted, or heard. It is essentially active. All thinking, doubting, willing, and emoting occur in this substance. Matter, conversely, has extension and is inert or lifeless. In isolation, considered independently of mind, it has no significance or value.

Human beings form a unique composite of mind and matter where these two distinct sorts of substances interact. When a pin pricks your hand, for example, you normally feel pain. A modification in your body has effected a change in your mind. Conversely, hearing an embarrassing story may cause a person to blush. Here a mental event causes a bodily change. Still, despite all these continual interactions, there is never any doubt that the spiritual mind has absolute priority over the corporeal body. Our minds are our essences; without them we cannot exist. Our bodies are ours only contingently; we can exist without them.

Descartes conceived of animals as nothing more than relatively complex machines. They lack minds or souls and as a result cannot think, feel pain or pleasure, or even be conscious. Descartes, of course, had personal experiences around animals, just as we have. He knew that horses yelp when whipped and that dogs groan when beaten. These and many other animals certainly *seem* to feel pain and react to it. Descartes's ingenious rebuttal was to compare the agonizing sounds of the whipped and beaten animals to the noises emitted from machines when their gears grind. Just as we hear unpleasant sounds when we insert a stick into a machine, we hear unpleasant sounds when we beat a dog or horse. But just as we do not and should not credit machines with minds and the capacity to feel pleasure and pain, we ought not to conceive of animals as having these capacities. To Descartes, then, animals are no more moral patients than are clocks.

Descartes's view does not contest the PGS. On the contrary, Descartes believed as do we, that it is wrong to intentionally inflict gratuitous pain or suffering on another. Descartes diverges from common sense, however, in believing that nonhuman animals lack consciousness and so cannot feel pain or suffer.

The almost automatic response to these Cartesian reflections is that they prove too much. If nonhuman animals are nothing more than complicated automatons and the noises they emit have no connection to anything mental, then why cannot the same be said of human beings? The point can be put picturesquely. Imagine a group of intelligent aliens visiting earth. They see and hear both human and nonhuman animals. What method can these aliens use to distinguish conscious humans from nonconscious animals?

Descartes anticipates this type of response and suggests two observable differences between humans and animals. First, no machine can have the ability to use language in the varied ways that humans can. Descartes concedes the possibility of machines that can utter the sounds "that hurts me" when they are poked with a sharp stick. Nonetheless, they cannot carry on a far-reaching and spontaneous conversation, as can even "men of the lowest grade of intellect." Second, machines, although able to perform some functions with even more precision than humans, can never act "from knowledge" but only react from impressions on their bodies.[6] The idea is that only rational creatures can respond appropriately in an indefinitely large number of different situations. Machines, however complex, will never be powerful enough to formulate appropriate responses to an indeterminate number of situations.

We should not be persuaded to abdicate our commonsense belief that many nonhuman animals are conscious, can feel pain and suffer, and so are moral patients. Of the many available responses to Descartes, one of the simplest is to imagine a human infant who suffers from a disease that will cause its death just a few weeks after birth. This baby cannot use language in the varied ways that most adults can. Further, by supposing that the infant will die shortly after birth, we rule out any appeal to its *potential* to use language. Unfortunately, this particular baby has none. Nevertheless, I trust that no one doubts that this child has the capacity to feel pain and suffer. If he or she were my child and required an operation to relieve some obstruction, I would insist on supplying anesthesia. And, I submit, so would you.

The same unfortunate situation can be used to rebut Descartes's second sign of a moral patient. A baby a few weeks old reasons no better than a chimpanzee; indeed, contemporary science tells us it reasons less well. And, again, the inevitable, imminent death precludes any appeal to a potential for rational action down the road. So once again, unless one is willing to concede that this unfortunate child is incapable of feeling pain and suffering, one must allow that some animals are moral patients.

Being a moral patient—being an individual with the capacity to feel pain and suffer—requires consciousness or having a mind. It is most profitable to define mind functionally: whatever it is that enables individuals to feel pain and suffer. I need not say exactly how this mind is constituted. For my purposes, it is unimportant whether the mind is a purely immaterial, spiritual substance, as Descartes and many religious people believe, or a physical object constituted of nerve cells, as many contemporary scientists believe. Moral patients are minded beings with welfares.

Virtually all humans are moral patients. Some fetuses are moral patients, but some are not. A one-day-old conceptus lacks any nervous system and is thus, according to current biology, thoroughly incapable of mental life. At a minimum these early conceptuses cannot feel pain or suffer. A great many nonhuman animals are moral patients. All nondeficient mammals fall in this category, and birds, reptiles, and fish apparently are moral patients as well. We are uncertain about oysters and termites. We are quite certain that amoebas and paramecia have no minds. There are many animate but nonminded individuals. Trees, rosebushes, and tomato plants have no minds, no consciousness, and no welfares. A similar verdict befalls natural but inanimate objects such as rocks, stars, and waterfalls. And at least at this juncture in our history, no artifacts are moral patients. Pencils, cola cans, and automobiles fall into this category.

Most people will probably agree with this general taxonomy, but some may worry that it is unduly restrictive. By eliminating an object from the realm of moral patients, I am saying that this object cannot have a welfare; it cannot be made better or worse off. Nevertheless, many would suggest that trees, rosebushes, rivers, and cars can be made better or worse off, even if they cannot feel pain or suffer. It may seem obvious that trees are made worse off when they receive limited water, waterfalls are made worse off when they are used as repositories of waste and debris, and cars are made worse off when other, larger vehicles crash into them.

Although popular, this way of looking at the matter is wrong. Certainly trees die if they receive too little water, and waterfalls used as repositories for waste become ugly and unhealthy for their inhabitants. Wrecked cars become unusable. Nevertheless, none of this should incline us to believe that these things are moral patients.

Consider the damaged car. Why would we think that being struck by another vehicle makes the car worse off rather than better off? It is certainly worse for the car's owner. He or she can no longer use the car as intended; it no longer serves as a means of transportation. But the question is why dents and broken glass make things worse *for the car*. Lacking consciousness, the car cannot feel any pain or endure any suffering. The crash itself, then, does not matter to the car, nor does its dented state bother, frustrate, or depress it. From the "perspective" of the car, nothing can matter to it; the car has no perspective or point of view from which it situates itself in the world.

Similar reflections attach to waterfalls and trees. The waterfall does not care whether it is filled with trash. It cares about nothing. It is true that the debris may affect the health of those who use its water for drinking and washing. The filth may trouble those who have an aesthetic sense. But note that their lives can be made worse only if the waterfall's users are conscious creatures. They must care about the conditions in which they find themselves. Trees do not care whether they are given insufficient water. They may die, of course, but trees do not care about dying. Trees do not care about anything; nothing matters to them. Like the automobile and the waterfall, they lack any perspective or point of view. Of course, the death of the tree may matter a great deal to some creatures. Squirrels may lose their homes and travelers may lose a shady place to rest. Squirrels and travelers have welfares that can be affected by the death of a tree.

There is no doubt that we automatically think of damaged cars, filthy waters, and dying trees as being bad states of affairs. In general I fully agree with this common assessment. The mistake lies in ascribing the badness to the car, waterfall, or tree. To do this is to assume the implausible position that items in the world that lack consciousness can care about anything, let alone care about their own lives or careers. Rather, these circumstances are (rightly) construed as bad because damaged cars, filthy waters, and dying trees typically make the lives of conscious creatures worse off than they would otherwise be. The squirrel and human have their well-being diminished when they live in a denigrated environment.

Lest there be any misunderstanding, I am not saying that since cars, waterfalls, and trees are not moral patients, we have moral carte blanche concerning our treatment of them. We certainly cannot do just anything to them. Although destroying any of these items would not affect them per se, their destruction most assuredly would affect creatures that do have welfares. Those who chop down a redwood willy-nilly, for example, are doing wrong, although they do not—because they cannot—do anything wrong to the redwood. They are destroying the homes, protection, and food sources for many creatures, as well as deeply offending the many of us who gain great pleasure from seeing such magnificent creations.

If we use the term *sentient* to describe those things with the capacity to feel pain and suffer, with the capacity to have their lives made better or worse off, then we can characterize moral patients as all and only those individuals who are sentient. All and only sentient creatures have welfares; all and only sentient beings care about what happens to them. From the moral perspective, in the last analysis, it is only with the sentient that we normal, adult human beings need concern ourselves. When we revisit the PGS, we can now see that we do wrong insofar as we negatively affect the well-being of innocent sentient creatures by causing them pain or suffering.

This way of looking at the matter may seem to ease our ethical burden or moral responsibility. After all, we ultimately need to worry only about the effect our behavior has on the sentient. Fair enough. But we must understand that the domain of moral patients extends far beyond the borders of our species. We must realize, in other words, that our moral community includes many nonhuman terrestrial animals and may well include many extraterrestrials as well. To realize that our moral responsibilities and obligations are not restricted to humans is the first step in a moral revolution whose scope and significance should, and hopefully will, eclipse those of all previous generations.[7]

# CHAPTER TWO

# THE VALUE OF HUMANS
# AND THE VALUE OF ANIMALS

## Instrumental and Inherent Value

The argument up to this point suggests that, by virtue of their sentience, many nonhuman animals ought to be included in the moral community. They have welfares and so can be made better and worse off. They are also innocent and, as I will later document, are subject to enormous intentional infliction of gratuitous pain and suffering. Thus, it is morally incumbent on us to initiate widespread revisions in the ways we live our lives.

To put it mildly, attempts to broaden the moral arena to include nonhuman animals have not been enthusiastically received. One common line of resistance rests on the idea that human beings have a special kind of *value* that nonhuman animals lack. Advocates of this strategy generally admit that many animals do have welfares, and so can be made better and worse off, but argue that the possession of sentience is not sufficient for inclusion in the moral community. Many of these advocates deny the PGS by claiming that the disparity between human and animal value is so great that it makes the *gratuitous* infliction of pain and suffering all but impossible. Indeed, even the notion of disparity is misleading, since it suggests that the value of humans and that of animals are comparable, whereas they are not. Rather, they differ fundamentally, not just in degree. Proponents of this view reject Descartes's categorization of animals as insentient, complicated machines, yet they ascribe a special type of value to humans, effectively denying any significance to the feelings of nonhuman animals.

To enter this dialogue I must introduce the notion of *instrumental* value. This familiar sort of value or worth refers to the value something possesses as an instrument or means for accomplishing some task or goal. The greater help it provides in meeting a particular task, the greater the object's instrumental value to its employer. Money is a paradigmatic example of something with instrumental value. It serves as a means to gather items that are useful to us, such as food, shelter, and clothing. A hoe, too, has instrumental value. Its value is almost solely a function of what it can do for us. Hoes facilitate digging into the earth, expediting our planting. There is nothing novel or mysterious about the idea of instrumental value. It is simply the garden-variety kind of value we ordinarily mean when we speak of certain items as having value or worth.

Since instrumental value is a functional notion—the instrumental value of an item is determined by how well it functions as a means toward reaching our goals and aims—items with merely instrumental value are interchangeable. The green dollar bills with pictures of dead presidents have instrumental value only insofar as they can be used in commerce. From this perspective, one five-dollar bill is exactly as good as any other. A ten-dollar bill has more instrumental value than a five-dollar bill because it can do more for us; it buys us more food and better shelter. Conversely, a one-dollar bill has less instrumental value than a five; one-dollar bills lack the purchasing power of their five-dollar cousins. Moreover, we are largely indifferent as to whether coins or beads replace these green dollar bills. As long as the instrumental value is the same, the material vehicle matters little if at all.

Those who claim a special value for human beings emphasize its contrast with instrumental value. I will follow them by calling this special value "inherent value," a term reflecting the claim that this value inheres within (at least) human beings (i.e., is a matter of the nonrelational or intrinsic properties of human beings) and is independent of any service it may provide for others.

What are the characteristics of inherent value? This special value is not a functional notion, so that, unlike items with instrumental value, humans are irreplaceable or nonsubstitutable. Inherent value is not aggregative; one cannot add and subtract this value as one can with instrumental value. Moreover, this value is understood as identical for all human beings. The intelligent, rich, and successful have neither more nor less of this value than the unintelligent, poor, and unsuccessful. Inherent value, for humans at least, is a fully egalitarian type of value.

The consequences of having this value conform to many of our common beliefs about human beings. For example, we do not generally think that human beings are merely instrumentally valuable. Most of us do not conceive of one fruit picker as having more value—as a human being—than another because he can pick more fruit per hour. Nor do we think that a better pianist has more value—as a human being—than another, less talented musician.

Also, most of us claim to think of humans as irreplaceable. If the cotton picker or pianist dies, we comment that this is a loss to the world, one for which the birth of some other picker or pianist cannot compensate. More poignantly, consider your reaction if you were offered the trade of your mother for another woman who appears identical. They look precisely alike, their culinary skills do not differ discernibly, and they have identical intelligences and senses of humor. Suppose, even more fancifully, that they will care for and love you equally. I gather that none of us would entertain the thought of swapping our mothers with such clones and that anyone would feel a great personal loss knowing that his or her mother had died even if her doppelganger tried to fill the void.

It seems bizarre to quantify human values. It is not as if the slower fruit picker and the more talented pianist can be said to be more (or less) valuable than the faster picker and less talented pianist. At best we think of them all as having equal value, and so any comparison becomes trivial. Finally, relationships among humans do not seem to affect the value we impute to them. While we may think of our brother having more value to us than some stranger, we acknowledge that the stranger's brother would have more value to him than to us. *Sub species aeternitatis*—from a God's-eye perspective—we think that the two men have equal value as human beings.

These considerations are just the beginning of an argument for this special human value and not a demonstration of its existence. At best this discussion shows that there are grounds, in the ordinary ways we conceive of human beings, for thinking of humans as bearing a particular value. Unfortunately, our ordinary conceptions of things have hardly proved infallible. At certain times in our past, virtually everyone thought the creation of a heavier-than-air flying machine was impossible and that no human could run a mile under four minutes. Creationism, not Darwinian evolution, was the accepted explanatory hypothesis of humankind's origin. I trust that we now find that all but the last claim clearly false, and many of us take issue with our predecessors' view of our origins. The moral is that we cannot rest content with our belief that humans have special value merely because the idea is deeply entrenched in our common ways of thinking about ourselves and our relationship with the world.

The claim that humans have inherent value is not an empirical claim. Neither its supporters nor its detractors believe that the issue can be settled by our sight, hearing, or touch. Rather, the debate can be resolved only on the basis of arguments. Only if there are good reasons for accepting the existence of this special value should we countenance it as part of our ontology.

For my purposes, such inherent value is important because it purportedly makes us morally superior to nonhuman animals. Because we possess inherent value, our lives are said to be more important than the lives of animals. Diminution of human pain and suffering takes precedence over lessening the pain and suffering of animals, and the enhancement of the pleasure and enjoyment of humans has priority over increasing that of animals. Possessing inherent value makes a human death a greater loss than the death of an animal, and so, all else being equal, the maintenance of a human life has priority over that of an animal's. In sum, the possession of inherent value gives us a superior moral status that justifies treating our welfare preferentially.

Certain examples can clarify this idea of superior moral status. Suppose that a human and a chimpanzee have recently broken their arms. The fractures are equally serious, and the two experience the same sort and amount of pain. The chimpanzee is harmed to the same degree that the human is. (Undoubtedly these qualities are difficult to compare, but the intelligibility of such a comparison is all that is required to give content to the notion of superior moral status.) Suppose, further, that they are both rushed to the hospital and arrive at the emergency room simultaneously. Finally, imagine that the only available physician can treat both human and nonhuman animals.

The advocate of a special human value, whom I will call the "inherentist," believes that the physician ought to treat the human before treating the chimpanzee. This is not the relatively tame position that the physician may choose which patient to treat first or that he or she may treat one before the other. Rather, the inherentist makes a stronger claim, namely, that the physician has a moral responsibility or obligation to treat the human prior to treating the chimpanzee. The human deserves better care in virtue of having this special sort of value lacked by the chimpanzee.

Once again, the inherentist's concept of human moral superiority resonates with most persons' commonsense views. A poll would undoubtedly show that most believe the physician to have a moral obligation to aid the human before the chimpanzee and that this priority is a function of the unique value that the human has. Generally people endorse the idea that the pains and pleasures of humans should count more heavily in our moral deliberations than those of nonhuman animals. Perhaps in cases where there is a great disparity in pain or suffering—where, for example, the chimpanzee is experiencing a heart attack and the human a hangnail—the animal ought to be treated first. Still, whenever the suffering for both is within the same quite broad boundaries, the human deserves priority.

If the alleged superiority of humans is to be explained by the unique possession of inherent value, certain tests must be passed. It must be shown that all and only humans have this sort of value. After all, if animals have this value as well, then the factor that supposedly distinguishes human from nonhuman lives cannot confer privilege on humans. And if some humans lack this value, then presumably there are occasions when these persons do not merit preferential treatment over animals.

Alternatively, the inherentist might allow that both animals and humans have inherent value (and so retract the supposition that animals lack this sort of value) but base the hierarchy on the amount of this value. So, were any human to have more inherent value than any animal, the fact that animals have this value would not in itself vitiate the distinction. But this reduces to verbal haggling. We can call the minimum amount of inherent value necessary to confer moral superiority "maxi-inherent value." We can then demand the inherentists to show that all and only humans have maxi-inherent value. Better we forgo the ugly and potentially confusing language and phrase the problem in the more comfortable idiom.

Inherentists also need to explain the constitution of inherent value and establish that this makes its possessor worthy of preferential treatment. To clarify this demand, assume that all and only human beings have fingernails. This property, then, can be used to demarcate human from all nonhuman animals. But certainly we would find it farcical if the inherentist went on to say that this differentiating attribute justifies giving humans special care and treatment. Inherentists must show that what they claim to constitute this special value really does have the significance they place on it. They must demonstrate not just that all and only humans possess the property but also that this quality can bear the heavy burden they place on it. This latter point is easily overlooked. We must not forget that this special value is reportedly sufficient to decide major, even life-and-death decisions. Thus, we need not only a morally relevant property unique to humans but also a property potent enough to justify treating humans and animals in drastically different ways.

The importance of this investigation can scarcely be exaggerated. We eat, hunt, and experiment on animals without their consent, but we never treat humans in these ways. We wear the skins of animals and use them purely as means for recreational purposes. We do not act thus toward human beings. When asked to justify this difference, almost everyone will reply that human life and well-being are far more significant than the lives and welfares of animals. The difference between animals and humans is one of kind and not degree, so that we are permitted to treat animals differently than we treat humans. But is this difference in behavior is justified? Do certain qualities unique to human beings warrant our disparate practices toward humans and animals?

## The Secular Quest for Moral Uniqueness

The leading candidate for inherent value no doubt comes from the Western religious heritage. By virtue of its historical significance alone, the contribution from the Judeo-Christian tradition deserves singular attention. I hope to give the theological response the careful and full discussion it merits. First, however, I should investigate the leading secular candidates. Are there, then, any secular or natural properties that are shared by all and only human animals and that can account for the special regard with which we think of and treat human beings?

Unquestionably, the secular candidate that has garnered the most support is rationality. The lineage of this suggestion begins almost 2,400 years ago with Aristotle, who defined humans as rational animals. For Aristotle, definitions of species are best given in terms of genus and difference. In the present case, the species human is defined in terms of the genus animal and the difference of rationality. Aristotle's definition thus manifests his belief that humankind is distinguished from the rest of the animals by rationality. Our ability to reason makes us special. According to Aristotle, rationality is the essence of humankind, where essence is to be understood as those essential or necessary qualities that are unique to humans.

The belief that rationality grounds inherent value remains prevalent, but a little reflection shows that rationality cannot do this. Fortunately we need not haggle over an acceptable definition of rationality to recognize that not all human beings are rational. The most obvious examples of such people are anencephalics. These tragically stricken humans are born absent a brain except for its stem. They simply lack the biological necessities for having any thoughts at all. Fortunately, they usually live no more than a day or two. There is no doubt that these individuals are human beings; their human parentage is not up for debate. We thus have an incontestable example of humans incapable of thought, and so rationality cannot serve as a satisfactory account of inherent value, since it is not present in all humans.

Other humans, too, are either largely or wholly nonrational. Severely retarded, senile, and brain-damaged humans form a large and tragic part of this sector of the human population. Victims of Alzheimer's disease, especially when the illness has progressed to an advanced stage, constitute perhaps the fastest-growing segment of these unfortunate humans.

Conversely, advances in science have confirmed that many animals are capable of reasoning. The great apes (which include humans) clearly can reason, as their complex social interactions and general behavior show. Their ability to use tools and communicate in American Sign Language should convince any open-minded person that chimps and orangutans think. Many scientists place ape intelligence at least on a par with a toddler's and believe these primates have an IQ equivalent to 60 or above. Indeed, although this point is more contentious, many researchers maintain that some nonhuman primates create works of art. Virtually anyone with a dog or cat will assure a skeptic that his or her animal thinks and will be able to recall scores of incidents where the animal's behavior is best explained by making this assumption. It is obvious to anyone who has spent much time with companion dogs and cats that they are rational creatures. They learn the location of their food bowls, remember the approximate times for their walks to the park, and recognize some people as friends and others as enemies.

Similar assurance comes from those familiar with dolphins, pigs, horses, cows, and chickens. In fact, it is likely that at least all (normal) mammals and many birds are capable of some reasoning, a speculation that accords well with Darwinian evolutionary theory. Moreover, at least some of these have better reasoning powers than do some human victims of the horrible afflictions already adumbrated.

The Aristotelian apologist faces other challenges. For the sake of discussion, assume what seems plainly false—namely, that all and only humans are rational. We still need proof that this property is morally relevant, that its possession makes one's life morally worthy of superior attention and treatment.

Rationality has obvious instrumental value. Reasoning ability has worth insofar as it allows us to satisfy aims that range from getting our next meal to building a suspension bridge. It is a rare situation where having the ability to reason cannot aid its possessor attain some goal or satisfy some desire. Nevertheless, this should not incline us to believe that the possession of rationality confers inherent value.

To see this, consider Bob and Sally, who simultaneously arrive at a hospital bearing similar wounds and suffering similar pain. By fiat we make Bob a victim of advanced senility and Sally a woman of average intellectual abilities. Other than this difference, Bob and Sally are relevantly identical. The question then becomes whether Sally deserves priority. If we cannot attend to both at the same time, does having greater rationality in and of itself make Sally's welfare more valuable than Bob's and so morally obligate us to tend to her interests prior to his?

Surely Sally's intellectual superiority does not mean that her life has greater value. Consider how strange—and unfair—it would be were the hospital staff to consider relative intelligence as a factor in attending to suffering patients. Surely if two people walked into a hospital at the same time with equally severe injuries, a person who has a 140 IQ ought not—for that reason alone—have his injury treated before someone with an IQ of 100. And if this is so, then it does not matter whether the lower IQ is negligible. Anyone who agrees must thus believe that reasoning power has no connection with the significance we place on one's welfare.

This conclusion harmonizes with the inherentist tenet that all humans are equally valuable as human beings. In fact, unless the inherentist is willing to forgo this characteristic, rationality will inevitably fail as the distinctive quality that morally differentiates humans from animals. Since it is inarguable that humans have different degrees of rationality, were rationality to constitute the special value imputed to humans, not all humans would be equally valuable. This tension in the inherentist position makes it impossible to maintain that all humans are equally valuable as humans and that rationality is what accounts for this fact.

The second-most popular candidate for humankind's unique status requires returning to Descartes. Recall that Descartes viewed animals as nothing more than automatons, relatively complex machines incapable of any consciousness whatsoever. The sounds animals emit when hit or cut are not indications of suffering. Rather, they are akin to the sounds of machines when their gears are impeded. As the clock has no thoughts, sensations, or feelings, neither do cats, dogs, and all other nonhuman animals. The Cartesian sign of consciousness is linguistic ability. While we may be tempted to dismiss these conclusions as consequences of an unsophisticated science, the rationale behind Descartes's view has exhibited staying power. The ability to use language is the Cartesian candidate for inherent value.

Apes such as Washoe and Koko have learned sign language, which seems to answer the suggestion that all animals lack linguistic ability. A dissenter, however, may present a somewhat technical sense of language that precludes classifying such ability as linguistic ability. In the ordinary sense of the term, where language is understood as a form of intentional communication using signs, there is little doubt that not only do rather specially trained apes such as Washoe and Koko qualify, but animals far lower down on the phylogenetic ladder, such as birds and bees, also pass the test. Still, we need not cavil, for it is clear that not all humans have linguistic ability. Again, we need only remind ourselves of the "marginal" humans who suffer from severe mental disabilities. In addition, some young infants not only do not communicate but also lack the capability of communication. Some unfortunate infants are born with neurological disorders that will prevent them from ever learning even the most rudimentary language.

Although linguistic ability clearly has instrumental worth, the notion that it provides inherent value is far from obvious. Consider Phil and Jane, whose only relevant difference is that Jane lacks linguistic ability. We do not believe it right to give priority to alleviating Phil's pain and suffering. We would think it odious if a hospital based its treatment schedule of equally ill patients on communicative ability. It approaches the surreal to think that, on average, we should alleviate the pain of English professors before that of mechanics and cab drivers. Decreasing the patient's linguistic ability dramatically, even to the point where communication is nonexistent, should not yield a different verdict.

Obviously, I cannot canvass all the candidates for inherent value. I am confident, however, that virtually all other candidates can be approached in a similar manner. Either not all humans have the proffered attribute, or some nonhuman animals do. In fact, usually both are the case. In addition, it is usually doubtful whether the property in question suffices to enhance the relative importance of the agent's welfare.

Some emphasis should be given specifically to the idea that some animals have a proposed morally relevant quality to an equal if not greater degree than do some human beings. This strategy, often referred to as the "marginal-case argument," turns on unfortunate humans, including those suffering from debilitating conditions such as Alzheimer's disease and advanced senility, who do not reach the competence of some animals regarding any plausible natural candidate for conferring inherent value. Therefore, if one believes that the possession of this property, at least some degree of it, suffices for inherent value, then many nonhuman animals have this special worth. In practical terms, this would mean that if we think it morally repellent to eat, skin, hunt, or experiment on marginal human beings—as presumably we do—it is likewise wrong to practice these activities on many animals.

This is not the venue to create a full-blown defense of the marginal-case argument, but one common misconception requires address.[1] Some people object to the strategy on the grounds that it is illicit to use marginal human beings, who constitute a relatively small segment of the human population, to draw conclusions about all humans. Virtually all humans are more rational and have greater linguistic ability than all animals, they say, and so the case for humans having special value is far more compelling than might be gleaned from allusions to marginal humans.

This objection is misdirected. Those who use the marginal-case argument freely admit that most humans are more intelligent and have better language skills than do nonhuman animals. The point of the argument is to demonstrate that any natural candidate for conferring inherent value will not be species specific. If we continue to tether ourselves to any of these properties, then from a logical point of view, our treatment of marginal humans and animals ought to be the same. Either we should treat both of them as having merely instrumental value and so think of them as replaceable commodities whose value resides only in their servicing others, or we should treat both marginal humans and animals as having inherent value and so commanding the respect that this value is said to give its owner. Undoubtedly few would choose the first option. It is a rare person who thinks it morally permissible to eat, hunt, or experiment on his or her senile mother. It is morally incumbent, then, that we behave toward animals as we should behave to any creature with inherent value.

One candidate cannot be routinely managed and is therefore worthy of separate discussion. Some have claimed that the property of *being human* is what confers inherent value on human beings. Obviously, humans uniquely have this property. In this case, unlike those where the proposed candidate is rationality or linguistic ability, no human can lack it and no nonhuman animal can have it. One who proposes this suggestion is a *speciesist*. Speciesists claim that species is a morally relevant category. Although strictly speaking one may be a speciesist without granting the human species moral priority, this position is never advanced. In practice, a speciesist believes that merely being a member of the human species (*Homo sapiens*) gives human beings a special value that warrants considering their well-being to be categorically different from and superior to that of all other animals.

A suspicious air surrounds this proposal. We are searching for those attributes endemic to human beings that bestow a special moral status on them. We are told that the property we seek is the property of being a human being. What makes humans special is that they are human. At first blush this does not seem like much of an answer. In trying to discover what it is about humans that makes them special, we are told that it is their membership in the human species. This appears to beg the question.

Perhaps we are being too rash. The speciesist may remind us that this proposal, just as those of rationality and linguistic ability, is offered as a *fundamental* mark of moral demarcation. If there were more fundamental facts about humans that made rationality or linguistic ability a morally relevant criterion, then there should be no impediment in explaining moral boundaries in terms of these more basic facts. Were there more basic facts, rationality and linguistic ability would need to be understood merely as intermediaries between the true basis for human moral superiority and the privileged position of humans. But fundamental features have no such underlying aspects. Thus, it would be unfair to require the advocate of rationality or lin-

guistic ability to identify more basic human properties, and it is equally unfair to demand this of the speciesist.

This speciesist response is well taken. We should not dismiss the speciesist
account simply because there are no further reasons to explain why species
has this moral significance. However, a serious problem with the proposal
does arise when we recognize that speciesism precisely parallels racism and
sexism.

A prowhite racist claims that membership in the white race confers moral
priority; a promale sexist, that membership in the male sex confers privilege. Prohuman speciesists claim that membership in the human species confers moral privilege. These positions appear precisely analogous. For those
of us who are adamantly opposed to racism and sexism, parity of reason
compels us to dissociate ourselves from speciesism.

The analogy becomes even more powerful when we recognize that the
course of action employed by the speciesist is open to the racist and sexist.
The racist may claim that it is a fundamental fact—and therefore not susceptible to explanation—that having white skin confers moral privilege. In
a similar vein, the sexist can claim that membership in the male sex is the
bedrock fact that grants moral privilege to its fortunate members. This tactic makes it illegitimate to ask the obvious question: why does membership
in the white race or the male sex confer moral priority? The racist and sexist can answer with equanimity that there is no more basic reason that these
characteristics have the power they have. It is just a basic fact. A question
of consistency then arises: how can the speciesist justify an abhorrence to
racism and sexism while maintaining that species membership is the fundamental moral attribute that bestows inherent value on only human beings?

Bernard Williams, a contemporary British philosopher, has suggested that
the analogy of speciesism to racism and sexism is illicit.[2] While agreeing that
concern for animals is an appropriate attitude for humans to cultivate, Williams emphasizes that our moral relations must derive from our ineliminable
human perspective of the world. Nonhuman animals, lacking this point of
view, necessarily stand in a moral relationship with us that differs from the
one we share among ourselves. Thus, the only moral question regarding animals is how we should treat them. Contrariwise, there is no ineliminable
white or male perspective, and so it is wrong to believe that the only moral
question is how to treat nonwhite or female humans. To think that this is
the only question is already to be prejudiced against them.

But this argument proves too much and too little. Not all humans have a
human perspective of the world; not all humans "know what it is like" to
be human. We need only recall the examples of the severely marginal. More-

over, it is far from obvious that only humans can have a human perspective. Surely extraterrestrials might have or learn to have a human point of view. Undoubtedly, all and only humans are humans, but this trivial truth entails nothing of moral import. At the same time, the claim that all and only humans have a human perspective is a substantive proposition from which certain truths about moral relationships *may* be derivable. Unfortunately for Williams but fortunately for the marginal, animals, and extraterrestrials, this proposition is not true.

Finally, it is worth exploring arguments designed to show that the speciesist criterion is arbitrary. The property of being human has been explicated in two ways. The dominating conception has been an Aristotelian one, where species is taken to express an individual's essential nature. This idea should not be summarily dismissed as a vestigial remnant of a long-discredited metaphysics. Consider, for example, the reasonable naturalistic proposal that an individual's species is constituted by its DNA structure. This structure is something knowable only by scientific investigation; only with the aid of biologists and geneticists do we have any hope of discovering the pattern of DNA that makes humans human. It is also plausible to believe that such a discovery yields the essence of an individual, that property necessary and sufficient to make an individual a token of a particular type. It would then be a biologically necessary, empirically discoverable truth that humans have a DNA pattern of a particular kind.

The other account of humanity takes its cue from relatively recent considerations about ontology in the philosophy of science. The central point concerns the status of so-called natural kinds—the "objects" of scientific laws. According to this line, there are no natural kinds in biology; that is, the categories of lions, tigers, and humans do not reflect how the external world is "really like." These groupings are just conventional devices based on individuals' superficial similarities that are pragmatically useful to us; there is nothing more to the group than its name (thus people espousing this view are sometimes called "nominalists"). Species' distinctions have no more metaphysical importance than do our imposed differentiations between sweet and tart oranges. We would do better to understand species as interbreeding populations subject to evolutionary change.

The speciesist who subscribes to the Aristotelian, biological account must explain why the piece of deoxyribonucleic acid essential to humanness has this extreme moral significance. One hopes that even the speciesist will find it bizarre to suggest that the presence of this molecule morally justifies preferential treatment. That the same type of consequence faces the racist and sexist may also have salutary effects. To be told that an extract of melanin or a Y chromosome morally justifies superior or inferior treatment may strike at least the undogmatic racist and sexist as cause for reconsideration.

The second account situates humanness in the fact that humans beget other humans. Although there is "nothing under the skin" that makes us alike, we humans are made a family via our ancestors and progeny. But of course, the same can be said for dogs, cats, lions, and chimpanzees. Perhaps it is unfair to ask the speciesist to explain why our procreative chains have moral import, but it is a different and seemingly fair question to ask why the same logic cannot be used to support canine or feline moral superiority. We are in the throes of a moral relativism; humans are justified in treating humans better than all other species, while dogs and cats have the same warrant concerning their conspecifics. We ought to treat our species with special concern, while other species ought to act similarly toward theirs. Again, the same question can be transferred to the areas of race and sex. Do we want to say that blacks owe it to their race to consider "their own" prior to whites and Hispanics? Should women show moral preference to females? How far do we extend this idea? For all I know, left-handedness is an inherited trait. Does Whitey Ford owe something to Bill Clinton that he may not realize? Where do a white, right-handed human male's obligations lie? Should he help a right-pawed albino male lion before coming to the aid of a black, left-handed human female? The litany of absurdities could continue indefinitely.

The fact that nominalists (unlike the essentialist Aristotelians) admit that species' distinctions do not carve nature "at its joints" makes for other intractable problems. What ought humans or chimpanzees do with offspring created from the genetic material of both? Are we to treat sterile humans less favorably than fertile ones? When biological techniques that were all but unimaginable in the times of Aristotle are conjoined with the biblical pressures exerted over the last two millennia, it is not surprising that species membership has been thought an immutable characteristic that captures the essential nature of every individual. Scientific advances throw this orthodoxy into grave doubt and give rise to the real possibility that we have been basing moral priorities on conventional and not natural distinctions.

Perhaps the speciesist will be moved by considering the imaginary scenario where we receive visitors from another galaxy. They don't look human, their DNA structure is quite different from ours, and they cannot reproduce with humans. After a period of time, clever linguists develop a means of communicating with these aliens. During this period of getting to know and speak to each other, we earthlings come to realize that these visitors are quite extraordinary. They are very much like us in that they endure physical and mental pain and distress. They become sad or depressed when their important desires are thwarted. They love their families enormously and would do almost anything to protect them and to ensure their future welfare. Still, they differ from us noticeably. They are far brighter than we are; have better language skills; and more important, are far kinder, wiser, more courageous, and more peace loving than we are. In fact, we are able to determine that they outstrip us in all the qualities that we hold dear and identify in the members of our species whom we esteem most highly.

There is no reason, other than chauvinism, to withhold from these visitors the moral status or standing that we attribute to members of our own species. Thinking ourselves to be morally privileged relative to these visitors seems purely arbitrary. Being human, then, seems to be insufficient to confer superior moral status vis-à-vis members of another species. Being human cannot have the moral significance that some have attributed to it.

Speciesists of a different stripe, however, base their claims on an interpretation of Judeo-Christian texts. They may accept the naturalistic arguments against speciesism but view religious truths as showing that human beings deserve superior care and treatment. It is to the religiously motivated speciesist that I now turn.

## The Religious Search for Moral Uniqueness

There is little doubt that the Bible has been an important source of differing attitudes toward human and nonhuman animals. Statements and parables found throughout the so-called Abrahamic scriptures suggest that humans have a special place in God's drama and that animals play a merely auxiliary role. In a way that parallels my characterization of the instrumental/inherent value distinction, human life is seen as unique and irreplaceable, while individual animal life is granted no importance in itself. Most scholars find this interpretation of biblical evidence obvious and ineluctable. It is this instrumentalist conception of animals that led the nineteenth-century German philosopher Arthur Schopenhauer to acerbically comment: "It is pretended that the beasts have no rights . . . , that our conduct in regard to them has nothing to do with morals, or (to speak in the language of their morality) that we have no duties towards 'animals': a doctrine revolting, gross, and barbarous, peculiar to the West, and which has its roots in Judaism."[3]

Western religion is more ambiguous than the dominant voices would have us believe. Still, before I entertain some challenges to the orthodox interpretation of the Bible in matters animal, I need to examine the scriptural bases for the traditional view.

## Dominion and the Image of God

The evidence for the uniqueness of humans begins early in Genesis, which offers the first expression of two foundational ideas of human superiority over nonhuman animals. The passage tells us that humans are given dominion over the rest of creation and that humankind, and humankind alone, is created in God's image.

> And God said: "Let us make man in our image, after our likeness; and let them have dominion over the fish in the sea, and over the fowl of the air, and over the cattle, and over all the earth, and over every creeping thing that creeps upon the earth." And God created man is His own image, in the image of God created He him; male and female created He them. And God blessed them; and God said unto them: "Be fruitful and multiply, and replenish the earth, and subdue it; and have dominion over the fish of the sea, and over the fowl of the air, and over every living thing that creeps upon the earth." (Gen. 1:26–28)

The dominion motif is repeated soon afterward when Noah and his children become the new progenitors of humankind: "And the fear of you and the dread of you shall be upon every beast of the earth, and upon every fowl of the air, and upon all who teem on the ground, and upon all the fishes of the sea: into your hand are they delivered" (Gen. 9:2).

There is no doubt that these passages bestow on humans a singularly significant position in the divine drama. Indeed, some scholars, including Isaac Abarbanel, have imputed great importance to the scriptural language that is used to introduce humankind into the world. When God creates the light, stars, and nonhuman animals, the introductory locution is "let there be . . ." But the announcement of humans utilizes the plural "let us," which in idiomatic Hebrew suggests deliberation and attention. Although we should probably not place too great a burden on this syntax, since the plural-pronoun locution is used to indicate things other than deliberation and attention (cf. Ezra 4:18), the text clearly grants humankind a type of superiority over the rest of God's creation. The real task is to elucidate the nature of this hierarchical relationship. In the context of these oft-quoted passages from Genesis, we need to know how best to understand what it means to be created in God's image and given dominion over the animals.

At the outset it is important to acknowledge that the Hebrew Bible is a historical document and can be accurately understood only by recognizing the times in which the text was inaugurated. If it was to be understood, accepted, and transmitted, it had to be presented in terms familiar to its original audience. This comprehension involved far more than just understanding the words, terms, and phrases; the text had to resonate with its audience deeply and fundamentally. The word of God, if it was to ground a new way of life, had to be particularly relevant to the concerns and hopes of a people at a particular time in their evolution.

This point should not be too contentious. Although it conflicts with a nonhistorical interpretation that allows no special significance to the fact that the original audience received the earliest parts of the Hebrew Bible close to six millennia ago, it is consistent with the generally held notion that the moral principles purveyed by the scriptures are timelessly applicable. There is no reason to deny the pervasive belief that the Ten Commandments, for example, are to be followed as scrupulously now as they were to be then; it is not as though they are now merely suggestions and not imperatives. Still, the fact that the Bible is a historical document serves as a caveat. We should be careful about reading and interpreting the work without paying careful attention to the climate of the times in which it was initially received.

The importance of historical context first comes into play when we recognize that invoking the "image of God" language was not an attempt to set humankind above the animal kingdom. Rather, it was a means to eradicate the distinction, so common in prebiblical times, between royalty and the populace. Kings and emperors were thought to be either descended from deities or capable of having direct access to the commands and desires of gods. This difference evaporates if all humankind is created in God's image. Very much like the Declaration of Independence, this scriptural passage declared all humans to be equal in an important way: no longer were some humans thought to be innately more worthy of divine dispensation than others.

Previously a few human beings, separated from the rest by their quasi-divine status, had merited riches, glory, and reverence, whereas the new dividing line separated all humans from the one true lord and savior. The passage was intended not to position humankind over the rest of the animal creation but rather to unify human society. We are now to understand that all humans share a special place in a divine plan and that they are all subservient to a unique God. This special status is introduced in the same passage—in fact, the same sentence—that introduces the notion of dominion. The contiguity of these two ideas makes it natural to believe that they are intimately related. We, alone of all the species, are given dominion over the rest of God's creation. But what does this amount to?

There are two major competing interpretations. On the traditional view, *dominion* can be seen as essentially synonymous to *domination*. This implies that animals exist merely to serve our human purposes. The domination articulation of dominion grants animals only instrumental value. If we have been granted the right to dominate animals, to all but unrestrictedly use our power over them, very little behavior will be ruled ethically out of bounds. We should exercise prudence for our own sakes, but we need not fear that any of our acts may violate divine commands. On this interpretation, to be created in God's image is essentially to be granted God's unlimited power, albeit in a restricted sphere. Unlike God, we lack the power to create the universe from nothing or make the stars rotate as they do, but we are given the divine gift to do with animals as we please. We have the right to make the lives of animals conform to our wishes.

The popularity of the domination interpretation can be traced to Aristotle, a mainstay of philosophically minded Jewish and Christian theologians, especially in the Middle Ages. Aristotle believed that nature forms a sort of hierarchy. Although Aristotle was not a true dualist—one who believes that there is an immaterial human soul working with a corporeal human body—we can employ "soul talk" to understand how this natural order is constituted. Aristotle believed that there are three kinds (stages or gradations) of soul. Plants, animals, and human beings all possess a nutritive, or vegetative, soul. This type of soul allows the organism to use food for energy and growth. Sensitive souls are reserved for nonhuman and human animals. These souls allow sentient creatures to perceive the world. The sensitive soul lets one see, hear, touch, smell, and taste. Finally, of the animals only humans have rational souls. This kind of soul permits its owner to think, contemplate, deliberate, and act freely in the world. Evidently, those with rational souls are of a higher order than those who have only the other kinds of soul or lack any kind of soul at all. Furthermore—and here I use the idiom of Aristotle's greatest medieval apologist, St. Thomas Aquinas—the imperfect is made for the use of the more nearly perfect. In virtue of our rational souls, we humans are the most nearly perfect beings who are not divine. The raison d'être of the nonhuman part of God's creation is effectively to serve us on our journey to salvation with our Creator.

Further, this ordering is natural—a reflection of God's desire to shape the world in a particular way—not a contrivance that humans invented to allow them to dominate and utilize everything else in the natural world. It is a divinely created natural order, one that is discernible to all who use their senses and reason about the world. Thus our superior position vis-à-vis animals is warranted by the source of all morality: God. Aquinas epitomizes this uncompromising instrumentalist view of animals when he tells us that "it matters not how man behaves toward animals because God has subjugated all things to man's power. By divine providence, animals are intended for man's use in the natural order and it is not wrong for man to make use of them by killing or in any way whatsoever."[4]

Even charity does not extend to irrational creatures, since "they have no fellowship in the rational life."[5] The only possible reason for compassionate behavior toward animals is that, in certain circumstances, it may have a salutary effect on human affairs. For Aquinas, writing in the spirit of Aristotle, nonhuman animals have no inherent value. To speak of humans having any (direct) duties or obligations to animals is simply silly.

The Apostle Paul's comment as to why we are enjoined not to muzzle an ox threshing corn provides the perfect Thomistic precedent. "Does God care for oxen?" he asks. "Of course not; the purpose of the law is altogether for our sakes" (1 Cor. 9:9–10). Augustine expresses a similar position when he interprets Jesus' sending swine to their deaths and cursing a fig tree that bore no fruit as showing that "to refrain from killing animals and destroying plants is the height of superstition."[6] Calvin refers to humankind as "lord of the world," adding that God gave Adam and his descendants dominion over animals so that "none of the conveniences and necessities of life may be wanting to men."[7] Luther reaches the same instrumentalist conception by a different route. We are to exercise power over animals principally for the admiration of God and a holy joy that is unknown to us in this corrupt state of nature. In this postdiluvian state animals are subjected to humans, just as humans are oppressed by tyrants, with absolute power over life and death. This relationship between human and animal is warranted because our tyranny is an extraordinary gift from God that reflects his favorable inclinations and friendship toward humankind.

These sentiments find a scientific mirror in Francis Bacon, who speaks of the rational element properly dominating and subjugating the emotional, passionate, and nonrational (i.e., animal) segments. In addition, the nineteenth-century Jesuit Thomas Rickaby endorses the Thomistic perspective by virtually reproducing St. Thomas's words: "We have no duties of charity nor duties of any kind to the lower animals, as neither to sticks and stones." Rationality, as usual, is the secular criterion of demarcation: "Brute beasts not having understanding and therefore not being persons, cannot have any rights."[8] There is, then, little doubt that all these thinkers subscribe to the domination interpretation of the "dominion passage" in Genesis.

This traditional Thomistic picture could not be more conducive to an extreme instrumentalist conception of animals. To those steeped in this tradition, questions about the morality of eating meat, wearing fur, or using animals for recreation, cosmetic testing, and scientific experimentation appear odious, if not blasphemous. Clement Markert, a biologist at Yale and elsewhere, recently seconded this understanding of animals when he described them as the raw materials of the laboratory, having no rights whatsoever;

according to Markert, anyone thinking that animals have any rights suffers a mental deficit.

The second interpretation understands dominion as stewardship. On this interpretation, we are not granted a power to rule the animals; rather, we are burdened with a responsibility to care for them. The fact that humans are blessed in being created in God's image makes us uniquely qualified to care for the rest of his creation. The stewardship interpretation compares our role toward animals to the role loving parents play regarding their children. As we conceive of children as having inherent value, we are to think of animals as having value in themselves as well. Whereas the domination interpretation glorifies power as the central aspect in which we are created in God's image, the stewardship interpretation emphasizes the intelligent, caring, and compassionate dispositions that we uniquely share—to a lesser degree—with a supreme being.

## Considerations for the Stewardship View

Evidence for the stewardship view begins with etymological considerations. The key Hebrew term *yirdu,* while not one that readily translates into English, has a root meaning of "leading about" rather than "dominating" or "ruling." This suggests that our divine charge is to guide, care for, or shepherd.

The literal and metaphorical senses of shepherding are always used in a laudatory manner. Moses is portrayed as catching a runaway sheep from his father-in-law Jethro's flock and carrying it back on his shoulders, not realizing that the sheep ran because of thirst. God rewards this compassion by promising Moses that he will tend to Israel, God's flock, as long as he lives. David is appropriate for kingship in part because of his sensitivity as a shepherd. Rebecca is deemed suitable for Isaac's wife not only because she gives Eliezer, Abraham's servant, water but also because she provides water for his camels (Gen. 24:11–20). Jacob is pictured as conscientiously caring for his flock, where this is meant to refer to both his cattle and children (Gen. 33:12–14). Jacob instructs his son Joseph to discover the welfare of the flock (Gen. 37:14). And Joseph, who joins Noah as the only two explicitly named *tsadiks* (righteous men) in the Bible, are so described because of their service to animals. Joseph helps animals in emergency conditions, including famine, and Noah is portrayed as being unable to sleep because he must continuously feed all the animals on the ark. Finally, God himself is portrayed as a shepherd in the justly famous Psalm 23.

Plausible interpretations of other passages early in Genesis support the stewardship view. While we are enjoined to subdue the earth, an act akin to dominating, we are allowed only dominion over the animals. This gives some reason for believing that our attitudes toward animals should not be assimilated to domination. God's strikingly similar interactions with humans and animals suggest a kinship that is antithetical to a domination relationship. Although there is no distinct divine blessing for land animals, there is one for the fishes and birds, which were created the day before God created Adam (Gen. 1:26). It seems most unlikely that the land animals are any less deserving of being blessed. The idea that part of God's creation—especially a blessed part of it—can be treated without care or concern seems disrespectful, if not blatantly inconsistent. Furthermore, the fact that humankind and land animals are created on the same day must be significant.

The many important elements common to both humankind and animals make the domination elucidation strained. God explicitly makes five covenants with the animals, including some with Noah and the animals (Gen. 9:8–10; Ezekiel 34:24–25). These covenants bind them into a community that is confirmed by many other significant biblical events. In addition to being created on the same day and being offered the same blessing (Gen. 1:22, 28), both humans and animals have their Sabbath days and years, when they are ordered to rest in emulation of their same Lord (Exod. 20:8–11, 23:12). And consider this telling passage in Ecclesiastes (3:19–20): "For the fate of the sons of men and fate of beasts is the same; as one dies so does the other. They all have the same breath (spirit) and man has no advantage over the beasts; for all is vanity. All go to one place; all are from dust, and all to dust again."

We should also think of animals and humans as sharing a bond simply because both were created by God. That animals and humans have the same source provides the rationale behind the kinder sentiments of St. Francis and St. John Chrysostom, both of whom emphasize the brotherhood between animals and humans and urge that, in virtue of this, we should show kindness and gentleness to animals. In fact, St. John goes so far as to ask that we demonstrate altruistic love for animals, suggesting that Christianity has the resources for a stance toward animals far more compassionate than the one usually attributed to it. Acting altruistically is acting for the sake of another rather than for one's own sake. St. John's thoughts thus support two claims. First, animals do have "sakes," that is, welfares that need to be taken into account when we act; second, animals should not be considered only instrumentally, as mere means whose reason for existence is to serve humankind.

The fact that animals and humans share the same divine source is reason to believe that they both have a similar sort of value. This theocentric theory of value, which situates value throughout God's creation simply because

God created it, poses a threat to those who believe humans have virtual carte blanche in their interactions with animals and the environment. To maintain their old and comfortable ways, some traditionalists suggest that the natural world is a product of creaturely and environmental generation and so deny that all value originates with God. This is an ineffective evasion. Even if we accept, for the sake of discussion, that God is not the (proximate) cause of the natural world, he is still required for sustaining it. There is no reason to believe that the objects in the world would continue to exist without God's continuous oversight and maintenance. Not only is there is no scriptural support for this natural view, but we should keep in mind the psalmist's reminder that animals as well as humans are dependent on God's providence for everything that happens to them.

Although some, such as Albert Schweitzer, have interpreted theocentricity as undermining any objective basis on which to differentiate our duties to all living things, including plants, there is theological support for limiting human obligations only to other humans and animals. Animals possess greater value than God's inanimate creation because God gave spirit only to human and nonhuman animals. The Hebrew, Greek, and Latin terms for spirit (*ruach, pneuma,* and *spiritus,* respectively) all mean breath as well, and the fact that only animals breathe has been imbued with great moral significance. The scriptural foundation is best found in Joel (2:28), where the beasts, suffering in a barren land, cry out to God, who responds by saying, "I will pour out my spirit on all flesh." And it is appropriate to remind ourselves that God has made a covenant with every creature of flesh and not with vegetables or rocks.

None of this contravenes the point that humans hold an exalted position in God's creation. Only we can fully appreciate and love what God does, and only we can knowingly cooperate with God to complete his divine plan. Cardinal Manning (a nineteenth-century archbishop of Westminster and vice-president of the Society for the Protection of Animals from Vivisection) argues not that we have direct duties toward animals but that we have obligations to God, their creator, to act with *eternal* mercy. In practice, however, there is little difference between the advice of Cardinal Manning and the suggestion that we need to treat animals as creatures with noninstrumental value. In either case vegetarianism, the abolition of fur wearing and hunting, and the eradication of animal experimentation would be called for. While St. Basil the Great, St. Isaac the Syrian, and St. John Chrysostom might have been more receptive than was Cardinal Manning to an inherent-value rationale behind these changes in lifestyle, all four would have urged us to faithfully follow divine dictate by being good stewards for all God's creation.

I have suggested that the major purpose of the image-of-God metaphor is to provide solidarity for all humans; all are equally created in God's image and so are potential subjects of divine dispensation. Investigating what constitutes this common human thread further buttresses the case for the stewardship interpretation. The best accounts of this metaphor assign to those created in God's image one of the following properties: (1) the capacity for eternal life; (2) the possession of a spiritual component (soul); (3) the capacity to act morally and immorally; (4) the capability of acting justly and mercifully; (5) the ability to act freely; (6) the capability of knowing, loving, praising, and worshiping the Creator; and (7) the capacity to act from and according to reason. Of course, these alternatives are not exclusive; indeed, some of them are mutually supporting. For example, many theologians and philosophers argue that only autonomous agents can act morally, so that condition 3 will guarantee condition 5. Having the capability to perform just and merciful acts, moreover, seems to require the more general capacity to act morally. Significantly, none of these usual explications of the image-of-God metaphor assigns a special role to power or force, a fact that will surprise no one familiar with the divine qualities stressed in the Hebrew Bible. The idea that power is central to divine action is a nineteenth-century invention. Suspicions that this addition is more politically than theologically motivated gain force from the recognition that identifying a dominating God with an all-powerful one is antithetical to Judaism.[9]

Consider first the claim that being created in God's image consists in participating in an eternal life. Accepting this conception of our unique status renders the domination interpretation especially ironic. However poor our earthly lives have been, however we have been ravaged by disease, poverty, and sadness, we will have the opportunity of spending eternity in blissful communion with God. According to the orthodox understanding, however, earthly existence is the only possible life for animals. Since they are not created in God's likeness, they cannot enjoy postmortem bliss. It would be egregiously despicable to exploit individuals who cannot look forward to a joyful life after their lives here end. If we alone have the opportunity for eternal life, it would speak well of us to make the limited earthly lives of other creatures as pleasant as possible.

To be sure, opinions regarding the possibility of animal salvation and redemption take various forms. The psalmists, Isaiah, and verses in Ecclesiastes speak approvingly of animal salvation. Support also comes from many Christian sources, in whose work allusions to an afterlife play a far more dominant role than they do in Judaism. Among these are Henry More, John Bradford, Samuel Clarke, Bishop Butler, Matthew Henry, John Wesley (the founder of Methodism), and Lord Shaftesbury. Perhaps most famously, we have St. John the Divine's prophetic vision pictured in the fourth and fifth chapters of Revelation, where he speaks of animals joining in a heavenly chorus. Bishop Butler believed that animals can be redeemed and expressed grave doubts about the scholastic tradition of making rationality a criterion for heavenly membership. Commenting on Augustine, who believed that animals lack "spiritual bodies," the resurrection of which was a requirement for salvation, Butler prudently cautions that we do not know the "latent capacities of brutes" and reminds us that "a great part of the human species go out of the present world before they come to the exercise of these (rational) capacities in any degree at all."[10] (Think of humans who die as infants.) Perhaps most remarkably, St. Paul, normally no friend to animal welfare, wrote a letter to the Christians of Rome expressing hope for the redemption of all nonhuman animals. Two more likely saintly apologists, Irenaeus and John of the Cross, also allow for redemption.

Conceiving our likeness with God in terms of ensoulment also makes the domination interpretation unfathomable. Essentially, the argument just adduced works here, too, since a major benefit of possessing a soul is that it grants its owner the possibility of entering into an eternal relationship with God. More generally, however, having a soul offers a superior quality of life—be it during our natural life span or beyond—our good fortune therein suggests that we should extend the greatest concern to those less fortunate.

If being created in God's image amounts to the ability to reason and deliberate about moral matters, we again have strong reason to adopt the stewardship account. Lacking the capability to perform moral or immoral actions, animals cannot do anything that deserves moral censure. They are moral innocents, not moral agents. It is therefore difficult to understand how any harm, injury, or suffering inflicted on an animal could be anything but gratuitous. This does not imply that there may not be appropriate occasions when wild or domestic animals need to be restrained and perhaps even put to death. There may be times when, because of disease or temperament, they pose a significant danger to either themselves or others. Still, the animal does not deserve punishment even on these rare occasions, for its inability to think and act morally precludes it from intentional wrongdoing. Consequently, under no circumstances should the animal be subjected to any more pain or suffering than that which is necessary to eradicate the danger it presents.

This parallels the way our legal system treats those humans who cannot distinguish right from wrong. The people who are labeled "legally insane" are not subject to the same sanctions as those who perform evil acts knowing them to be evil. Rather than imprison the legally insane, we send them to mental institutions, since punishment is inappropriate to those who truly have no sense of morality. These people are ill, not evil. Undoubtedly, distinguishing those who are amoral from those who are wicked is an inexact science, but this only bolsters the major point. If we agree that only humans have the capacity for moral reflection, then we should never punish animals for their actions. (The notion that our uniqueness resides in our ability to act justly and mercifully inherits these same considerations.)

We will reach a similar conclusion if we focus on the properties of free will, knowledge, and reason. A creature without freedom can do nothing other than what it does. Its movements and "actions" are no more its own than are the movements of a clock's hands. To blame an animal for its behavior, therefore, would be as senseless as blaming minute and hour hands for their movements. Moreover, if we conceive of animals as incapable of knowledge or reason, they cannot be held responsible for their inability to understand the difference between right and wrong. In this way, our treatment of an animal should parallel our treatment of a human who, in virtue of a brain lesion, cannot learn proper conduct. We do not believe that these unfortunate humans can be used instrumentally. Consider how you would feel if scientists experimented on humans who, in virtue of poor genes, were unable to reason anywhere nearly as well as average human beings. We all would condemn, I believe, the practice of experimentation on those humans who are legitimately classified as profoundly retarded or extremely senile. Once again, we generally believe that we have an obligation to extend special care and concern to the people who suffer from these intellectual disabilities.[11]

In the end, common sense prevails. Only a twisted logic could support the idea that we may treat an intellectually or spiritually inferior creature as a mere instrument. In fact, we should reach the opposite conclusion. It is toward these unfortunate individuals that our most serious and concerted efforts should be made. Reasonable scriptural interpretation confirms this result. It is only when we construe being created in God's image as a license to use power that we are disposed to the domination view of dominion. We should never forget that God's omnipotence is always tempered by justice and mercy, a fact that is continually reinforced in both Jewish and Christian scriptures. It is best that we think of our likeness to God as being constituted by these moral virtues.

### Biblical Expressions of Animals as Persons

The Hebrew Bible contains numerous examples suggesting that animals act with reason, free will, and moral responsibility. These qualities imply that animals have minds and deserve to be categorized at least as moral patients.

Defenders of the traditional religious view have two choices. They may suggest that all these portrayals of animals should be understood metaphorically and so do not entail that animals have moral status. Alternatively, they may suggest that the attributions are to be taken literally but that these qualities still fail to warrant including animals in the moral community. The latter alternative loses any attractiveness once we recall that these and similar properties have historically been used to argue for the inherent value of humans. The former alternative seems strained given the large number of examples and the function they play in the biblical narrative. To address this alternative, we need only to look at some salient instances of animals acting with qualities that we often associate solely with humans.

There would be no justice in condemning the serpent for its role in the Garden of Eden unless we conceive of the snake as acting freely and intentionally. Just as it would be farcical to condemn a boulder for crushing your car, it would be absurd to blame an unfree snake for its behavior. Like humans, animals are threatened if they touch Mount Sinai during God's revelation to the Israelites, yet verbally threatening an individual makes little sense if the individual threatened cannot think or reason. The litany of narratives that are intelligible only if animals are ascribed cognitive and affective abilities similar to humans often includes the ultimate punishment. The ox that gores and kills a human is stoned to death. In interspecies sex the members of both species are punished, with the animal rape victim being subject to even more punishment than the human rapist. Egyptian cattle are killed along with their owners (Exod. 9:6, 10, 25), the first-born cattle of Egypt are killed (Gen. 6:12), and Jeremiah condemns beasts to die with the defenders of Jerusalem (Jer. 21:6). The sharing of bloodguilt derives from an admonition in Genesis (9:5): "And surely your blood, and the blood of your lives will I require; at the hand of every beast will I require it." It is extremely difficult to understand how a totally just God can condone the deaths of these creatures if we do not attribute some capacity for free, deliberate, and intentional action to them.

Animals are given special roles and responsibilities that seem to require intelligence. Ravens are asked to feed Elijah; lions are sent to kill a rebellious prophet and new Samarian inhabitants. Cocks, fish, frogs, and sparrows are portrayed as praising God and, in *Perek Shira* (a section of some Jewish prayer books), pictured as competing for most devoted and pious. Sometimes the deliberate actions of animals are viewed as effective and decisive; one rabbi explains the defeat of the army of Sennacherib and deliverance of Jerusalem by claiming that prayers uttered by beasts caused the attackers to flee.

Animals are also described as having beneficial powers that humans either lack or have only partially. Isaiah contrasts Israel's failure to acknowledge God with a beast's unerring knowledge and recognition of its master (Isa. 1:3). Jeremiah extols birds' unerring homing instincts, which he contrasts to Israel's inability to follow in God's path (Jer. 8:7). We learn that animals can perceive spirits that humans cannot (Job 12:7–8) and that Balaam's ass can detect the presence of God although its master is oblivious (Num. 22:25).

## Reconciling the Stewardship View with History and Practice

A powerful objection to the idea that the scriptures conceive of animals as having inherent value derives from directives concerning vegetarianism and sacrifices. If Judeo-Christian religion serves as an imprimatur to the stewardship interpretation, it is difficult to understand how meat eating and animal sacrifices could be condoned. The task becomes more taxing when we review biblical passages that seem not merely to allow these practices but to encourage and even mandate them. These two practices seem to undermine the stewardship view, not the domination view. This poses a serious challenge to those who wish to argue that the orthodox scriptural interpretation of nonhuman animals ought to be revised.

VEGETARIANISM — If the Abrahamic religious heritage explicitly allows flesh eating, then how can it grant animals noninstrumental or inherent value? Nevertheless, it seems obvious that we have divine permission to eat meat: "Every moving thing that lives shall be food for you; as the green herb that I have given you all" (Gen. 9:3); "When the Lord will enlarge your border, as He has promised, and you will say: 'I will eat flesh' because your soul desires to eat flesh; you may eat flesh, after all the desire of your soul" (Deut. 12:20). These apparently unambiguous statements permitting rampant carnivorism need to be understood in context: "And God said: 'Behold, I have given you every herb yielding seed, which is upon the face of all the earth, and every tree, in which is the fruit of a tree yielding seed—to you it shall be food; and to every beast of the earth, and to every fowl of the air, and to every thing that creeps upon the earth, wherein there is a living soul, [I have given] every green herb for food'" (Gen. 1:29–30).

There is a change from a vegetarian edict in the ideal, Edenic state to permissible meat-eating in the postdiluvian state. What causes this drastic change from the time of Adam and Eve to the time after the Flood? Significantly, God permits humans to eat meat only after Noah's forty-day travail. Some scholars have suggested that the postdiluvian world contained no food other than animals, since all plant life had been destroyed. The permission to eat meat came from dire necessity. If this reason is accepted, are we still allowed to eat meat now that nonflesh foods have reappeared? The contemporary rabbi Abraham Isaac Kook, a leading scholar on Kabbalism and Hasidism, says that humans ought never to forget that meat eating was but a temporary concession.[12] He further speculates that the permission to eat meat was the only way to avoid the presumably worse fate of humans eating humans.

Another possible explanation is that Noah, having successfully fulfilled his divine charge to save God's animal creation, now becomes a partner with God in the preservation of species. But it is difficult to understand why such a partnership would dispose God to allow Noah and his descendants to eat the progeny of the very animals they indefatigably helped to preserve. Perhaps we are to understand this as a sort of reward that God conferred on Noah for his good work, permitting him and his children to enjoy the taste of meat. But why presume that Noah has such a taste? Anecdotal evidence has convinced many that children, far from having a taste for flesh, have a natural aversion to it. Why should Noah be any different? Furthermore, it would require a somewhat quirky personality to think of this as being a *reward* for his work. Having fed and looked after these animals for forty days and nights, he would naturally have developed strong bonds with them. Surely none but a depraved person could then, even with divine permission, eat those whom he has grown to know and care for.

Combining theological speculation with health claims, Maimonides suggests that humans were weakened after the Flood, so that God permitted them to eat meat to regain their strength. Meat, along with vegetables, become the natural food of humankind. The rabbis Nachmanides, Yochanan, and the Hida, who echo Maimonides' sentiments, are instrumentalists regarding animals' value. Still, even they express reservations. These three Talmudic scholars explicitly add that meat is solely a requirement for keeping up one's strength and that God does not permit its consumption for pleasure. Moreover, all four suggest that we should partake only rarely, with Maimonides going so far as to describe those who eat in excess as "scoundrels with a Torah license."[13]

The scriptures often associate meat with gluttony, self-indulgence, and disaster, perhaps most notoriously at Kibroth-hattaavah, the wilderness site where the Israelites rose in rebellion because of a lack of meat and were subsequently punished. Of course, people can maintain their strength and live healthy lives without eating meat, and so *any* eating of meat can be deemed excessive or unnecessary. Once this is realized, Maimonides' calling for pity and mercy to all living creatures "except when necessity demands the contrary" becomes especially poignant. The monastic St. Benedict echoes the same idea when he tells us that only the weak should eat the flesh of four-footed animals. The idea is given contemporary expression by the moral philosopher Stephen Clark, who uncompromisingly says that "eating animals is gluttony. Those who still eat flesh when they can do otherwise have no claim to be serious moralists."[14]

In fact, not only are meat and dairy products inessential to good health; they tend to damage it. They are the sole dietary sources of cholesterol, the primary cause of atherosclerosis. Furthermore, it has been proven that those who eat no meat have far less incidence of various forms of cancer, heart disease, and digestive-tract disorders. Of course, this is not meant to imply that earlier Jews were not warranted in believing that meat is the sole dietary source of strength. After all, it is only within the last several decades that science has overturned this dogma. The point, rather, is that the aforementioned rabbis might have adopted a less instrumental approach toward animals had their dietary knowledge been greater.

Another explanation for this change of divine plan involves the speculation that God had to acknowledge human nature to be inevitably corrupt and that the newly given freedom to eat meat is a concession to this unfortunate fact. God has become resigned to the fact that creatures with free will inevitably commit evil and act against his original precepts. This is the price to be paid for giving individuals the freedom to choose and act, a freedom that is part and parcel of humanity's special status of being created in God's image.

There are two lines of response. First, note that, although condoning meat eating, this interpretation hardly views God as encouraging it. On the contrary, the best way to lead one's life would still to maintain vegetarianism or something close to it. Eating meat does not conform to God's original intention, and resorting to carnivorism merely accentuates an unattractive part of human nature. Rabbi Kook reminds us that the merciful God of Israel would never decree that humankind's survival should be eternally contingent on butchering animals. Slaughtering animals appears inconsistent with the God-given deep feelings of kinship with and compassion for all forms of life.

The passage in Deuteronomy (12:20) also suggests that God does not look approvingly at carnivorism. Here the permission is predicated on our desire for flesh, a point that would need no mention unless this desire held a negative connotation, since we give permission for an action only when there is a prima facie reason to proscribe it.

The second, stronger response is the observation that carnivorism is not inevitable. Millions of vegetarians attest to this fact. We may grant that our free will ineluctably causes us to do some evil but deny that eating animals must be part of it. There is no reason to believe that the inevitability of evil acts in general justifies any particular evil act. This reasoning would subvert morality altogether.

Rabbi Kook's speculative comparison of murdering animals and humans should not be summarily dismissed as gross overstatement. He predicts that someday we humans will look back at our carnivorous past with great shame and remorse, for we will view the eating of animals as we now view the eating of humans.[15] It is fascinating to see this point expressed some four hundred years earlier by Leonardo da Vinci in his *Notes:* "I have from an early age abjured the use of meat, and the time will come when men such as I will look upon the murder of animals as they now look upon the murder of men."[16]

A close reading of Genesis 9:3 reveals that it does not explicitly give us permission to raise or slaughter animals for food. This is important, since the ethical motivation for vegetarianism rests almost exclusively on the idea that it is wrong to harm or kill another sentient creature for mere carnal pleasure. Few ethical vegetarians would object to eating flesh if the animal lived unconfined, pleasant lives and died natural deaths. (Admittedly, some may find this practice to be disrespectful of the animal's life or likely to result in the harm and killing that they deplore.) Thus, it is not the eating of meat itself that causes the ethical problem with Genesis 9:3; rather, it is the natural inference that God is permitting us to slaughter these beasts for food.

Admittedly, the Torah later reports a prohibition against eating animals who die naturally or from wild animal attacks. Some may thus conclude that slaughtering animals is permissible, for although Genesis 9:3 permits only eating animals, eating them requires slaughtering them. In practice, then, God's permission to eat meat carries with it the permission to slaughter the animals who are its source.

But it is incongruous that an all-knowing, all-powerful, and all-good God would create sentient creatures whose major raison d'être is to be fodder for another segment of God's creation. This difficulty does not extend to plant life, which lacks the capacity to experience pain and pleasure. Unlike cows, chickens, and lambs, plants are incapable of enjoyment or suffering. Having no interior life, they care about nothing, and so killing and eating them does not raise any problems with God's omnibenevolence. We are left with a conundrum regarding God's creation of sentient food animals. Surely, given his omniscience and omnipotence, he could have made some creatures with the texture and taste of chickens, cows, and lamb but without any experiential life. Alternatively, God could have created plants with the taste, texture, and nutritive value of meat. In either case the amount of pain and suffering in the world would have been greatly reduced. If this line of thought is right-headed, it presents a puzzle that survives an explanation of the disparity between the earlier and later passages in Genesis. We also need to explain why Genesis 9:3 forms part of the creation narrative in the first place. Even if God permits the eating of flesh as a concession to humankind's fallen nature, why create innocent, sentient creatures who suffer in virtue of our moral weakness? We have an enigma that calls for an ingenious response.

The Hasidic scholar Shneur Zalman of Lyady and the Kabbalist Sherira Gaon offer a mystical suggestion to those who wish to reconcile Genesis 9:3 with attributing intrinsic value to animals. They deny what I have taken as self-evident, namely, that the death of an animal constitutes a harm for it. These Jewish mystics believed that if an animal is slaughtered and then consumed by a righteous man either in performing a good deed or gaining the strength to perform a good deed, the animal will be transformed into a "higher being," one that better serves its divine purpose. The theory's apologists differ as to the mechanism for this transformation. For some, notably the apologists of Isaac Luria and his version of Hasidism, the animal's soul can migrate to another body (even, on occasion, an inanimate body), giving it its only chance for an elevated status. This idea harmonizes well with attributing intrinsic value to animals. It is for the sake of the animal and not for our human benefit that we eat it.

A different tactic is used by those who believe that in eating meat we return sparks of holiness that were trapped in material things during Creation. It is not transparent exactly who or what enjoys the benefit of the returning sparks, but regardless, these Kabbalist speculations cannot be used to vindicate meat eating today. The Kabbalist rabbi Yonassan Gershon says that all the holy sparks have long since been returned. With trapped particles of holiness no longer awaiting release, Rabbi Gershon suggests that vegetarianism should now be practiced.

Admittedly, these latter two responses are not mainstream. This is to be expected. Since orthodox scriptural interpretation accepts an instrumentalist interpretation of animals' value, it should come as no surprise that these serious responses are relegated to the religion's "fringe" elements. This derision, although unfair, is understandable. Traditionalists cannot avail themselves of the migration response since they do not accept the phenomenon of transmigration of souls. Indeed, the very notion of a nonhuman animal's having a soul is typically (but not universally) denied in Judaism. More basically, Judaism makes no clear ontological distinction between soul and body. The idea that the soul is our spiritual component and that the body is the corporeal or material component becomes religiously significant with the advent of Christianity.

The righteousness response, not based on any ontological distinction between soul and body, bypasses this traditionalist objection but must explain why a cow or chicken, no longer with an individual consciousness, is really better off by being consumed. It is sensible to claim that the animal has (involuntarily) sacrificed itself for the good of a greater being, but this is a far cry from showing that the slaughtered animal itself is made better off through being consumed by a righteous man. I would not consider it a personal benefit if I were killed and turned into compost that was used to grow plants from which a person, far more righteous than myself, sustained himself. I suppose that some people might so offer themselves, and in appropriate circumstances such self-sacrifice is no doubt admirable, but this does nothing to offset the commonsense belief that, all things being equal, the death of a creature is bad for the creature itself.

Regardless of the ultimate theological and logical viability of these quasi-mystical ideas, they all attempt to reconcile carnivorism with a noninstrumental account of animals' value. On these Kabbalist-Hasidic renditions, the permission (and even injunction) to eat meat becomes a way of providing service to the animals rather than to us. The justification for Genesis 9:3, then, is that carnivorism is the only way that animals can fulfill their spiritual potential or reach their ultimate communion with God. By eating animals, and of course by inducing the least possible pain in bringing about their deaths, we are being good stewards. We are acting in ways that eventually promote the welfare of the animals we eat.

The mystical tradition should be applauded for its efforts to reconcile the apparent contradiction of an all-good and all-merciful God who permits killing and eating animals. For those with more traditional attitudes, I suggest that the reconciliation take the form of recognizing the relevant historical context. Fully cognizant that flesh eating is not required for life or even good health, we lack any legitimate basis for acting in accordance with the baser part of our nature. We should strive to return to the Garden, whose two original occupants feasted more than adequately on plant-based foods. This is the way that God would prefer us to behave. The *Sifre* admirably summarizes the point when it tells us that inasmuch as animals possess a certain degree of intelligence and consciousness, it is a waste of a divine gift to damage or destroy them.

INJUNCTIONS TO EAT MEAT — It is one thing to reconcile a vegetarian, noninstrumental, stewardship ethos with God's permission to eat meat; it is quite another to reconcile it with God's commands to eat meat. Meat is apparently mandated on special occasions such as the Sabbath and other holidays, most notably Passover. There is a historical rationale for focusing on meat. Meat was seen as a luxury or extravagance; the average Jew at the time the Second Temple was torn down (70 A.D.) ate meat only about twice a month. As previously mentioned, it was also viewed as a "health food," one that provided nutrition and strength to its consumer.

Some rabbis thought that these injunctions applied only to the times before the Temple was destroyed. Rabbis Yehudah and Yishmael suggest a compromise of sorts by saying that wine—another food that is biblically linked with joyous occasions—but not meat should be used for culinary celebration. They believed that the rabbis failed to sanction vegetarian laws because regulations imposed on a community that is not ready to accept them are fruitless. Once again, the failing results from our less than perfect natures holding sway in a relatively unsophisticated historical period.

A more radical idea supported by various scholars is that meat eating was not required even during the Temple period. Rabbi Nissim describes meat eating on holidays as *mitzvah min ha-muvchar,* that is, the best but not necessarily only way to satisfy a commandment. Rabbi Moshe Halevi Steinberg believes that meat eating is merely a symbolic way of expressing our enjoyment. According to Rabbi Steinberg, individual sensibilities should guide each person in celebrating the Sabbath. Keep in mind that the Judaic God desires his subjects to enjoy life. In fact, it is considered a sin (*averah*) not to enjoy appropriately pleasurable things. Since carnivorism was viewed by many as one of life's great pleasures, it is not surprising that the commandment contains a reference to meat. However, we should be careful not to conflate a contingent historical situation with the rationale behind the commandment.

Not everyone enjoys eating meat. For some people, the taste or texture of flesh produces nausea. For others, the knowledge that virtually all animals raised for slaughter suffer the deplorable conditions found in intensive farming is sufficient to dispel any desires for flesh.[17] It is difficult to imagine how anyone with a compassionate sensibility could enjoy eating the products of such cruel practices. It seems mistaken, therefore, to think that the commandment to enjoy pleasurable things implies an injunction to eat cows, chickens, and fish. Maimonides, like Steinberg, recognizes that the key concept here is rejoicing and that people rejoice in different ways; after all, children enjoy nuts and sweets whereas women enjoy clothing.

The *Shulchan Aruch,* the foundation of normative law for Jews today, does not insist on eating meat on *Yom Tov* (Sabbath and other holy days). This further supports the idea that we should not understand the injunctions to eat meat literally. It is merely an accidental historical fact that meat (and wine) symbolized good times. In our modern times the thought of what transpires to our food animals should be enough to defeat any gustatory pleasure we might otherwise have.

Even the consumption of the Paschal lamb on Passover can be forsworn. The Talmud explicitly tells us that boiled beet can be substituted for the meat, demonstrating that the mind of the believer, not the unthinking following of ritual, plays the pivotal role in the righteous or holy life. Passover is a joyous holiday celebrating the Jews' escape from their Egyptian slavemasters. The feast commemorates the Hebrews' freedom. The means of commemoration is of secondary importance.

One might argue that vegetarianism prevents its practitioners from fulfilling the many commandments (*mitzvot*) that deal with carnivorism. Vegetarians will bypass the good deeds that can be performed in the slaughter, preparation, and consumption of meat detailed so meticulously in Leviticus. But this objection comes with its own problems. One might argue that the stringent rules that deal with carnivorism are a not-too-subtle hint that meat eating would not occur in a perfect world. Moreover, divine regulation for an activity should not be read as condoning that activity—better to view them as making the best from a bad situation. It would certainly be absurd to believe that God endorses war and slavery (although an Alabama state senator recently suggested this latter point), despite the presence of biblical prescriptions for these activities. These injunctions are best conceived as reflecting God's acknowledgment that some evil inevitably results from the creation of autonomous creatures and that these practices are therefore better regulated than not.

Vegetarianism also has the benefit of making the violation of some commandments impossible. No longer need one be concerned about prohibitions regarding the mixed consumption of meat and dairy, eating nonkosher animals, or eating the blood and fat of animals. At the same time, many food-related *mitzvot* are still observable. The blessings said prior and subsequent to meat meals are identical to those said for soup and juice, and *mitzvot* for other food-oriented activities concerning Kiddush and the Passover seder would be unaffected.

Ultimately one observes laws of *kashruth* (dietary laws) to attain holiness, not to ensure health or hygiene. Given the *mitzvah* of taking care of our own health and our current state of knowledge, vegetarianism makes following *kashruth* easier yet not trivial. Baked goods and cheeses, for example, may not be kosher. Still, there is historical precedent of Jews turning to vegetarianism in an effort to maintain the dietary laws. Some Jewish priests at a trial in Rome ate only figs and nuts to avoid eating flesh that was used in idol worship. Some Maccabees, in flight from Syrians, ate only plant foods to avoid becoming "polluted." Rabbi Robert Gordis of the Jewish Theological Seminary crystallizes the point when he says that vegetarianism "offers an ideal mode for preserving the religious and ethical values which *kashrut* was designed to concretize in human life."[18]

According to believers, the immutable issues are religious values; the means of practicing and perpetuating these values can and inevitably do change. In this way, the increased knowledge and ethical sensitivity of the times affect morality. If we believed, as did some in previous centuries, that nonhuman animals are incapable of any sensations and emotions, then it would make no sense to be concerned about their well-being. They simply would not have any welfare, and one who tried to make their lives better would be foolish or mad. But now we know better. Science has shown us beyond any reasonable doubt what most of us accept as prosaic common sense. Most of the animals we eat are sentient. Judeo-Christian values are better preserved in a vegetarian ethos.

SACRIFICES — Leviticus details several injunctions that seem to require animal sacrifices. This poses yet another obvious challenge to the view that animals have value in and of themselves. Is there any way we can reconcile animal sacrifice with the proposal that we humans are divinely commanded to be stewards of inherently valuable creatures?

I begin by drawing some significant differences between biblically sanctioned sacrifices and others. First, human sacrifice was forbidden, a point gleaned from the fact that God did not permit Abraham to sacrifice his son Isaac. Second, there was no licentiousness involved in Jewish sacrifices. Third, there is no hint of magic or demonology in the service. Fourth, the scope of the practice's efficacy was quite limited. While sacrifices were required for those witnesses who failed to give testimony, for those who contacted impurities, for those who failed to fulfill vows, and for those who breached the trust of others (Lev. 5:1, 20–26), sacrificial atonement applied generally to unwitting sins. One could not knowingly and intentionally harm another and then clean one's moral slate by offering a sacrifice to God.

Considerations concerning sacrifice further support the idea that a vegetarian ethos is consistent with Judaism. Although the Bible commands sacrifices, it does not require eating meat. Rather, eating meat required a sacrificial ritual. Eating the dead animal was of secondary importance. Of primary significance was celebrating the glory and goodness of God. The blood, identified with life, was always returned to God, the life giver, as was the fatty or choicest parts of the animal. The carcass was salted and soaked in water several times, a process that tends to diminish the taste of the meat. No utensils, pots, or serving dishes that were used in the preparation of dairy foods were usable in the ritual. No milk or cream was permitted on the table during the meal, and one had to wait hours after eating meat before eating dairy. None of these restrictions is conducive to enjoying the meat meal.

Animal sacrifices were first and foremost religious rituals. Before the destruction of the Second Temple, the slaughters were performed only by the holiest men in the community and only at a specified area of the Temple. These Temple priests were under strict guidelines governing the slaughtering procedure. They were charged with looking after the health and cleanliness of the animal and causing it the least possible suffering.

Carnivorous animals were considered unfit for sacrifice. Some scholars interpret this restriction as implying that a double contamination attaches to anyone who eats something that has itself consumed meat. One might, then, interpret the permission to eat only grazing quadrupeds (hoofed feet being an indication of a grazing animal) as a nod toward vegetarianism (see Lev. 11:3–8; Deut. 14:4–8). There are additional limitations on eating other animals as well. Only fish with both fins and scales are permissible for food, and all insects except for some locusts are proscribed. Land creatures that either crawl on their bellies or move on many feet are prohibited, as are waterfowl and predatory fowl.

No universally accepted view explains the divine dictates regarding sacrifice. Judaic scriptures never formally explain the rationale behind sacrifice. Many scholars readily admit this but suggest that since sacrifice is an explicit divine command, no rationale is necessary. This response is unappealing. Effectively it "resolves" a problem by evading it or—what amounts to the same thing—consigns its solution to an incomprehensible mystery. One would hope, given Judaism's high regard for reason, that we can do better.

There are three prominent hypotheses.[19] Some, like Hallevi and S. R. Hirsch, accept the traditional symbolic interpretation that understands sacrifice to symbolize humankind's gratitude and devotion to God. Abraham's substitution of a ram for his son as sacrificial victim reflects this view. The juridical interpretation, favored by Nachmanides and Ibn Ezra, views sacrifice as a way of transferring guilt and sin from oneself onto another, innocent party. The rationalist approach espoused by Maimonides and Abarbanel sees sacrifice as a means of weaning an unsophisticated religious group from the primitive and wicked rites of false religions (see Lev. 17:7). Maimonides explains God's decision to allow sacrifices by claiming that a command to discontinue this virtually universal practice would have caused tension with an entrenched practice. The contemporary rabbi J. H. Hertz echoes this thought, arguing that a sacrificial cult was essential to religious practice at the time. Thus, if the laws of Moses had omitted this "universal expression of religious homage," Moses' mission "would have assuredly failed, and his work would have disappeared."[20] It is almost as if the renunciation of idols and polytheism was as much as this newly anointed group would be able to bear. Abarbanel, emphasizing the point that Jews customarily witnessed sacrifices in Egypt, avers that the Jews needed to be slowly and gradually led away from sacrifice. God initiated this change by ordering that all animal offerings be performed at the Temple, thus making it impossible for private sacrifices to occur at a faster rate. This fits well with the general acceptance of the idea that sacrifices were superseded by prayers and good deeds after the destruction of the Second Temple. On this view, sacrifice is necessary only in virtue of the instability of those patrons of a new religion. The rationalist interpretation sees idolatrous religions still capable of great influence at that juncture in Judaism and worries that a complete severing of a rite as entrenched as sacrifice would likely have instilled confusion and chaos among the recently religiously enlightened.

The rationalistic interpretation comports well with history. The loss of the Temple was already accompanied by social chaos; people lost jobs, homes, goods, and hope. The conditions were ripe for the creation of revolutionary sects, as the emergence of the Nazirites, Essenes, Rechabites, Zadokites, and Theraputae bears out. These sects shared an ascetic supposition: with the end of the Temple, there is no cause for rejoicing or celebration. To enjoy oneself in this most dire of times is grossly inappropriate.

These rationalistic seeds give birth to a historical argument for vegetarianism. Since meat was viewed as a luxury, these sects advanced vegetarianism as the only proper way to manifest the mourning state all Jews should be in until and unless a new temple is built. Biblical precedent for this comes from Daniel's abstention from flesh, wine, and "pleasant bread" for a mourning period (Dan. 10:3). The Talmudic rabbis saw this as a serious argument, ultimately rejecting it on the grounds that God created humankind to be happy and enjoy life. To be eternally mournful would be a sin against God. This same attitude is manifested during *shiva,* the week-long mourning service for a loved one who has died. After this very solemn period, a period in which one is meant to be uncomfortable even when sitting, there is a timetable for life to get on normally. The wife of a deceased husband, for example, is urged first to leave the house and take short walks and gradually but steadily increase her normal daily activities.

Although their position was ultimately deemed unacceptable, the ascetics had their apologists. Rabbis Ishmael ben Elisha, Simeon ben Gamliel, and Joshua thought that Jews should abstain from both meat and wine (thought to be the sources of the major pleasures of eating) but should not formulate this as a legal dictate since society in general would not obey this rule. (Not coincidentally, this is the same logic that propels the rationalist understanding of sacrifice.) Some hypothesize that a more significant reason for rejecting vegetarianism was the notion (justified or not) that many of these ascetics looked sick and that their adherence to a vegetarian diet was the culprit. Given our present knowledge of vegetarianism, one may speculate that the fears of malnourishment and deficiency diseases that concerned the general populace were no more than projected rationalizations to defend their customary meat eating. Perhaps a more real concern was that these sects advocated celibacy, not a particularly popular option. Somewhat as a compromise, the rabbis made the nine-day period prior to the anniversary of the Temple's destruction a time for vegetarianism. Some very religious Jews still advocate continuous vegetarianism for those Jews living in Jerusalem waiting for the day that the Temple is rebuilt.

The difficulty of justifying the institution of sacrifice with an all-good and all-merciful God was not lost on the later prophets. In effect, they believed that reconciliation was not possible and that the only legitimate course of action was to put an end to sacrifices. Consider their vehement denunciations of the slaughter.

> I hate, I despise your feasts, and I will take no delight in your solemn assemblies. Though you offer me burnt-offerings and meal-offerings, I will not accept them, neither will I regard the peace-offerings of your fat beasts. Take the noise of your song away from Me and let me not hear the melody of your psalms. But let justice well up as waters, and righteousness as a mighty stream. (Amos 5:21–24)

> To what purpose is the multitude of your sacrifices to Me? Say the Lord; I am full of the burnt-offerings of rams, and the fat of fed beasts; And I delight not in the blood of bulls, or of lambs, or of he-goats. Whenever you come to enter my presence—who asked you for this? No more shall you trample my courts. Bring no more false offerings. It is an offering of abomination to me. (Isa. 1:11–13)

> He who kills an ox is the same as he who slays a person. (Isa. 66:3)

> Add whole-offerings to sacrifices and eat flesh if you will. But when I brought your forefathers out of Egypt, I gave no commands about whole-offering and sacrifice; I said not a word about them. (Jer. 7:21–22)

> Loyalty is my desire, not sacrifice, not whole-offerings but the knowledge of God. (Hos. 6:6)

Perhaps most tellingly and most beautiful of all is Isaiah's prophecy regarding the messianic era, the time at which universal peace and love will extend throughout all God's creation.

> And the wolf shall dwell with the lamb,
> And the leopard shall lie down with the kid;
> And the calf and the young lion and the fatling together;
> And a little child will lead them.
> And the cow and the bear shall feed;
> Their young ones shall lie down together;
> And the lion shall eat straw like the ox.
> And the child shall play on the hole of the asp,
> And the weaned child shall put his hand on the viper's nest.
> They shall not hurt nor destroy
> In all my holy mountain;
> For the earth shall be full of the knowledge of the Lord.
> (Isa. 11:6–9)

This spectacular picture shows humans and animals coexisting peacefully in the future. The corrupt, carnivorous human disappears. The natural enmity among certain animal species is a thing of the past. And significantly, these events happen together, suggesting an intimate link between the salvation of humankind and humans' attitudes toward and treatment of animals.

The final line of this passage is pivotal. The point is not, I suggest, that this loving and peaceful state arises from full knowledge of the Lord. Rather, this blissful state, this state that mirrors life in Eden and so provides symmetry to the divine plan for God's creation, *is* the state where we know the Lord. The knowledge consists not merely in knowing what God wants from us (knowing the commandments and good deeds) but also in acting as God wants us to act. Knowing the Lord is acting holy in virtue of recognizing that this is the way God prefers us to be. Part of this holy life reflects the nonviolent, vegetarian lifestyle that existed in Eden. When this time occurs, our natures will no longer be debilitated and no more repugnant concessions will be necessary. We should constantly aspire to be the best our divinely given natures allow us to be. The messianic era returns us to the idyllic, Edenic state of Adam and Eve, a world without carnivorism and without any reason whatsoever to engage in the practice of sacrifices. At this wondrous time, both meat eating and sacrifice will strike us as alien and repellent.

We can synthesize the insights of Maimonides and Abarbanel with those of Isaiah. Sacrifices are allowed, even commanded, not because they are good practices in and of themselves but because they speak to both the historical and personal situations in which Jews found themselves. Like carnivorism, which was permitted after the Flood, sacrifices are a concession to a people who are trying to adapt to a new religion and new way of life. Unfortunately, human nature prohibits most people from making sharp breaks with their past, especially with their religious and social institutions. In realizing this, God allowed sacrifices to take place to facilitate the transition to Judaism. It is a necessary evil from which we eventually need to be weaned.

Presumably we have been at this stage for a long time. Few of us now believe in the necessity of sacrifice; prayer and acts of righteousness became the primary vehicles for accomplishing the goals of sacrifice after the Temple fell. The efficacy of prayer becomes more closely tied to the state of mind of the supplicant. Without a pure mind, without good intentions, prayer is empty. The sacrificial behaviors can be seen as merely contingent accompaniments of what is truly necessary for a good relationship with God.

This hypothesis is compatible with the general thesis that scripture accords animals inherent value. Even though animals are full-blooded members of our moral community and deserve the consideration and respect that we ordinarily restrict only to humans, extraordinary times sometimes require that their rights be violated. Recall how tenuous Judaism's existence was at this time, and you may agree that the violation of personal rights was necessary. Consider a contemporary analogy where the sacrifice of a human being would be necessary and sufficient for the eradication of heart disease. If we could cure heart disease and therefore prevent the pain, suffering, and deaths of millions of persons, it is at least arguable that we are warranted (perhaps even obligated) to sacrifice the one innocent human. If we compare the significance of sustaining an entire religious way of life with the importance of ending heart disease, we at least have a model showing how even the inherent value of an individual may be compromised in extreme circumstances.

One may reasonably ask why *human* sacrifice was never given divine sanction even in these most perilous of times. The answer may be simply that human nature reacts differently to human sacrifice than it does to animal sacrifice. That is, humans and animals have equivalent inherent value, but whereas animal sacrifice allowed this great religious journey to continue, human sacrifice would have stopped it in its tracks. Another plausible reply is that God holds humans in higher regard than animals. This is consonant with the traditional belief that humans hold center stage in God's plan.

There is another fascinating avenue of response to the injunctions for sacrifices. Perhaps we need not concede that God commanded sacrifices. Although voicing a minority opinion, some influential Judaic scholars have, drawing mainly on verses in Isaiah and Jeremiah, argued that sacrifices were not commanded but chosen by the Israelites. Rashi bases this on Isaiah 43:23, where God says that he has not burdened the Israelites with a meat offering. David Kimchi bases the same conclusion on Jeremiah 7:22–23. Kimchi notes that the Ten Commandments never mention sacrifice. More significantly, when discussing rules for sacrifice Leviticus (1:2) uses the expression *when* (i.e., *if*), suggesting that animal sacrifice is a voluntary practice. It cannot be denied that Leviticus employs the language of obligation and not choice regarding sacrifices. It is worth recalling, however, that many passages from the later prophets (see Amos 5:21–24) emphasize that sacrifice is primarily symbolic and that the Lord's goal is for the Israelites to live a more holy life, a life of lovingkindness and justice. This rendering brings us close to the "symbolic" interpretation of sacrifice favored by Hallevi and Hirsch. This interpretation is further supported in Proverbs 21:3, which states that "to do righteousness is more acceptable to the Lord than sacrifice."

The evangelical minister J. R. Hyland suggests that sacrificial rituals were foisted on the populace by high priests who acted self-interestedly. These priests typically received the choicest cuts that remained after the sacrifice and, he claims, utilized these rituals to sustain their power and prestige in the community.

Again, the fact that sacrifice is introduced without negative comment does not imply that God condones it. Renunciation of disreputable behavior may come from others, as when Isaiah, Jeremiah, and Hosea denounce Esau for cheating Jacob of his birthright. It may be more than coincidence that these later prophets also railed against sacrificial offerings.

While the Hebrew Bible neither states nor implies a simple, univocal view regarding animals, I have argued that a conception of animals as bearing inherent value best harmonizes with the concept of an all-merciful God full of lovingkindness. It should from the outset strike us as queer that such a God would condone, let alone encourage, treating a huge part of his sentient creation with relative disregard. Again, the idea that sentient animals—creatures with the capacity to feel joy and pain—can be used as resources to satisfy our desires conflicts with our reflective sensibilities. I have tried to show that these sensibilities can be given scriptural sanction. Not only can the instrumentalist evidence be deflected; in addition, we can plausibly interpret much of scripture as supporting the view that animals have value beyond the instrumental.

## Precepts for Leading the Holy Life

Four of the essential Old Testament guidelines for a holy life suggest that we should treat animals far better than we normally do in our society. At some places the interpretation attributes only instrumental value to animals, while at other places it seems to base its claims on inherent value. From a practical point of view, however, both bases would provide virtually identical consequences; most of our ordinary practices regarding animals would be drastically modified if we were to follow the spirit of these key precepts.

The first principle, *tsa'ar ba'alei chaim*, enjoins us to prevent and alleviate the unnecessary suffering of living creatures. This attitude circulates throughout the Torah, Midrashim and other rabbinical commentaries, legends, codifications of Jewish law, stories, and poems. Maimonides and Judah ha-Hasid ground this injunction on an angel's statement to Balaam: "Wherefore hast you smitten your ass?" (Num. 22:32). In Exodus 23:5 we are commanded to assist burdened animals ("If you see the ass of someone you hate [i.e., your enemy] lying under its burden, you should not pass by him; you should unload it with him"); this command is so stringent that the Talmud tells us it overrides rabbinical ordinances on keeping the Sabbath. Further confirmation is found both in Deuteronomy 25:4, where we are ordered not to muzzle an ox while it is threshing, and in the Talmud, where we are informed that we have the duty to relieve the pain of an ownerless or enemy animal.

Since Jewish law regarding animal cruelty is derived in part from biblical verses, *tsa'ar ba'alei chaim* is said to be *d'oraita;* that is, it has the force of Torah behind it. Rabbi S. R. Hirsch perspicaciously notes that the precept tells us not only to prevent but also to alleviate pain and suffering, which suggests that our role in helping be active. This command has frequently been elucidated as prohibiting both wantonly torturing and killing animals. In *The Guide to the Perplexed* Maimonides summarizes this position when he tells us that "we should not learn cruelty and should not cause unnecessary and useless pain to animals but should lean toward compassion and mercy."

As its name suggests, sport hunting does not presume to serve any need, let alone a legitimate one. In fact, Jewish law prohibits hunting for sport. This prohibition is based primarily on Psalms 1:1, which tells us "not to stand in the way of sinners"; Talmudic interpretation has us being compelled to disassociate ourselves from hunters. While Rabbi Landau's classic late-eighteenth-century responsum allows "non-Jewish" men to hunt as long as some utility ensues, the rabbi points out that "in the Torah the sport of hunting is imputed only to fierce characters like Nimrod and Esau, never to any patriarchs or their descendants. I cannot comprehend how a Jew can even dream of killing animals merely for the pleasure of hunting. When the act of killing is prompted by that of sport, it is downright cruelty." Nodah Bi

Yehudah agrees that sport hunting is unconscionable. Using animals for sports is also forbidden; the Talmud thus similarly condemns bullfighting, cockfighting, rodeos, and fox hunting using dogs.

In the same vein, there is no reason now, especially in the civilized world, for killing animals to obtain their fur. We can make warmer clothing at a lower cost. Cosmetic testing also is unsalvageable under this Old Testament precept. We currently sacrifice tens of thousands of guinea pigs, mice, hamsters, and rabbits to produce a new shade of mascara or a better whitener in our laundry detergent. It can hardly be considered miraculous that the ancients and moderns survived without these niceties.

Most important, meat eating can no longer be considered a necessity. Unlike those Hebrews and others who believed that a certain amount of meat is necessary for strength and good health, we know better. Virtually all recent studies emphasize that at least some kinds of meat are major factors in heart disease and some cancers and that a diet primarily consisting of fruits, vegetables, legumes, and grains is far better for most persons than a diet that makes flesh the main component of the meal. *Tsa'ar ba'alei chaim* urges us to return to our vegetarian roots.

The second precept, *bal tashcit,* orders us not to destroy. This is derived from Deuteronomy 20:19–20, where Jews are expressly ordered not to destroy trees around a city under siege. Although the original passage differentiates food-producing from non-food-producing trees, Talmudic scholars have extended this notion to any sort of destruction or vandalism, exploiting the common tactic of generalizing from a particular example.

*Bal taschit* is both narrower and broader in application than *tsa'ar ba'alei chaim*. It is narrower in that the precept does not address itself to torture, maiming, and injuring. One might attempt to argue that as far as *bal taschit* is concerned, we violate no commandment when we trap or confine animals, even when these practices create great suffering. As long as the animal survives, the act satisfies *bal taschit*. Its application is also broader than that of *tsa'ar ba'alei chaim,* however, for the item need not have the capacity to suffer to fall within its compass. Since trees, for example, do not suffer pain as humans and nonhuman animals do, the wrongness of their destruction requires *bal taschit*.

In practice, however, the two principles coincide where animals are concerned. Most of our uses of animals involve first causing them great pain then killing them. Although animals used in entertainment (e.g., circuses, aquariums, horse and dog racing, and rodeos) are typically not destroyed, most major forms of exploitation cannot claim compliance with *bal taschit*. Obviously the cows, chickens, pigs, and fish that we eat are killed. The same fate awaits those we hunt, trap, and vivisect. Virtually all animals used in cosmetic testing are killed. Researchers do not apply antidotes after pouring toxic substances in the unanesthetized eyes of rabbits, creating horrible ulcerations and abrasions. Sometimes the rabbits are subjected to another set of incredibly cruel tests, but whether they face additional painful experiments or not, they are eventually murdered. A similar fate awaits mice, hamsters, ferrets, and guinea pigs used in research.

The broad Talmudic interpretation need not be understood to mean that we do wrong by destroying a rock or a copper rod. This is surely far too stringent. If so, however, where should we draw the line? Indeed, we can look at this slippery slope from the other direction, too. Since scholars tell us that *bal taschit* derives from biblical passages about trees, why preclude rocks and copper rods from falling within the command's domain?

I see no simple response to this dilemma. Perhaps some uneasiness can be removed by recalling that similar problems arise when we consider some of the Ten Commandments. We are ordered not to kill; there is no addendum of exceptions or qualifications. Even so, no Judaic or Christian scholar has suggested that we are violating an injunction from God when we kill a tomato plant and then eat its fruit. (We may feel less comfortable if we were to kill the plant wantonly—if, that is, we were to kill it and completely waste it.) Context no doubt explains why most scholars agree that this commandment applies only to human beings. The requirement of understanding commandments contextually allows us to reconcile God's postdiluvian permission to kill and eat some nonhuman animals with *bal taschit*. Still, at the very least, most would agree that something would be morally amiss were we to kill a nonhuman animal without a good reason or purpose, where what constitutes a good reason is intentionally left vague. It is in this context that I propose that *bal taschit* include nonhuman animals within its domain. The salient difference between trees and rocks is that trees have life and organic unity. Animals obviously have more sophisticated lives and greater organic unity than trees. Most important, animals, unlike rocks and trees, have an interior life, a life that includes feelings of pleasure and pain. It would be perverse, therefore, to believe that trees fall within the scope of *bal taschit* but nonhuman animals do not.

Moreover, our reactions toward the gratuitous destruction of animals, trees, and even rocks and copper rods can be justified by early passages in Genesis that portray all God's creation as having value. This theocentric (God-centered) account of value derives primarily from the passage where God beholds his creation and judges it good. The theocentric theory of value is neither anthropocentric (human-centered) nor instrumental because every part of the natural world has some inherent value or worth independent of any use that humans may make of it. This does not imply that all things have equal value, but it does suggest that we ought not use anything wantonly, without good, biblically sanctioned reasons. Wanton use is exploitative and violates the sanctity of God's creation. This does not mean that we are sinful if we use lumber to build houses or use water to quench our thirst. Still, we owe all God's creation prudent and thoughtful treatment. Without a compelling need, we should let God's creation be. As Father Zossima says in Dostoyevsky's *Brothers Karamazov*, we should not "trouble creation."

The third injunction that leads to a more exalted status for animals is *pikuach nefesh*. This precept enjoins us to guard and care for our own health. Aforementioned points are obviously pertinent here as well. Given our present state of knowledge, we ought to be vegetarians. We now know that the risks of heart and cardiovascular disease are greatly increased by eating some kinds of meat. Many types of cancers—colon, stomach, and prostate, among others—are also more prevalent in those who eat meat. Much of the increased risk of heart disease can be traced to cholesterol and saturated fats that abound in meat products. Plants contain no cholesterol whatsoever. Moreover, obesity is far less common in vegetarians (and even less common in vegans) because they consume fewer calories. Nutritionally, virtually everyone can do without any meat. Even vitamin $B_{12}$, which was once thought to be derivable only from meat, can be procured from nonanimal sources. One's mental health also forms part of the domain of *pikuach nefesh*. I am reminded of Einstein, who admitted that he ate meat but felt guilty about it. I do not mean to suggest that Einstein's mental health was compromised by this realization, but it does seem likely that the more one is aware of the sort of inhumane practices one endorses by eating meat, the more one—at least if one is sensitive and reflective—should be troubled. It is difficult not to be both mentally and viscerally affected when witnessing the treatment of chickens, cows, and pigs subjected to the intensive production methods used in the United States and other developed nations.

The fourth commandment is *tsedakah,* or charity. Eliminating meat production would let us do a far better job of feeding all the hungry and starving people (and animals) of the world. Approximately one-half of the water used in this country goes to animals that are slated for slaughter. Protein from meat sources requires eighteen times the amount of land that vegetarian sources need. The litany of advantages of a vegetarian diet to humans, especially those who live in poverty, is almost unending.[21]

## An Instrumentalist Objection

As a principle derived from the Torah, *tsa'ar ba'alei chaim* ostensibly governs universally, but there is debate regarding its rationale. Again, I cannot prove that this precept (or any of the others) is motivated by a conception of animals that bestows inherent value on them. The scriptures certainly allow the standard instrumentalist interpretation of animals under *tsa'ar ba'alei chaim*. The instrumentalist can claim that the principle enjoins us to prevent and alleviate suffering among animals not for the their sake but for our own. Although cruelty and lack of concern are to be avoided, causing animals to suffer does not itself hinder our odyssey to salvation. Rather, the problem is that these attitudes and practices incline us to act cruelly toward our fellow humans. This is *tsa'ar ba'alei chaim* understood in an instrumentalist manner.

I believe that the inherent value interpretation has as much biblical support as the traditional view. Still, in the spirit of cooperation, why not consider the possibility that this injunction may have more than one rationale? No incoherence need attach to the idea that these precepts might have more than one motivation behind them. It is wrong to treat animals unkindly because cruel behavior will incline us to act inhumanely toward our fellow humans *and* because creatures with inherent value should not be treated as mere resources. In addition to its indirect effects, gratuitously inflicting harm on animals provides serious, if not insuperable, obstacles to attaining holiness.

Consider, in this vein, the two animal injunctions perhaps most popular for founding proanimal sentiments. The first, in Deuteronomy 25:4, tells us that we ought not to muzzle an ox treading corn. The Apostle Paul interprets this injunction to be aimed at the benefit of humans. In 1 Corinthians 9:9–10 Paul says that God's concern here is only for humans, not for oxen. The suggestion is that muzzling an ox increases its stubbornness and fatigue, so that less corn will be threshed. Even though an unmuzzled ox would no doubt eat some of the corn while it worked (and, presumably, gain strength), forgoing the muzzle would benefit the owner in the long run. Nevertheless, the Christian scholars James Gaffney and J. R. Hyland deny this interpretation and read the scriptural passage in a way that makes oxen a direct concern of God. After all, oxen work hard, and the great majority of their labor benefits their human owners, so it seems only right to allow the ox some food. On this view, it is a point of justice and not compassion or kindness to leave the ox unmuzzled while it treads the corn.

The second injunction comes from Deuteronomy 22:10, which enjoins us not to plow with ox and ass together. The instrumental interpretation makes this a practical injunction: to maximize the yield, avoid such a mismatched partnership, since their wildly different strengths would make for inefficient plowing. The animals would be working less as a cohesive tandem than as adversaries. Nevertheless, one can easily read this injunction as manifesting direct concern for the animals. The unequal partnership would likely result in injury to one or both. It would prove cruel to the ass, which would be dragged by the far stronger ox, and cruel to the ox, which would need to work against its instinct to move more quickly. The ass and ox have done nothing to deserve the pain and suffering that would likely ensue from their mismatch. Once again, one may read this as a command for compassion and humane treatment of animals or in a stronger moral sense as a question of justice or desert. Under either interpretation, we should not be misled into thinking that the precept is narrowly applicable only to oxen and asses. The example should be understood, as I have shown before, as a model from which to generalize. We can expand this idea to interspecies animal partnerships and even more broadly to animals of different physical capacities.

While there is nothing incoherent in suggesting two rationales behind these injunctions, other evidence supports the contention that scriptural evidence favors the inherent-value reading. The psalmists speak of God's creating things for the sake of animals. The trees are created for birds; high hills, for wild goats; and the deep and wide sea, for innumerable things both big and small. Indeed, darkness is created so that forest dwellers can safely leave their abodes at night. An excellent example of this attitude appears in the concluding section of Job (38:26–41), where God ordains some natural events that do not benefit humankind. This passage tells us that God "causes it to rain on a land where no man is or wilderness wherein there is no man." It is difficult to make sense of this unless God grants value to the land itself or to nonhuman animals that graze on it.

### Additional Torah Laws Regarding Compassion to Animals

I have documented cases where we are commanded to benefit nonhuman animals. I have spoken of the paradigm cases of leaving a threshing ox unmuzzled and not yoking an ox to an ass to plow a field. There are other cases that merit notice. Deuteronomy 11:15 ("I will give grass in the fields for your cattle, and you will eat and be satisfied") has typically been interpreted as an obligation to feed and water one's animals before oneself. The duty is so stringent that one is permitted to interrupt a rabbinically commanded activity to ascertain whether the animal has been fed. Although presumably Gandhi was not influenced by this directive, a famous story of a meeting between Gandhi, Roosevelt, and Churchill has him interrupting the proceedings so that he could feed and tend to his goat. Churchill apparently found this behavior more than a little odd, but it is an excellent, if unintentional, example of the Talmudic interpretation of this scriptural passage.

Animals were given both a Sabbath day and year (Exod. 20:8–10 [part of Ten Commandments], 23:12; Deut. 5:12–14; Lev. 25:6–7). This is a powerful indication of how closely the human and nonhuman animal worlds are related, since the Sabbath is the holiest of days. Commenting on Exodus 20:10, Rabbi Hertz extols Judaism as being thousands of years in advance of other religions in fully recognizing our duties to animals. Furthermore some scholars, including Rashi, interpret the application of the Sabbath to animals as ordering us not only to give them rest but also to provide for their contentment. Once again, the notion of stewardship rather than domination is best suited to ground these duties.

It was forbidden to sacrifice a newborn ox, sheep, or goat until it had enjoyed at least seven days of warmth and nourishment from its mother (Lev. 22:27). Using the Talmudic principle of natural extension to include cows within the province of this injunction means that this command is broken frequently and violently. Veal calves—male calves that are essentially viewed as a waste product of the dairy industry—are separated from their mothers at birth. They are led away screaming for their mothers and pushed into tiny wooden stalls where they are unable to turn around. The tenderness of veal depends on the calf's not building any muscles, so growers prevent any physical activity. The veal calves are fed a horribly deficient diet, especially low in iron, so that their meat is white, the color thought best by veal connoisseurs. Housed indoors, never to see the sun, feel the wind, or play in the fields, they are killed after three or four months. It is difficult to fathom how one would begin to reconcile this institutional cruelty with the Leviticus injunction.

The very next passage of Leviticus (22:28) speaks of the impermissibility of killing an ox or ewe and its young on the same day. Philo Judaeus tells us that it "is the height of savagery to slay on the same day the generating cause and the living creature generated." Yet are routinely killed on the same day as their children. In factory farms that deal with "layers" (hens who are used only for their egg production), male chicks are disposed of immediately. Often they are summarily thrown into dumpsters, the weight of those subsequently tossed crushing those dumped before them.

An injunction somewhat similar to the second of these prohibits killing a mother bird together with its young. The mother is to be sent away before the young birds are taken (Deut. 22:6–7). Nachmanides and Kol Bo (thirteenth century) understood this as merely good prudential, anthropocentric advice. Acting otherwise would threaten the species with extinction. Others interpret it in the usual instrumental way, telling us that the command will make us more sensitive and kind in human dealings. Curiously, this is one of only two of the Hebrew Bible's 613 commandments that offers a reward. (Honoring one's parents is the other.) Good fortune and a long life will accrue to one who obeys the rule. Why this command proffers a reward while the similar and in ways more demanding commandment concerning oxen, ewes, and their young does not is not clear. Perhaps mother birds were thought to be more sensitive to the deaths of their children than are mother oxen and sheep. They would be prone to suffer more intense grief and sorrow. This interpretation supports the view that God bestows inherent value on his non-human animal creation. He cares about the mother bird's feelings without any reference to any benefits birds may bring to other species.

We are also prohibited from removing eggs from a nest in the presence of the dam. Maimonides says we send away the bird out of compassion for animals. Nachmanides says we do so out of compassion for human sensibilities. An explanation more compatible with the stewardship view characterizes this command as a divine reminder that God lets us eat eggs only as a concession to our fallen state. Ideally we would eat no eggs whatsoever. After all, there was no egg eating in the Garden of Eden. The Torah never mentions eggs anywhere else, which supports this interpretation; some significance should be placed on the fact that the only reference to eggs involves a prohibition.

Exodus 23:19 and 34:26, Leviticus 22:28, and Deuteronomy 14:21 tell us not to boil a kid in its mother's milk. Rashi surmises that since this injunction appears in three biblical passages, a threefold ban is implied. Milk and meat should not be eaten, cooked, or mixed together. This restriction makes meat more difficult to eat and perhaps less appetizing. Maimonides saw boiling of this sort cruel, barbaric, and insensitive. Others plausibly see this injunction as a stark example of keeping the natural order pure and unalloyed, for mixing the kid with the mother's milk is metaphorically to mix life and death. Less severe commandments of purity occur frequently throughout the Hebrew Bible, with perhaps the most temperate instance being the command not to wear linen (a vegetable product) with wool (an animal product).

While discussing *tsa'ar ba'alei chaim,* I already referred to scriptural passages that order us to help ease the burden of even our enemy's ass. Deuteronomy 22:1 tells us that if we see our brother's oxen or sheep driven away, we should bring them back to him. The Talmudic expansion imposes an obligation to care for any lost animal. We are bound to feed, water, and shelter the animal until we can find its owner. This precept certainly lends itself to an interpretation that grants inherent value to the animal. The instrumentalist rendering would explain the command in terms of the owner's benefit, but this would make little sense where the owner is an enemy. The Jews in ancient Egypt would hardly have wanted to do anything that would have benefited their slavemasters. We tend to the animal's sake, even though an enemy owns it, simply because the animal's welfare matters in its own right.

### Stories, Tales, and Folklore regarding Compassion to Animals

Hebrew folklore includes countless narratives regarding compassion shown to animals. They range from the comical to the poignant, but like all good stories, they make or emphasize an important point. In the case at hand, the point is that we should cultivate compassion toward animals.

Consider the tale about Israel Salanter, a nineteenth-century orthodox rabbi. He failed to appear at a Kol Nidre service, which closes Yom Kippur, the holiest holiday of the Jewish year. His congregation was fearful, believing that only great illness or injury would cause him to miss the service. Instead, the rabbi had ventured passed some lost calves (belonging, incidentally, to a Christian neighbor) who had become tangled in brush. Being sensitive to their distress, he led them through a long and hilly journey home.

The Talmud often refers to the notion that the Lord is good to all and that his tender mercies pour over all his works. Proverbs 12:10 offers this directive to mirror God's divine compassion: "The righteous man regards the life of his beast." This is beautifully exemplified by the tale of Rabbi Zusya, who patronized an inn that housed caged birds. Hearing the call of "tender mercies," he freed the birds only to be assaulted by the innkeeper. The rabbi nevertheless left serenely, content in the knowledge that these birds were free to live their lives. The story was echoed in contemporary times when the Nobel laureate Isaac Bashevis Singer recognized that his caged parakeets deserve freedom and let them go.

Not all rabbis learned the lessons of compassion quickly. Rabbi Judah the Prince, who compiled the Mishna, the fundamental redaction of the oral law that constitutes the basis of the Talmud, is said to have suffered great intestinal pain after treating a frightened calf cruelly. The calf had apparently escaped from a slaughterhouse and ran to the rabbi; Judah ordered it returned to the slaughterhouse, reasoning that it had been created to be killed for food. Moreover, a thirteen-year-long toothache finally terminated when he stopped his daughter from killing a weasel. Here Judah alludes to the notion that tender mercies apply to all God's work.

It is instructive to compare these two tales, since the intestinal problem is frequently interpreted as a punishment not for Judah's attitude toward slaughter but his lack of pity toward the frightened calf. The usual interpretation of the weasel story, however, vitiates an instrumentalist rendering of the calf tale. The former attributes his awakening regarding the weasel to an understanding that objects have inherent value simply because they are part of God's creation. Weasels have less value to humans than calves, however; we neither eat nor milk them. Furthermore, the rather low regard in which weasels are generally held would minimize the effect that killing them would have on subsequent intrahuman behavior. The story, therefore, is best understood as confirming that nonhuman animals have value simply because they are sentient parts of God's creation.

A Midrash story tells of the evil city of Ninevah, whose inhabitants escaped divine punishment by separating parents from young animals and threatening God that they would be cruel toward the animals were he to take no pity on their city. Unlike the above tales, this is surely allegorical; undoubtedly God cannot be blackmailed. Still, it is not unreasonable to interpret this as a powerful reminder of animals' importance to God.

The story in which God tells the Israelites to kill all the wicked Amalekites and their animals (see 1 Sam. 15:3–23) provides more evidence that animals have inherent value. God says the animals are to be killed because they are really disguised warriors who transformed themselves by sorcery. The point here may be that the innocent—epitomized by nonhuman animals—are never divinely punished. A similar rationale may be used to answer David's plaintive query regarding God's killing his sheep (see 2 Sam. 24:17, 22:6–7). Our sense of divine justice requires an explanation along these lines, since bringing about the torture and death of the innocent is antithetical to God's nature as all powerful and all good.

I end with the moving Hasidic tale of a young *schochet* (the person who performs the ritual slaughter, *schechitah*) who expertly replaced his recently retired predecessor. Despite his technical skill, some of the elders of the religious community find his performance lacking, for unlike the elder *schochet*, he fails to moisten the blade with his tears.

## Animals and Rights

Theologians and others contentiously debate whether being a product of God's creation suffices for being a right-holder. Some, like St. Paul, suggest that the language of rights is antitheological. He rhetorically asks how the created can have rights against the Creator and suggests that this makes as much sense as believing that clay can have rights against the potter. But Paul is mistaken. Bracketing God as the ultimate creator of everything, children have rights regarding their proximate creators—their parents. This commonsense attitude is reflected in our laws, which make child abuse a criminal offense. Indeed, it seems that even God lacks the moral freedom to treat us in any way whatsoever. Like anyone else, God would be wrong to cause us unjustified pain and distress. Of course, he would never do so. Since God is omnipotent, omniscient, and omnibenevolent, we can rest assured that he will never act unjustifiably.

Furthermore, Paul's analogy misses the point somewhat. Even if it is true that the created cannot have rights against their creator, the more relevant question is whether one part of God's creation can have rights regarding another part. Conceding Paul's claim concerning rights against God scarcely obviates talk about animals having claims against us. The theocentric view of value—a view that has substantial scriptural and commonsense support—sustains this idea. It seems appropriate to speak of animals as having, minimally, the right to be treated kindly, caringly, and graciously by us. Accepting that animals are part of God's creation and as a result have inherent value makes the language of rights not only intelligible but natural.

Some have suggested that talk of animal rights, although not antitheological, is oxymoronic. Rights holders must have the capacity to acquire duties, and since it is obviously unintelligible to attribute duties to animals, we cannot ascribe rights to them. This claim, however, seems inconsistent with other applications of the notion of rights. Human infants lack mental abilities sufficient to incur duties, and yet we surely think of them as having some rights. Once again, the commonsense idea, and one reflected in our legal code, is that infants have the right not to be tortured and the right to be cared for by their parents. The capacity for reciprocity is not required for having rights.

The central Christian idea of helping those who most need our help is best instantiated by a loving stewardship relationship toward animals. C. S. Lewis puts the point nicely when he says that we ought to show ourselves to be better than beasts by acknowledging duties to them that they do not acknowledge to us. Our special position in God's creation imposes special responsibilities on us. That is, we bear responsibility to animals precisely because we are superior to them.

The Reverend Andrew Linzey, a professor at Oxford, attributes rights to animals on the same basis that he attributes rights to humans. God is the creator of both and so God has the right to have his creation treated respectfully. Respecting and honoring animals is one way in which humans give God what he deserves. In 1977 Archbishop Donald Coggan said that animals have rights; that same year the General Synod of the Church of England resolved to respect the "due rights of all sentient creatures." In the end, I believe, the applicability of the language of rights is really a pragmatic issue. Having its origins in the seventeenth century, talk of rights is a relatively recent political development, and we can probably translate virtually everything we mean to say from a language of rights into a language without these terms. Still, there is nothing either logically or theologically untoward in implementing the language of rights.

## Conclusions

Judeo-Christian heritage has both the room and the motivation for conceiving of nonhuman animals as having inherent value. Scriptural support can be gathered for this conception. Scholarly commentaries can be garnered to support this conception. Reflective thought about the omnibenevolence of God suggests this conception. Thinking of ourselves as stewards rather than rulers of another segment of God's creation more closely aligns our earthly existence with the one we wish ultimately to reach.

Let me summarize the conclusions to this point. There are no good reasons for conceiving of human beings as having a special value that confers privilege only on them. The secular candidates for providing humans with inherent value cross species borders. Rationality, linguistic ability, moral agency, and so forth are qualities some nonhuman animals possess and some humans lack. Furthermore, and more significantly, these properties lack the moral relevance frequently attributed to them. Attempts to use Judeo-Christian religion to morally segregate humans from animals also fail. Virtually all scripture can be legitimately interpreted in ways that grant animals inherent value. Most important, our institutionalized abuses of animals in factory farming, vivisection, and hunting are irreconcilable with the conception of a God whose most salient attribute is lovingkindness.

# CHAPTER THREE

# THE HOLOCAUST OF FACTORY FARMING

This is not a chapter for the squeamish or weak of heart. Understanding what happens to animals before we bite into a steak, taste some pork, or munch some chicken is not pleasant. Still, it must be done, for it will show just how much gratuitous pain and suffering we inflict on innocent creatures. Applying the PGS to these data will demonstrate that we are morally obligated to end all our factory (intensive) farming. Since factory farms produce some 95 percent of the flesh we consume, fulfilling our ethical obligations will call for drastically changing how we live our lives.

One may object to this discussion by accusing me of appealing to sentiment, not reason, to make my case, playing with people's emotions much like the antiabortionists who protest by carrying pictures of early-stage fetuses. Some may further suggest that if I had a good case against intensive farming or for vegetarianism and veganism, I would not need to resort to these unfair methods of persuasion. I would avoid emotional appeals and simply put forth reasons to demonstrate that eating meat and dairy products is wrong and should be abolished.

I absolutely will appeal to your emotions and feelings, but not from a need to be manipulative or unfair. Indeed, the dichotomy assumed by the objection is a false one. Properly understood, reason does not stand opposed to the emotions. In fact, without emotions or feelings, reason cannot gain a foothold on moral issues.

Consider a totally reasonable, intelligent individual who is completely devoid of emotions; a futuristic robot would fit the bill. It sees persons starving to death in sub-Saharan Africa but cannot react to them emotionally. The robot has no sympathy or empathy for these people. It cannot feel sorry for what they are going through or put itself in their shoes. The robot does not *care* about these people at all.

Were human beings like this, we would think of them as leading lives far less rich than our own. Regardless of how intelligent they are or how well they can reason, this lack of sentiment excludes them from the realm of moral agents. Our emotional lives are what trigger our thinking about ethical issues. If we could not care about others, morality simply could not be an issue for us. This is not to say that reason has no place in morality or even that it has a diminished significance in our moral lives. Reason and argument are crucially important to morality, for without them we could not intelligently converse about any moral issue. For example, both prolife and prochoice advocates have reasons for their positions, and any participants in this debate must give each side a fair hearing and then evaluate the relative strengths of the views. If people did not feel deeply about this issue, however, the debate would never have begun.

I thus raise emotionally charged issues not because I need to manipulate my readers unfairly but rather because this debate is possible only if one starts caring about the abuses ubiquitous in factory farming and slaughterhouses, and caring can begin only if there is some state of affairs that bothers, annoys, frustrates, or repulses. It is thus essential to document what transpires on factory farms and in abattoirs. I limit the discussion to the treatment accorded cattle, hogs, and chickens because these compose the overwhelming majority of the animals we consume. I give the plight of the chicken the most sustained attention for two reasons. First, the travails of chickens are perhaps worse than those of cattle and hogs (although this is a bit like saying that time spent in Auschwitz was worse than time spent in Bergen-Belsen). Second, chickens suffer and are killed far more than happens with any other farm animals. In fact, far more chickens are killed for food than are all other farm animals combined. These facts suggest that, contrary to popular opinion, forgoing chicken and eggs as food prevents more pain and distress than does declining beef.[1]

## Cattle

### The Dairy Cow

Small dairy farms with ten or fifteen cows face a limited future. The number of dairy farms has been halved over the last fifty years, and the evidence suggests that this trend will continue. Replacing these family farms are enormous factory farms owned by huge conglomerates. Farmers spend far less time with any particular cow than they did in the past. This has dire consequences for the cow.

Milking is done by machine on these factory farms. This in itself is not especially harmful to the cow, but malfunctions are. Since farmers spend little time with any cow, a malfunctioning milking machine will probably not be discovered for quite a while. Poorly functioning machines can worsen preexisting udder problems and, more seriously, lead to mastitis by injuring an udder. Mastitis, an udder inflammation that affects 20 percent of dairy cows, invites infection.

Most of the dairy cow's life-threatening conditions have resulted from genetic "advances." The dairy cow on a factory farm is an unnatural freak, created solely to produce as much milk as possible. As a result of genetic manipulation, cows suffer deficiency diseases such as ketosis. Cows won't produce milk unless protein has been extracted from their blood. Huge demands for milk leave cows without sufficient protein for their own nutritional needs, thus compromising their metabolisms.

Shortly after a cow gives birth, its milk production declines. Since less milk translates into less profit, the farmer tries to keep the cow pregnant as much as possible. The dairy cow is thus artificially inseminated after only a two- or three-month respite. This constant parade of pregnancies often causes problems for the cow. Great stress ensues, and the cow often becomes too weak to walk or even stand. These "downers" receive no treatment for any broken bones or diseases they may contract. Instead, they are herded onto trucks and sent quickly to the nearest slaughterhouse. Since federal law allows downers to be slaughtered only if they are breathing when they reach the slaughterhouse, time is of the essence; the cow's physical condition not.

After the cow turns three its milk production drops precipitously. After about five years the cow no longer produces enough to justify keeping it. These animals, whose natural life span is some twenty years, are sent to a slaughterhouse having lived only one-quarter of that. (Discussions of factory farming often fail to include the unnaturally short lives virtually all farm animals live.)

The plight of the veal calf has filtered down to the general public. These male offspring, being of no use to dairy farmers, are sold to veal houses as "waste products." To get the more expensive "milk-fed" veal, farmers separate the young calves from their mothers almost immediately after birth and pen them in tiny wooden crates for the rest of their lives. The crates make it impossible for the calves to turn around. The less the calf moves, the less his muscles develop, resulting in more tender veal. To provide the white color that some consumers prefer, the calf is denied any iron. Calves naturally need and crave iron, and in earlier times they could obtain some by licking the metal bars of their cages, but the wooden crates now housing them during their entire lives prevent even that. After four months the calf is relieved of his frustrated life by being slaughtered.

Interestingly, many meat-eating humans draw the line at veal. They believe, correctly, that by eating veal they are perpetuating enormous suffering among male calves. As I will show, hogs and especially chickens suffer nearly as much. Parity of reasoning may suggest to these "circumscribed" carnivores that they eliminate other animal products from their food choices.

*Beef Cattle*

Of all the farm animals, beef cattle probably lead the best lives. Unfortunately, this does not mean that their lives are good. Although allowed to roam and enjoy some semblance of freedom, beef cattle, like all other intensively farmed animals, are treated purely as a means to an end. The beef cow (I use the term generally to refer to cattle of either sex) is seen as an instrument to maximize the production of meat (and some by-products) with minimal cost. As always, economic considerations dictate the treatment of the animal.

There are three major stresses that face a beef cow: branding, dehorning, and (for males) castration. Until 1995 there were no federal regulations against face branding. It is difficult to imagine how much pain a fully conscious cow feels when someone firmly presses a scalding-hot branding iron against its face. The body branding now currently in vogue for livestock is somewhat less painful, because the body has fewer nerve cells than the face, but it is still an extremely painful and terrifying experience for the cow. Typically branding and castration are done at the same time. Workers on horseback rope the calves and pin them to the ground. One worker rips the scrotum with a knife while another tears out the calf's testicles. A third simultaneously brands the calf. Its shrieks and frenetic movements inarguably show the suffering that the young calf endures. Dehorning is performed either by a paste that dissolves the horn or by workers who saw it off. We should not be misled into thinking that this is a painless operation. The horn contains many nerve cells, so that pain is virtually a certainty. Usually neither branding, castration, nor dehorning is accompanied by anesthesia.

Growers seek to fatten the beef cow as much as possible at the lowest possible cost. To this end, they feed the cattle anything from blood to manure to chicken waste—a significant divergence from the cow's natural diet of grasses. When the beef cow is heavy enough for slaughter, he is urged onto a truck for transport to the slaughterhouse. Some forty to fifty cows may be crammed into a truck that travels some 1,500 miles. Heat exhaustion commonly ensues in the summer, when temperatures often reach well into the nineties. Cows become too weak to stand, and those who don't die from heat exhaustion may be trampled by other cows weighing in excess of 900 pounds. The animals fare no better in the winter, however. They travel in open trucks at some fifty-five miles per hour in a season when subzero temperatures are common throughout much of the United States and Canada; the wind-chill factor may plummet to fifty degrees below zero. The cows urinate and defecate in the trucks, and the waste quickly freezes in such frigid conditions. This, too, can cause the cows to fall, allowing them to be either severely injured or trampled to death by their truckmates. Be it from great heat or great cold, a cow who falls and is trampled for perhaps ten or fifteen hours endures a harrowing plight. In either case, many are severely injured by the time they reach the slaughterhouse, only to be chained and dragged to the kill area so they can be slaughtered.

## The Cow Slaughterhouse

The federal Humane Slaughter Act dictates how cows are to be slaughtered.[2] This affects the approximately 40 million cows that are slaughtered in the United States each year. Workers begin the procedure by ushering the cows into a "knocking box" or to a conveyor-restrainer that carries them to a stun operator. The knocker, usually called a "stunner," has the task of killing the cow using a compressed-air gun that projects a steel bolt into a small area on the cow's forehead. If the gun shoots the bolt powerfully enough and the stunner hits the appropriate spot, the cow is killed or at least rendered unconscious. The bolt is then retracted so that it can be used for the next cow in line.

The stunned cow then passes to the shackler, who wraps a chain around one of its legs. After being shackled, the cow is automatically hoisted to an overhead rail. The cow, now upside down and hanging from one leg, is next met by the "sticker," who cuts the carotid arteries and jugular vein in the cow's neck. In the vernacular, the sticker slits the dead or unconscious cow's throat.

The cow is then allowed a few minutes to bleed out, emptying its blood into a pit below the overhead rail. The dead carcass is next met by workers who skin its head and cut off its head and legs. Further down this (dis)assembly line, the cow has its remaining skin removed, is eviscerated, and cut in half vertically.

This scenario, unappetizing as it may be for most of us, describes what *ought* to happen according to federal law. What commonly *does* happen is at odds with these guidelines. Almost anything that can go awry in this process does.

Many problems result from the speed of the entire operation. Large slaughterhouses can slaughter over three thousand cows daily. The stunner is often

too hurried to hit the correct spot on the cow's skull. Any of several possible results can ensue. Sometimes the cow escapes from the chute and runs
wild in the plant. More frequently the stunner simply tries again. It may take
anywhere from four to ten or more blows of the steel bolt before the cow is
knocked out or killed. Sometimes the cow is stunned but not knocked out.
In this case a dazed but conscious cow is shackled and hoisted on the overhead rail. The frantic cow bellows and stretches in all directions while enduring unimaginable pain. This is not a rare occurrence. Some former
slaughterhouse workers have claimed that 25 percent of the cows were conscious while being shackled and hoisted at their plants.

Stickers who meet one of these writhing cows seldom get a "good stick."
That is, the cow's arteries and veins are not properly cut to allow the blood
to drain. Still, there is no stopping the line, and the cow is next greeted by
the head skinners, who literally skin the cow alive. There are times, that is,
when a conscious cow has its skin taken off. Sometimes a skinner dealing
with this situation will stick a knife in the back of the cow's head to sever
the spinal cord, but this only paralyzes the cow from the head down. The
cow is still conscious. So even if the skinner cuts the spinal cord, the cow
will still be conscious when skinned. Some leggers (those who remove the
legs of the cow when it is skinned) have reported that virtually *all* the cows
at their facilities were conscious when the removal took place. There have
been reports of incidents where a cow was not rendered unconscious until
ten minutes after it was improperly stunned.

You might wonder how this is possible. One might suppose that workers
would complain to the plant manager and request that the production line be
slowed. One might think that inspectors and even veterinarians are present in
the slaughterhouse to ensure that the slaughtering is done according to Hoyle.

Indeed, the U.S. Department of Agriculture has set up a chain of command. Slaughterhouse inspectors report to in-plant veterinarians, who report to one of the country's 200 circuit supervisors. The supervisors report
to one of eighteen district managers, who are accountable to the USDA's
Field Operations Department in Washington. If violations of the Humane
Slaughter Act occur, the details must first pass through the slaughterhouse
inspectors. The previously mentioned "mishaps" suggest that these inspectors should have their hands full.

Unfortunately, in most plants the in-house inspectors are located quite far
down the production line. As a result, they cannot see the slaughtering. This
is not surprising since their major function, especially as they see it, is to ensure not animal welfare but the safety and cleanliness of the meat (it would
take another book to discuss how well they accomplish this job). Not only

are inspectors not ordered to check on the conditions of the kill area; they are not even authorized to do so. If they did, they would be leaving their stations and committing a potentially actionable offense. Of course, the inspector could order the processing line stopped, but this would likely draw a strong rebuke from the plant manager and perhaps even lead to the inspector's dismissal. After all, an inspector who sees a violation must have left his or her prescribed station. We are left in a catch-22. The inspectors are the people who can verify compliance with the Humane Slaughter Act, and yet for all intents and purposes, they never are in a position to see any violations. In fact, several years ago Secretary of Agriculture Edward Madigan effectively endorsed this paradoxical position when he said that the hoisting area adjacent to the knocking box "is not an area where inspectors perform their tasks."[3] The Humane Slaughter Act is effectively nullified.

The veterinarians are typically not helpful. They are often otherwise retired and (like people in general) by and large want to be troubled as little as possible and to avoid any physical or unpleasant work. It is not pleasant to watch animals being stuck and drained of blood. The veterinarian should report violations to the plant supervisor, but there is strong disincentive to do this. Veterinarians who cause downtime eat into their plants' profits, which does not endear them to plant managers. The plant manager may take out his frustration by speaking to the circuit supervisor. As a result, the veterinarian may see his or her job rating plummet, suffer disciplinary action, or lose pay. The veterinarian will tend to take the path of least resistance and let the plant run as it illegally does. A vet who makes no waves enjoys increased chances of becoming a consultant. Consultants collect a USDA pension while working a relatively cushy job.

Going up the chain of command to the circuit supervisor provides little help. However well intentioned, the few circuit supervisors must cover such large areas that they often cannot make it to a given plant more than once every two or three months. If these visits are known in advance, the plant manager can keep things shipshape during the inspection. He or she can slow down the line or warn employees not to act inhumanely to the animals as they pass along the production line. Furthermore, supervisors typically relegate responsibility to their subordinates. If they hear of some animal-abuse complaint, they often tell the veterinarian and inspectors to work it out among themselves. Part of this attitude may be plain laziness, a condition pandemic in all fields. Like the veterinarian who does not rock the boat, circuit supervisors can improve their future job prospects by avoiding confrontations. They will have better chances of being hired as plant consultants, regional directors, or agency administrators when they retire.

# Hogs

As with the cow, the hog or pig has fallen prey to huge farms owned by powerful corporate interests. Lowering labor costs saves money. These farms employ few workers, each of whom spends little time with any individual hog. Thus, as with cattle, injuries and illnesses can fester and worsen before an employee notices a hog's deteriorated condition. According to some estimates, the average hog receives twelve minutes of human care during its entire life. In fact, in 1990 one-quarter of surveyed pig operations went the entire year without veterinary service. One should not conclude that the hogs were incredibly healthy. Rather, the obvious inference is that paying veterinarians is by and large not cost effective. It is usually cheaper to start again with a new piglet than to mend a sow's broken leg.

Economic considerations demand that pig sheds house as many pigs as possible in the most labor-efficient way. To accomplish this goal, farmers use concrete slats for the hog's floor. Concrete is easy to wash down, and the angled floors allow the excrement to fall down into a collection area. Since any straw would fall through the slats as well, the floor is left virtually bare. The hogs are forced to sleep directly on concrete, even though studies have shown that straw bedding enhances a pig's physical and psychological welfare. Concrete floors bring more than just discomfort, however. Joints swell, skin abrades, and feet get infected. This increases pain and frustration, which in turn lead to internecine fighting.

The poor-quality air that surrounds pigs their entire lives causes respiratory diseases. High levels of air-borne urea and ammonia leave as many as 70 percent of hogs with pneumonia at the time of their slaughter. Simply ventilating these houses by pumping fresh air from the outside has been deemed too expensive. It is cheaper to let some hogs die before reaching the slaughterhouse than to provide them with breathable air.

If allowed, pregnant pigs give birth by building nests that will house as many as ten piglets. The sow expends significant time and energy in picking the proper location and bedding material. In the artificial surroundings of the factory, however, the sow spends her pregnancy in a small crate inside the shed. In addition to frustrating her natural instincts, the crate endangers the newborn piglets, for the mother can suffocate them merely by turning slightly. Even after pregnancy, the sow is denied any freedom. Farmers find it cheaper to house the sow in a small crate for virtually her entire life; a four-hundred-pound pig is forced to live her life in two-foot-wide crate. The hog cannot turn around, let alone walk or play. These intelligent and psychologically complex animals manifest their frustration by launching themselves against their crates and fighting among themselves, including biting each other's tails. Although free-roaming pigs occasionally fight, tail biting rarely occurs. This activity seems to result from the pigs' extremely confined living spaces. Farmers solve the problem simply by cutting off the piglets' tails. No anesthesia is used. As always, the motivation for all this is economic. The smaller the "homes" are, the more pigs a shed can hold. Moreover, confinement lowers feed costs. Restrained pigs spend less energy, so that less food is required to maintain and fatten them.

The piglets who fail to grow rapidly enough—the runts of the litter—have no value, because uniform size is very important to meat packers. Workers separate these runts from the rest and "thump" them. That is, the workers pick them up by their hind legs and smash their heads against the concrete floor. Those unfortunate enough to survive the first thumping must endure a second one. Some piglets surviving a thumping have their throats stepped on until they die. In a single plant over one hundred piglets can suffer this fate in one day. Here, economic concerns may partner with sadism.

Factory farm pigs lead immensely depressing lives. Soon after birth their ears are clipped for identification purposes, their needle teeth are removed to prevent injuries in fights, and males are castrated (all without anaesthetic); some four months later they are slaughtered. Throughout it all they experience only unrelenting frustration, pain, and suffering. Pigs live in hierarchically structured groups. Some are dominant, some are submissive, and this order emerges only after they spend time together. Adding new pigs to the mix destroys the social structure and almost inevitably leads to vicious fighting. Because their confined areas leave no room for the more submissive or weaker pigs to retreat, these fights produce numerous fatalities. Frequently these battles occur when pigs are transported or awaiting slaughter.

In addition, factory farming greatly affects the pig's natural food-gathering and eating habits. Left to its own, a pig will spend half its waking hours searching for and eating food. The diet is rather varied, comprising seedlings, insects, and even very small animals. The factory farm subverts all this. The pig cannot search for food and is fed only a concentrated, protein-rich supplement formulated to fatten the pig as much and as quickly as possible. Eating time is reduced to twenty minutes, and although the pigs receive enough calories to maintain life, they suffer from hunger. The concentrated feed often causes liver abnormalities that go untreated. Since the pig will be slaughtered in a few months, medical treatment would just decrease profits.

It is occasionally said that foraging behavior is purely instinctual, so that the pigs do not really suffer from their confined quarters. The logic of this argument is twisted. If anything, thwarted instinctual behavior will cause more frustration than stifled learned behavior. If the behavior were instinctual, or "hard-wired," restricting it should be more problematic, not less. For example, breathing is instinctual in humans. Parity of reasoning would tell us that humans will not be frustrated (not to say suffer) when denied air.

## The Hog Slaughterhouse

About 100 million hogs are slaughtered annually in the United States. The prescribed method of slaughter is slightly different from that required by the regulations that putatively govern the slaughter of cows. Hogs are "urged" through a narrow angled restrainer and then electrically (rather than mechanically) stunned. Electrodes held at the rear of the pig's head and back for about 3 seconds ostensibly render it unconscious, if not dead. Then, in a step similar to one in cow slaughterhouses, they are shackled by one leg and hoisted onto an overhead rail. They then have their throats slit and bleed out. Next they are lowered into scalding water, after which they are eviscerated. Problems occur with great frequency everywhere along the production line.

The priority that plant managers place on speed again causes much of the unnecessary pain and suffering. At larger plants a hog is slaughtered every four seconds. Problems occur from the beginning, the chute leading up to the restrainer. Usually two or three men urge the hogs through. Unsurprisingly, many of the hogs are reluctant. They smell the blood, sense the terror, and frantically twist and turn, attempting to escape the chutes; some become crippled. Workers use violence to badger these hogs, which are kicked, whipped, and beaten with almost any imaginable object. Prods are shoved up their rectums. Meat hooks are stuck in their anuses and then pulled. Anything goes, as long as it speeds the hogs to the restrainer. A hog that cannot walk is beaten to death, shoved to the side, and hung up later.

The stunning operation tends to be farcical. The hogs are frenzied when they enter the restrainer—facing every which way, running with fear, and banging into one another. It is not surprising that the stunner often fails to solidly stun them. There are several causes for this. Sometimes hogs come by one on top of another, and the stunner doesn't see the bottom hog. Some stunners enjoy harassing the shackler, so they intentionally misstun the hog to make the shackler's job more difficult. Sometimes they doze off, letting live hogs pass by. Probably the major cause for unsatisfactory stunning, however, derives from orders of the manager.

Plant managers are notorious for requiring the stunners to use low voltage, because high voltage can tear up the meat. The diminished voltage can stun some of the pigs, but it often fails to stun a good size sow or boar. These larger hogs need to be multiply stunned, and even then they may still be conscious when they are shackled, hoisted, and stuck. Plant managers are fully aware that an improperly stunned hog may free himself from the overhead rail after being shackled. In fact, slaughterhouses address such escape attempts by incorporating pens below the overhead rail. These pens are usually small, large enough to hold perhaps two pigs. Sometimes, however, upward of ten or fifteen hogs—all of whom are thoroughly dazed and in excruciating pain—are crammed into the pen. Ostensibly the overhead rail is stopped when hogs fall into the pen, and a worker stuns the penned pigs with a portable stunner. When this task is completed, the hogs are to be reshackled, rehoisted, and stuck before the chain is restarted.

Shacklers often mercilessly beat the penned hogs with lead pipes until the animal is so dazed that he can be reshackled and hoisted. If there are many hogs in the pen, there may not be enough time to beat them. The shackler may chain and hoist an obviously conscious hog. Even those hogs that have been beaten often regain consciousness soon after they find themselves strung up on the overhead rail.

After having their throats slit, the hogs are dropped into scalding (140° F) water to remove their hair. But frequently live hogs are dropped into the water. Usually this is because a hog will tighten its muscles after having its throat slit, instinctively trying to keep the blood in its body. If the hog has not yet bled out or the sticking was performed less than adequately, the hog may be conscious when it hits the water. Sometimes live hogs are dunked into the scalding water because they haven't been stuck *at all*. The speed of the operation may make it impossible for the sticker to slit the throat of every hog that passes through. And sometimes hogs are chased into the scalding tank because some employees find it entertaining. Hogs scream from pain, thrash in the scalding water, and inevitably succumb and drown. This may take a couple of minutes. Plant managers are apt to get angry when a live hog is killed in the scalding tank, but not because of empathy; they realize that a meat inspector is likely to condemn the meat, so that the operation will lose money. The solution is to demand that the workers stick the living hogs and then proceed as usual.

Sadly, although I know of no statistics on the matter, some stunners are mean-spirited and sadistic. I have already mentioned how stunners harass shacklers by sending them conscious animals. There are reports of stunners moving the electric wand from the hog's head to his back without holding it for the required three seconds.[4] Apparently some of stunners receive perverted pleasure from seeing the hog jump and squeal from the pain. Stickers have also been known to beat hogs mercilessly with lead pipes, puncture their eyes, and cut off their noses. Stickers become annoyed at needing to stick conscious hogs, and the hogs become the innocent victims of their frustration. Also, continuously killing hogs every day may become a bit boring. Novel ways of causing pain, suffering, and death may spice up the day.

As it does with cows, transportation brings torture and death to hogs. Hogs packed into trucks are prone to heat exhaustion in the summertime. They may travel over a thousand miles and not be sprayed down for the entire trip. In the winter they die from the cold. Some, both the dead and the living, freeze to the steel railings of the truck. Workers then toss a cable around them to pull them off the truck and bring them to the slaughterhouse. That a leg may still be attached to the truck after the hog is dragged out is of no concern. At other times, workers use knives or wires to pry the hogs loose. That some of their skin is left on the truck is again of no moment. Since frozen hogs are valueless to the processing plant, they are usually left by the side of the facility. The living receive no care or attention. They are left to fend for themselves and soon die from exhaustion. The nominal power of the Humane Slaughter Act apparently does not apply to frozen hogs. Inspectors make no antemortem examinations, nor are there any regulations to guide their disposal. With frozen hogs—sometimes as many as fifteen or twenty in a truckload—there is not even the pretense of any concern for the animals' welfare.

Overcrowding kills some hogs but constrains costs by letting producers use fewer trucks, fewer drivers, and less fuel. As with cows, moreover, everyone in the chain of command has good reason to neither report nor correct inhumane practices. And so it goes, while the pigs pay the price.

## Chickens

Each year more than 8 billion chickens are killed in the United States. This number dwarfs the slaughter of all other farm animals combined. It may be difficult to grasp how large this number is, but it may help to realize that there are about 6 billion people on the planet. This means that every year U.S. factory farms alone annually kill one-third more chickens than there are people on the planet.

Chickens, like modern cows, differ radically from their naturally occurring counterparts, having been genetically manipulated to serve our lust for their eggs and flesh. Layer hens, manipulated to produce the most eggs possible in the least time, are confined to battery cages their whole lives. These small housing units are stored in huge warehouses in rows and tiers. Broiler chickens, raised for their meat, are not caged but are still confined to sheds for their entire lives. Chickens of both types are forced to lead lives completely at odds with their natures. The chickens in factory farms hardly count as chickens at all. They are aliens to themselves. As are cows and pigs, they are treated as things, instruments, mere machines whose sole purpose in life is to *produce,* be it eggs or meat. But of course they are not Cartesian automatons. They can suffer pain and frustration, and as I will show in some detail, they are submitted to ungodly amounts of both.[5]

## The Battery Hen: Childhood

Factory farming of chickens is among the most perverse of human activities. Virtually every stage of a chicken's life is altered to accommodate production goals. Consider, first, the thoroughly corrupted relationship between a mother hen and her progeny. Hens do not require roosters to lay eggs. Like other vertebrates, a hen periodically sheds eggs from her body. Still, when she is ready to lay an egg, a signal is sent out to her mate, if she has one, that the time has come to build a nest. This is a carefully planned activity. A proper place must be found, one that is relatively safe from predators and yet near enough to the twigs, leaves, and dirt that will serve as building blocks for the nest. The rooster is in charge of the search, but the hen has final say over the site's acceptability. Although chickens are polygamous, hens and roosters do not just breed but actually bond. For example, roosters perform dances for their special hens, and they exchange clucks of recognition and endearment throughout the day. In short, having a family is of great consequence to chickens.

When eggs are laid, the hen busies herself keeping her nest clean and rotating the eggs throughout the day to maintain the proper temperature. She will leave her nest for short periods during the day to forage for food, move around, and defecate, calling for the rooster to watch over the eggs during these times. Hens lay one egg daily over three to fifteen days. This group of eggs is known as a "clutch." After producing one clutch, the hen takes a day off before starting another. If the eggs are fertile, she will sit on them (i.e., incubate them), ensuring that the entire clutch will hatch the same day. After the eggs hatch, mother and children walk, eat, drink, scratch, and preen. Baby chicks are precocial, meaning that they exhibit these behaviors right after hatching, imprinting on a leader (typically their mother) who serves as a model for social activities. The mother hen's main job is to provide her children warmth, which she does by enveloping them under her wings. After a month or two the mother flies up to her perch, signaling that it is time for the chicks to strike out on their own. The metaphor that likens caring or even overprotective people to hens is well wrought.

Although a hen will be extremely protective of her brood, little aggression occurs within a flock. Chickens *play,* a fact that seems lost on almost all of us, factory farmer or consumer alike. (Another often unknown fact is that they fly. I suspect that if second and third graders were asked whether chickens fly, at least one-quarter would say they do not, so much is the true nature of chickens kept from us in our youths.) They chase each other and gently spar. Occasionally fighting occurs, but even then serious violence rarely ensues. Hierarchical relationships—pecking orders—are formed in flocks, and before too long chickens get to know their places and just how far they can tax their flockmates' patience and goodwill. Violent fighting does occur when chickens are confined to small cages, however. Tempers run short under these artificially crowded conditions, for there is no room to stretch, let alone run or play, and there is stark competition for the food in the feeder. This is not the first time that I have noted the dangerous consequences of overcrowding. Such consequences should not shock us; human beings act similarly. I can say from personal experience that the crowded conditions of jail cells increase the risks of fights. Although humans and chickens are both social creatures, neither species thrives in densely populated, confined conditions.

Before I detail the life of a battery hen per se, consider what happens at a commercial hatchery.[6] Hatcheries serve as artificial mother hens insofar as they incubate chicken eggs. A hatchery will contain many large incubators, each scheduled to yield newborn chicks on a particular day. Trays of chicks are gathered on carts and wheeled toward a window where workers remove each tray and toss the live chicks onto a conveyor belt. Speed is the key, and many chicks wind up on the hatchery floor. Instead of being picked up, the baby chicks are routinely squashed to death by the carts continually parading down the corridor.

Soon afterward, usually on the next day, male and some female chicks that are to be sent to breeding facilities have their toes cut off with an electric clipper. The future male breeders have their combs removed ("dubbed") by scissors or shears that are positioned perilously close to the backs of these newborn chicks' heads. All the other male chicks are worthless to a laying farm. As soon as the chicks are born, a worker manually determines their sex. Naturally, about half are male. Nationally 200 million of these chicks are immediately "disposed of"—that is, killed. The owner of a battery hen farm views male chicks much as the owner of a dairy farm views male calves. The newborns are an unfortunate and inevitable waste product of their industries.

Rather than expose the chicks to carbon dioxide gas, which would provide a quick, painless death, the hatcheries usually throw the male chicks into trash bags, where they die from suffocation. The ones on top squash the ones on bottom, who often suffer broken bones prior to their asphyxiation. Some hatcheries simply throw live male chicks into grinding machines to be turned into fertilizer. Some die immediately, but not all. The more unfortunate remain in eddies before they meet their end. Many of these chicks suffer broken bones and skulls before finally being ground to death.

The female chicks are debeaked at the hatchery or shortly after they arrive at the grow-out facility. While one part of a machine burns off one-quarter of the bird's beak, another part cauterizes the wound. Because beaks contain hosts of nerve cells, this burning hurts the frightened chicks, which they express through loud chirping and excessive defecation. Many die from shock and blood loss. In other cases, haphazard workmanship leaves beaks so disfigured that the chicks cannot eat and so die of starvation. Others who are improperly cauterized must endure the process a second time at a later date.

Vaccinations also occur at the hatchery. In some hatcheries workers hold the chicks while a machine automatically injects the chicks with the vaccine. This is done at breakneck speed—almost one bird per second. Puncture wounds are common, and infection frequently results. Moreover, needles are reused many times, creating a prime environment for contamination. Chicks destined for breeding are vaccinated again at the breeding facility. Common practice has workers catching three birds at a time, bending their wings behind their backs to expose the chest for inoculation. Birds are handled roughly throughout this procedure. Some die when caught, many have their wings broken when pinned behind their backs, and since once again needles are reused repeatedly, birds often become infected.

### The Battery Hen: Daily Life

I have alluded to the confined conditions in which battery hens spend their entire lives. It is now time for specificity. Warehouses routinely hold more than 100,000 birds at a time, and current plans call for megahouses that may hold five or even ten times that number. Space and time are at a premium. Arranging tiers and rows of cages in a circumscribed space means lower cost for rental, personnel, and feed. Federal regulations permit enclosing up to nine three- or four-pound hens with wingspans of thirty to thirty-two inches in a cage that measures fourteen inches high and eighteen to twenty inches across. Each hen has an average living space of forty-eight square inches. Imagine a six-by-eight-inch piece of paper. This is all the space that a four-pound bird may have for virtually her whole life.[7] The hens cannot stand normally, let alone perform normal activities such as walking, playing, preening, and flying. The chicken's natural life is utterly subverted in the name of economic gain. The welfare of the chicken counts not one whit.

These cages, which serve as homes for 98 percent of all egg-laying hens in the United States, are made of thin wire mesh triangles and designed to facilitate manure removal and egg recovery. The thin metallic footing is anathema to the chickens. Chickens are descendants of junglefowl that by nature continually scratch at the ground. Scratching on wire mesh results in cracks and deformities in the chickens' claws. Whereas constant scratching of the ground would keep a hen's claws short, the wire floors leave them long, twisted, and broken. Moreover, the claws often become entangled in the wire mesh, making it impossible for the hens to walk the tiny distance to get feed. When this occurs, they slowly starve to death. In tests where they were offered floors of wood shavings, peat, and dirt, hens unsurprisingly chose these over the metallic counterparts. This is not just a matter of comfort; the birds both pick at and dustbathe in these natural materials, two behaviors that are wholly denied them in battery cages.[8]

The ultraconfinement causes what is known as "caged layer fatigue," a form of osteoporosis stemming from the birds' complete lack of exercise. Bone density greatly decreases, making broken bones and paralysis much more likely when the hens are eventually removed for slaughter. This condition is exacerbated by the unnaturally high demand on the hens to produce eggs. Minerals that would normally be used to increase the hen's own bone density gets transferred to eggshells, a loss far greater than the hen can normally accommodate. The rate of heart attacks from stress greatly increases, because low serum levels interfere with calcium ionic exchange in the smooth-muscle tissue of the heart and arteries. Chickens become chemically unbalanced. In fact, soaring death rates due to this phenomenon became an economic liability. Geneticists and farmers had to do something to maintain profitability. Their solution was to add vitamins and other nutritional supplements to the feed, but this did not improve the chickens' well-being. The additional calcium required for bone maintenance still went primarily to form eggshells. As a result, the eggs we buy have pretty shells, but the epidemic of leg deformities and pain for the chicken continues unabated.[9]

Confinement also triggers facial cellulitis, an incurable disease more commonly known as swollen head syndrome. This disease arises from the filth that accompanies overcrowding. Tissue below the skin swells, pushing the face outward. The syndrome includes nasal discharge, mucous congestion, and increased nervousness.[10]

Confinement also provides an enhanced climate for pathogenic bacteria, perhaps the most notorious being salmonella. The incidence of salmonella infection has soared as cramped conditions have worsened. Previously salmonella appeared in eggs only when external sources contaminated cracked eggshells, but it now occurs in intact eggs. To combat these bacteria, antibiotics are administered to the battery hens. Seen from the farmer's perspective, this has the additional benefit of stimulating egg production and increasing growth rate. Virtually all factory hens in the United States regularly get antibiotics; consequently, many strains of bacteria have become drug resistant. More virulent strains, including a type of "super" salmonella, have become prevalent.[11]

On entering a battery farm, one cannot help but notice the acrid smell of ammonia. Unlike broilers, battery hens pass their entire lives in tiered cages, which greatly complicates manure removal. Tens of thousands of these birds will obviously create an enormous amount of manure. Troughs underneath the hens collect the droppings to expedite waste removal. The ammonia results from urea decomposing in the manure pits. In chickens the ammoniated air causes keratoconjunctivitis, an ulceration of the cornea that can end in blindness. Ammonia also irritates the mucous membranes of the hens' upper respiratory tracts, making it easier for disease to infiltrate the lungs and even the liver. Ammonia enters the blood stream, too, compromising the immune system and making it easier for diseases to occur. Thus ammonia presents far more than a merely aesthetic problem for the hens who are continuously subjected to it. The humane solution would be to give the hens room to walk about. When hen density decreases, so does manure density, and the waste would be dried by the sun and largely assimilated into the soil. The argument against this is the old refrain that such a change would lower profits.[12]

Coccidiosis, a disease caused by a protozoan parasite, becomes a problem in the confined spaces of intensive farming. The poultry industry itself admits that the parasite, normally situated benignly in the gut of a bird, becomes mortally dangerous among great concentrations of birds. It is the crowded environment that turns a benign parasite into a malignant one.[13]

The problems of confinement exceed an increase of disease. Behavioral disorders such as excessive pecking (known as "cannibalism") result from cramped conditions as well. Denied their natural activities, birds resort to pulling and picking on one another's vents, feathers, and toes. Pecking in chickens is normal, part of their natural foraging behavior. When hens are denied their normal ways of gathering food, however, it becomes a problem. First, pecking at another bird's feathers helps make up for lost nutrients.[14] This perverted pecking stems from the bird's inability to clean itself by dustbathing. Having no dirt to use, the chicken will turn to another hen's feathers, a poor substitute. Finally, birds peck more when they are afraid, and the hyperconfinement in which the hens find themselves clearly tends to increase fear. The farmers' solution to the pecking problem is debeaking.

Egg producers cut off about two-thirds of the hens' beaks in debeaking them. As mentioned earlier, the beak (including its tip) contains a host of nerves, so that the hen clearly suffers pain from debeaking. The worst pain may occur about a week later. Significantly, the birds often lose their appetites or are so mutilated that they cannot eat or drink. Nevertheless, the poultry industry defends debeaking by claiming that it is necessary to deter cannibalism. The industry compares debeaking a hen to trimming a human fingernail.[15] I have already shown that the first claim is spurious; several studies have demonstrated the second to be false, too.[16] Human fingernails lack nerve cells, a necessary condition for pain; not so for a chicken's beak. Just as bad, the poultry industry is disingenuous. Its members know full well that the procedure causes pain—their term "beak tenderness," which they use to describe the hen's feelings after debeaking, testifies to this knowledge.[17] In fact, poultry farmers build deep feed troughs so that the hens can eat without suffering severe pain; if the hens don't eat, they will die, often well before they can be used as productive egg layers. Debeaking in layers occurs twice, once at the hatchery and again in about four months, just before the laying cycle. The pace is extremely rapid, up to fifteen birds a minute. This ensures even more mutilation than would occur were all debeaking done with care. Although usually done with a hot electric blade, debeaking is sometimes performed with a knife or a pair of scissors. These are not precision instruments.

The genetic manipulation of the modern hen has exacerbated the suffering caused by debeaking. The hens produced via this manipulation not only mature earlier and produce more frequently but also suffer from an increased nervousness, which in turn increases pecking. The targets of a hen's pecking are by default her cagemates, who are constantly rubbing against her. All the caged birds are in the same impossible situation. They develop "caged layer hysteria," in which they wildly try to fly, hide, and squawk at the same time. The birds are driven mad.

I have already mentioned a humane solution to the "cannibalism" problem, namely, reducing confinement. Ironically, debeaking has created a novel sort of cannibalism. Constant mutual pecking produces blackened eyes and ear lobes, in addition to subcutaneous hemorrhaging below the eyes. One wonders whether the poultry industry is truly concerned with cannibalism, as it sometimes purports to be. Many farmers claim that even if science could create a calmer hen less prone to pecking, economic considerations might still dictate debeaking: debeaked birds eat less and so keep feed costs down.

I have alluded to the fact that confinement all but eliminates dustbathing. Dustbathing is an important activity for chickens, who use it to clean and refresh themselves, to keep their feathers healthy, and to stay cool. Confinement does not thwart this ingrained behavior, but it does eliminate the activity's beneficial results.[18] In fact, dustbathing under these conditions yields horrible results. Rubbing against thin metal mesh has only deleterious consequences for the claws, legs, and general health of the hens.

At the same time, the chickens face a threat from overheating. The high temperatures found in battery cage units, which generally stem from overcrowding, can be a real problem for the hens, who begin to suffer heat stress at about 80 degrees Fahrenheit. Birds do not perspire, so they help cool themselves by dustbathing, an avenue now closed to them. Egg factories generally use fans and sprinklers to cool down the birds and reduce the mortality rate. Comfort is not an issue, however. These cooling procedures may be just enough to keep the bird alive but not enough to provide even minimal comfort. When the fans and sprinklers break down—a not infrequent occurrence—the heat-sensitive bursal cells responsible for maintaining the hens' immune system stop functioning properly. The resulting immune system deterioration causes a condition in birds similar to AIDS in people. Every summer, millions of caged birds die of heat stress. In the heat wave affecting the East Coast in 1995, an estimated 3–5 million hens died of heat stress.[19] The problem is widespread, and the manner of death is especially horrid.

Another issue facing battery hens that has to some extent filtered into the public's consciousness is forced molting. At about eighteen months laying hens are either sent to slaughter or forced to molt. The forced molting process tries to fool the hen's body into thinking that it has entered another laying cycle, doing so by either completely starving the birds for two weeks or more or substantially reducing their food intake for the same period of time. The dietary constriction reduces hormones that inhibit egg laying. This technique, which also causes new feathers to push out old ones (hence the term *forced molting*), reduces the time between egg-laying cycles from four months to around one month. The natural four-month interval allows the chicken to maintain enough energy to produce new feathers and keep warm. In nature cold weather generally limits the amount of food available, so that evolution has tended to inhibit egg laying in cold weather. Since the egg farmers have no qualms about thwarting natural cycles, they prefer to deceive the hen's biology into thinking that winter, the time of decreased egg production, has passed.[20] But the farmers do not stop at starvation. A growing trend is to keep lights on in the warehouses *continuously* for two weeks, simulating a constant spring. Although starvation procedures have been banned in Great Britain since 1987, they are still legal in the United States.

Hens that are not "recycled" (or forced to molt) are nevertheless starved for about four days before they are shipped to slaughterhouses. This move is purely economic. Having virtually no monetary value, these "spent" hens are handled without care. Traveling in crowded trucks hundreds of miles without food or water, many have their wings, backs, and necks broken by the workers who round them up at their final destination. These hens are barely recognizable at the time of slaughter. Bruises, abrasions, broken bones, tumors, and hemorrhages are the norm rather than the exception. The birds are shredded and wind up either in cheap human foods (pot pies and institutional foods) or as feed for cows, pigs, and poultry. A coming trend is gassing the birds at the farm and feeding the remains to the other hens.

## The Broiler Chicken

Broiler chickens are raised for their flesh. Like most other farm animals used for human consumption, the modern broiler chicken is a genetically engineered product of "advanced" technology. The broiler chicken industry has a simple goal: to maximize the birds' weight and minimize production time. To gain some perspective, compare the 2.8-pound average weight of a four-month-old broiler chicken in 1935 to the 4.7-pound average weight of a seven-week-old broiler in 1994.[21] This is not evolution at work. This unnaturally rapid growth causes a host of problems. Since bone calcification cannot keep up with the growth rate, broiler chickens commonly suffer skeletal abnormalities. Legs become bowed and twisted, bones fracture and fissure, vertebra become dislocated, and cartilage grows in the lower back and protrudes against the spinal cord.[22] As a result, broiler chickens are in chronic pain.

The most serious affliction suffered by broiler chickens is heart failure. In fact, some chicken farmers take a high incidence of heart failure to indicate a good meat flock. The most common process for heart failure among broilers occurs in a disease called ascites, or pulmonary hypertension syndrome. This fatal problem directly results from manipulating chickens to grow far faster than they normally would. The perversion of the chicken's nature manifests itself early in the broiler chicken's life.

Because of premature rapid growth, the chickens' vascular systems are too undeveloped to adequately oxygenate their blood.[23] The lungs of birds normally develop more slowly than the rest of their bodies even in species free from genetic tampering, but the manipulation compounds this disparity. The heart tries to compensate by working harder to pump the blood through the body. Concomitantly, the birds' kidneys produce a hormone that stimulates red blood cells (which transport oxygen) and hemoglobin (protein in red blood cells). This causes the blood to become more viscous, and so the heart must pump even harder to get this "sticky" blood through the body. Eventually, either the heart fails or blood backs up in the lungs, causing the bird to suffocate. Incredibly, this disease process has been found to begin before the birds hatch. The chicken industry's demand for egg density and chick output has resulted in oxygen deficiency in newborn chicks.[24]

Problems increase as the chicken gets older and heavier. The increased demand for chicken meat has led growers to breed chickens that get heavier at an earlier age. "Roaster" chickens, the biggest of the lot, weigh between six and eight pounds when they are slaughtered after two and one-half months. Most chickens are somewhat lighter and get to live no more than two months. They are sent to slaughter at this early age, when they are still growing, because mortality rates increase precipitously thereafter. Birds as young as six to seven weeks are on the brink of heart failure or death from infection. One study delayed slaughter until sixteen weeks, still quite early in a chicken's life. More than one-quarter of this group died from heart failure, and another 10 percent were on the brink of fatal heart disease.[25]

Both roaster and typical broilers are crippled before slaughter, their weight being too much for their immature skeletons. Obese chickens have arthritic problems similar to those in obese humans. Their troubles go beyond chronic joint pain, however; the grossly overweight bird has trouble moving for other reasons, too. Their excessive weight pushes their bodies against the ammoniated floors that are covered with moist bedding and droppings. Additional ammonia results from the decomposing uric acid found in the birds' droppings. The ammonia irritates the birds' breast, feet, and whatever other parts are constantly in contact with floor, causing burning and ulcers. This environment invites staph infections in these exposed areas.

This ammonia causes further problems. The chicks live in filthy, dust-laden, ammoniated, oxygen-deficient sheds, which substantially hamper breathing for the twenty to forty thousand birds housed there. The ammonia produces irritations and burning sensations in their eyes and throat. Workers suffer similar effects, but unlike the chickens, they do not spend most of their lives in this highly polluted environment. When ammonia levels reach 60 ppm, a common figure in broiler warehouses, the chickens become susceptible to an extremely painful form of conjunctivitis. They literally cry out in pain, either unable or unwilling to open their eyes. Blindness may result, and if it does, eating and drinking obviously become more difficult.[26] Although this condition raises mortality rates, broiler farmers decline to improve ventilation, perhaps by installing air-conditioning or allowing the birds to spend some time outside the shed, dismissing such measures as cost-ineffective.[27] It is cheaper to lose birds than to improve their health.

Unfortunately for the broiler chicken, it can produce (i.e., gain weight in a short period of time) even when subjected to filthy, diseased conditions. Since the birds can do this, the broiler farmer sees no incentive to provide them with cleaner, less crowded conditions. In fact, overcrowding has become a science, one that seeks to get as many chickens as possible in the smallest possible space. Growers know that density increases mortality, but they also know that, on average, it increases the weight of a broiler during its first twelve months. Suppose that the farmer reduces the broilers' floor space from one to one-half square foot. Twice as many birds will die, but the survivors will have more meat on them at the time of slaughter. A breeding company has suggested that the best weight-to-space ratio is eight-tenths of a square foot per bird. This gives a bird about 115 square inches of room. This is not nearly enough space: a three- to four-pound chicken needs at least 74 inches just to stand, 197 square inches to merely turn around, 137 square inches to stretch, 290 square inches to flap his wings, 172 square inches to preen, and 133 square inches to scratch the ground.[28]

Life may become even worse for broilers. Heretofore leg problems, breast blisters, and especially poor growth have deterred farmers from placing broiler chickens in cages like those to which their laying counterparts are consigned. It is now alleged, however, that cages with plastic mesh floors and automatic manure and bird removal systems can cure this "problem." Farmers, of course, would welcome such an invention with open arms. This would enable them to set up a multitiered system like the one used for laying hens, enabling them to cramp even more chickens into limited space. As I write this book, such systems remain on the horizon, but the future may prove even more chilling to the broiler chicken.

## The Chicken Slaughterhouse

In the United States about 140 million broiler chickens are killed each week. In a year more than 100 million "spent" hens are killed and 250 million dispensable male chicks are killed at hatcheries.

Workers move into the broiler chicken shed at night. The relative quiet of the shed is shattered when they grab a handful of chickens—perhaps as many as four or five at a time—and load them into plastic crates. The birds are frenzied, desperately trying to escape the workers's clutches. The battle is futile. The birds will either get their skulls and bodies crushed before the workers can load them into plastic crates, or they will be forced into the crates, often with broken wings and legs. In theory the workers should exercise care when placing the birds in the crates so as to protect "carcass quality." In practice the workers, who are paid by their loading rate and not by the number of chickens that arrive at the slaughterhouse in good condition, scarcely care about the birds' welfare. There is not even the pretense of concern regarding "spent" hens, who are ripped from their battery cages, often leaving a wing or leg still attached to the wire mesh. The work continues until dawn, by which time some thirty thousand chickens have been either killed or shoved into crates. The crates are then loaded onto trucks that journey to the slaughterhouse.

In the summer some chickens die of suffocation, and in the winter some freeze to death while on the trucks. But the transportation is grueling for all. Heat stress is common, for ten to twelve four-pound chickens packed in 3.5 feet of cage space will experience significant heat even in only moderately warm outdoor temperatures. Trips may take ten or more hours. The birds' fear is enormous; tests have shown that their fear levels on these journeys equal that from high-intensity electric shocks. There is no food or water for the six to seven thousand birds on the truck. I have already mentioned that food is withheld from the spent hens to save money. In addition, food is denied to broilers for twelve hours before they are culled to reduce "intestinal splatter" and because it would not be metabolized into chicken meat.[29] To save even more money, battery hens are denied food for several days before slaughter.[30] The denial of food weakens their immune systems, resulting in a tenfold increase in the rate of salmonella poisoning. Fear, trauma, and stress make heart attacks responsible for half the deaths suffered during transport to the slaughterhouse. One looks in vain to find any federal regulations regarding poultry transportation by truck. The industry can do as it pleases without fear of legal repercussions.

On arriving at the slaughterhouse, birds may wait in their cramped conditions for many hours. The killing itself occurs in three stages: stunning (a term that I will show to be a misnomer), throat slitting, and bleeding. The millions of laying hens that are slaughtered annually are neither stunned nor paralyzed. After a year of intense egg laying, their brittle bones would shatter if placed in the electrified water. Often they are ground up while conscious. Most large plants stun broilers by hanging live birds upside down on a movable metal rack that passes their heads and necks through an electrically charged brine bath for about seven seconds. Broiler chickens (and turkeys) are forced to endure this to relax their neck muscles and contract their wing muscles, measures taken to facilitate their deaths by (usually) an automatic blade. It also supposedly diminishes the bird's struggle as the blood drains from its neck, promotes rapid (less than 90 seconds) bleeding, and loosens feathers.[31]

Chickens subjected to these electrical baths suffer body tremors, reduced heartbeat and breathing, and raised blood pressure. Most important, despite having been named "stun baths," these baths probably do *not* render the bird unconscious. In some cases a bird will arch its head, so that its brain is not sizzled with current. The bird is paralyzed but still fully capable of feeling pain and suffering. In other cases the current levels are too low. To produce unconsciousness, the current should be at least 120 μA; currents lower than 75 μA should never be used.[32] Most stun baths in the United States, however, produce unconscionably low currents, between 12 and 50 μA per bird.[33] The industry is loath to use more powerful currents because the higher voltage causes hemorrhaging, producing what is known as a "bloody bird." Ultimately, then, although stunning is supposed to render the bird unconscious for subsequent slaughterhouse operations, the electric shock frequently just immobilizes it.

The throats of chickens are slit either manually or automatically. In manual cutting the bird's neck is cut at a joint where it meets its head; in automatic cutting the neck is cut by one or two revolving blades. The fastest method to produce brain death is to cut the carotid arteries, which take blood to the brain. Cutting the jugular veins, which take blood away from the brain, prolongs the process. Worse still is cutting just one of the jugular veins, which can prolong death up to eight minutes. Problems arise from poor cutting and ignorance. Some believe, incorrectly, that cutting the jugular veins brings about the quickest death. Since the carotid arteries are located behind a muscular area in the chicken's neck, misplaced cuts can occur by not cutting deep enough.[34]

After bleeding out for about one minute, the birds enter a scald tank to loosen their feathers. They are supposed to be dead when dumped into the tank. Unfortunately theory yet again does not match practice. Around 4 million living, breathing broiler chickens are plunged into scald tanks every day in the United States. This is easier to confirm than one might think: birds who are killed in the scalding process emerge with red skins.[35]

\*　　\*　　\*

Mercifully, this brings my description of factory farming to a close. For the cows, hogs, and chickens, however, there is anything but closure. Their suffering continues apace. This documentation of intensive farming should suffice for persuading any fair-minded person that the industry violates the PGS. We are morally obligated to bring about enormous changes in the ways we relate to our food and its production.

# CHAPTER FOUR

# HUNTING

Recent feminist philosophers have rightfully made us more aware of the language that we use to describe women. The inordinate number of debasing terms for women clearly shows that our attitudes still need major repair. A similar point applies to hunting terminology. It is telling that hunters tend to characterize their practice as a "sport" and refer to themselves as "sportsmen" and "sportswomen." This is both misleading and repugnant. Sporting events involve voluntary participants. All the parties have some chance of winning, with the winner typically rewarded with money, a trophy, or a medal. But hunting has none of these characteristics. Obviously the animals do not voluntarily enter the sport. No doubt, given the choice, the deer, squirrel, or dove would opt out of the event. Nor does the animal have any chance of "winning." The best outcome is to leave the arena a free, uninjured creature. Conversely, the hunter cannot really lose. There is little or no risk that a deer, squirrel, or dove will cause physical harm. For the hunter, the worst outcome is failing to kill an innocent, defenseless creature. This is hardly a loss worthy of the name. Hunting is no more a sport than is bullfighting. It is nothing more than a rigged event where the loser is preordained and the loss is as serious as it can be. The animal can and often does suffer a painful, torturous death.

Annual animal populations are referred to as "crops"; killing members of what are deemed excessive crops is called "harvesting." Effectively, deer and other game animals are assimilated to nonsentient commodities. Killing an animal is like picking cotton. The covert implication is that, since harvesting cotton is thoroughly unobjectionable, taking animal life should be as well. As so often happens in exploitation, the victims are viewed as having no inherent value; they matter only as resources for their oppressors.

# The Arguments for Hunting

## Magnanimous Hunters

The argument hunters most common employ might be called the "kindness gambit." They begin by pointing out that animals in the wild are susceptible to starvation, predation, and disease. They then argue that it would be far preferable for the animal to find a quick and certain death from a hunter's gun, so that hunting becomes an act of kindness. The hunter thus construes his killing as an act of euthanasia.

In the greater public this argument becomes quite simple: hunters save animals, particularly deer, from starvation. Hunting is praised for saving deer from the slow and agonizing deaths they would otherwise suffer in the heart of winter. Promoted as agents of goodwill and mercy, hunters are portrayed as civil servants whose periodic "thinning" of the herds prevent deer from suffering horrible deaths when their populations overwhelm available food supplies.

Like any wildlife populations, deer populations fluctuate relative to available food, weather, and other environmental factors. They cannot increase indefinitely, however. When herds of deer surpass ecologically ideal conditions—when the population becomes too dense for a particular ecosystem—they succumb to stress, even if there is plentiful food and good weather. Advocates of the kindness gambit employ these ecological facts to show the magnanimity of hunters who, rather than allow deer to die slowly from stress, put them to a quick death.

To substantiate the horrors of an unchecked population, hunters frequently refer to the large management program conducted on the Kaibab Plateau in Arizona in 1908. This management program (actually an experiment) was designed to show whether deer populations would explode if natural predators were removed and the habitat was manipulated to provide additional food for the deer. To this end, hunters were asked to kill the cougars, wolves, and coyotes who were the natural enemies of the 4,000 mule deer that roamed the plateau. Conservation officers removed 200,000 sheep and 20,000 cattle so that the deer would have more food available. In fifteen years the deer population did explode, reaching 100,000. Afterward 60,000 died from starvation and malnutrition in a cold winter.

No one denies that animal populations increase in environments with plenty of food and space and few or no predators. As far as this is concerned, the Kaibab program was an expensive and superfluous experiment. Rather than confirm the paradoxical claim that killing deer benefits them, however, the Kaibab experiment suggests that we should not cavalierly tamper with nature. Leaving the predators and land as it was before human manipulation would have left the predator-prey relationship in harmony, as it had been before the study. Absent some cataclysm, no population explosion and no subsequent huge deer die-off would have occurred if the plateau had been left alone.

Paradoxically, hunting, especially intensive hunting, will increase the number of deer in an ecosystem and so maximize the number of deer deaths. When environmental factors are unfavorable, deer populations will occasionally plummet, or "crash," largely as a result of does absorbing embryos. After a crash deer fertility and reproductive rates rise in a natural attempt to return the population to an optimal level. Intensive hunting provokes a precipitous crash in the deer population. If the hunting continues annually and there is adequate food, the surviving bucks will impregnate most of the ovulating does. The does will typically give birth to two fawns rather than the usual one, not just for the initial pregnancy, but for subsequent ones as well. Studies have also shown that intensive hunting prompts unusually young does to become pregnant. Instead of ovulating and possibly becoming pregnant in their second or third autumn, does may be impregnated at their first fall. This mechanism increases the number of fertile does. Adding land manipulation that affords the deer more food than is common at certain times of the year yields a near-perfect scenario for a huge and quick increase in the number of deer.[1]

Whereas intensive hunting is likely to cause unusually high reproductive rates, predation will not. Many significant differences account for this. Nonhuman predators will kill the weakest and oldest of the herd. A wolf can catch an old, sickly deer more easily than it can a young, healthy one. In general hunters are not so discriminating; the healthy and the unhealthy are considered to be equally legitimate targets, so that they end up killing more fertile animals than, say, wolves do. Moreover, hunters like to shoot big bucks, since they provide a more impressive trophy and a better story. With a disproportionately low number of does killed, an abnormally large number of fawns will be born during rutting season. In a harmonious ecosystem predators will kill fewer deer than will hunters; less general stress will affect the herd, and so the deer will not undergo the reproductive changes that intensive hunting provokes. Moreover, hunting periods are short and concentrated. Many deer are killed within a month—in fact, an enormous number are killed within the opening days of hunting season—increasing the chances of a crash. Crashes are unlikely to result from predation, since predators hunt throughout the year at a far less hectic pace.

Over the course of centuries prey animals have developed ways of coping with their predators. Certain evolutionarily established behavior patterns—hiding, camouflaging, or running—allow the prey species to continue. But there are no natural behavioral patterns that can cope with a speeding bullet. Moreover, although prey animals no doubt experience stress when predators are close, hunters inflict needless additional stress. Since the loud noise of gunfire cannot be limited to certain animals, the stress it engenders affects all animals, not just the ones that are the targets.

These ecological facts are not lost on hunting groups. State wildlife agencies try to manage deer herds to present the "maximum sustainable yield" for hunters. Their own writings show how they do this. The following remark appears in the 1978 *Conservationist*, the official publication of the New York State Department of Environmental Education: "Ideally, if the desired number of antlered deer and antlerless deer are taken each year the herd will be comprised of the lowest number of males and the highest number of breeding females. As a result, a maximum fawn crop will be produced each year."

Statements such as this one undermine the notion that hunting is an exercise in compassion. If hunters were truly concerned about minimizing the pain and death attributed to starvation, weather, and other environmental factors, they would not seek to maximize the number of fawns. Such pronouncements instead support the widespread belief that state wildlife agencies aim to placate the powerful and rich hunters' lobbies by producing as many hunting opportunities as possible. In New York State, for example, this policy is implemented quite well. Each year up to 80 percent of the legal bucks and 15 percent of the does are murdered, along with 50,000 fawns.

Hunting disrupts family and social units, an issue that is infrequently discussed in debates about hunting. Game animals such as wolves, deer, coyote, and caribou have strong social structures and hierarchies, and social disorder often ensues when a leader is killed abruptly. Of course, leaders eventually die in any social group, be it from age, accident, injury, starvation, or predation, but they do so relatively infrequently. As an analogy, consider how much more turmoil and upheaval our nation would have suffered if Kennedy's assassination in 1963 had been accompanied by the assassinations of Vice President Johnson, Speaker of the House McCormack, and others in the line of succession to the presidency. Hunting can destroy many animals in a particular social group in a short period of time, which may partly explain why social game animals suffer large population fluctuations.

More specifically, young game animals are left far more susceptible to fear, harm, and death when hunters kill their mothers. We should not forget that hunters harm more than just the animals they hunt. Again, the analogy with humans is helpful. A murderer who kills the mother of a family wreaks havoc on the husband and children as well. Any animals with a family or social structure will suffer the same fate if one of their leaders is killed.

Habitat manipulation is another state ploy that argues against the sincerity of the kindness gambit. States clear cut hundreds of thousands of acres to enhance browsing for deer. More food opportunities for deer translates into more deer, which in turn results in a larger number killed by hunters. Michigan is one state that has employed this strategy successfully—successfully, that is, from the hunters' point of view. Stuart Free, the former chief of the Bureau of Wildlife of New York's Department of Environmental Conservation, was straightforward when, in a letter written in 1984, he said that "game species are managed for recreational hunting and trapping opportunities and to maintain population levels optimum for them." Each year hunters kill about 3 million deer, about 15 percent of the total population. Well over a half-million deer are left crippled, their deaths guaranteed by gangrene infection, starvation, or inescapable predation. State wildlife agencies artificially insinuate themselves into nature by removing or destroying natural predators (the wolf, perhaps, being the most common), manipulating habitat, and creating unnatural reproduction cycles; as a result, they and the hunters' lobbies that support them bear much of the responsibility for these deaths. Bob Lund, the former chief biologist of the New Jersey Fish and Game Commission, made this point in an understated way in 1980 when he said that he would not justify hunting as a means to save deer from starvation.

One final, more abstract point is worth making. Assume the best-case scenario for the hunter. Assume, that is, the clearly false claim that each deer is killed immediately and painlessly. (So-called wound rates, the percentage of deer shot or arrowed that die later, usually from infection, may approach an astounding 50 percent.) Even so, some of these deer would not otherwise have died from starvation, predation, or disease. In fact, many of these particular deer, being the healthiest, would have survived the coming winter. Hunters might agree but hastily add that these deaths will free up food so that other deer who would have starved to death now will not.

This response is telling in that it treats all deer as the same; one deer is as good as another. All that matters from the hunters' perspective is that the killing of one deer (allegedly) allows another to survive. The individuality of the deer does not count at all. This is to treat deer as *resources,* an attitude that pervades the notion of wildlife management. Resources are impersonal objects whose only value is their instrumental use to humans. But it matters very much *to the deer* whether he or she is the one who is killed or the one who survives. From the deer's point of view, which deer is shot makes all the difference in the world. When the hunter kills a deer who would have otherwise have survived the winter, he is acting wrongly *even if* such a death allows the continued existence of another deer who otherwise would have died. Surely we would think this way if the same hunting scenario were applied to humans, be they marginal or not. Since the deer has a perspective and welfare, his or her individuality and inherent value should be respected. To believe otherwise is to harbor bigotry against other species.[2]

## Hunters as Protectors of Human Interests

This second prohunting argument is premised on the idea that hunting is sometimes necessary to protect legitimate human interests. This argument does not require abandoning the idea that animals are sentient creatures with interests or even that some animals may have rights that limit hunting opportunities. "Nuisance" hunting is warranted if it is the only vehicle to protect our property. When an overabundance of crows destroys a midwestern farmer's crops or a large pack of coyotes kills a farmer's sheep, we should try to eradicate the prey animals responsible. Just as it is morally permissible to kill another human in self-defense or perhaps even to prevent theft, so too is it morally justifiable to kill animals who threaten our hard-earned possessions.

Proponents of this line tend to exaggerate, however, using it to justify hunting far beyond its supposed necessity. The best way to stop the fox from getting into the hen house is to make the hen house more secure, and small-scale farmers can secure their sheep by building fences (maybe even electrical fences) around their farms. Killing the predator thus fails to be a necessary means. Nor, typically, do animals present drastic threats. Coyotes and foxes have to eat, and it is foolish to suggest that a farm will collapse if it loses an occasional animal to a natural predator.

Neither should we overreact by attempting to resolve the problem using traps and poisons. Traps are a poor solution because they are nonselective. Traps cannot distinguish "target" animals from others. In response, trappers point out that traps come in different sizes, so that their appropriate use will avoid the problem. This response is not very compelling. Many animals fall roughly into the same size class, and so it is all but inevitable that traps will catch some nontargeted animals. In addition, there have been (admittedly rare) instances of humans—usually children—who inadvertently stepped into a trap.

Most important, trapping is inherently cruel. There is not even the pretense of a quick and painless death. If predators happen along, the trapped animal is completely defenseless. Trapped animals have no access to food, water, or shelter, problems that are exacerbated in a west Texas summer or a Vermont winter. Animals have been known to gnaw off their legs attempting to escape traps.[3] The pain of being clamped in a trap is greatly increased by the twisting and turning that inevitably accompanies an animal's attempt to free itself. Trappers are supposed to check their traps periodically to reduce the chance of these occurrences. Unfortunately, the period can be as long as thirty-six hours, and unsurprisingly, enforcement is virtually impossible. Of all the Texas Parks and Wildlife officials with whom I have spoken over a dozen years, none has told me of any trapper who was convicted of inattention to his traps.

Poisons, too, are nonspecific and can cause long-lasting contamination problems. The use of compound 1080 (sodium fluoroacetate) is a good example of the failure of poisoning. Although intended to reduce only coyote populations, it kills bears, foxes, wolves, mountain lions, eagles, and hawks. A predator that eats a poisoned animal may well become poisoned itself. In this way the poison can be "recycled" over long periods of time. As with trapping, poisoning usually harms the innocent as well as the "guilty" parties.

Still, animals can cause problems for humans. What of legitimate problems that are not exaggerated? Blackbirds, for example, eat the inner portion of corn kernels, causing farmers moderately large crop losses. Bracketing the highly questionable assumption that the farmer has greater entitlement to a livelihood than the blackbird has to a life, there may be rare occasions when hunting provides the only possible solution. Nevertheless, we need to be extraordinarily sensitive to the complexity of the ecosystem. Blackbirds devour an enormous amount of insects that, if left unchecked, can cause significant damage. Without the hungry blackbirds, the insects would destroy the plant cover that ducks and geese use as homes when reproducing. Perhaps more to the farmers' concern, they would damage crops extensively. The cure may thus be worse than the disease.

Similarly, sheep farmers who complain about losing sheep to coyotes should be made aware that these predators help keep the jackrabbit population manageable, eat destructive rodents, and keep ponds clean by eating sick fish and frogs. Chicken farmers, too, complain that coyotes kill dozens of chickens at one time, eating some and leaving the others to rot. But the major responsibility here lies with the farmer. As I have discussed, chickens are densely packed into sheds, which makes them easy targets of a coyote. Perhaps the coyote is confused and just attacks items randomly. After all, coyotes rarely find themselves in a shed with twenty to forty thousand chickens. It is also plausible that the coyote sees such a large group as a threat and is acting defensively. These considerations show that the reasons for allowing chickens more living space may be financial as well as moral. At any rate, the situation is almost always more complicated than the farmer or rancher would have us believe. Sometimes the predator acts in ways that are beneficial to humans but not immediately understood as such. At other times humans bring the distress on themselves. From an ecological point of view, nature is rarely so out of sync that hunting is the best or only solution.

## Hunters as Stewards of Nature

This stewardship argument revolves around the putative necessity of "habitat management" or "ecosystem maintenance." Hunters assert that frequent artificial manipulations of habitat are necessary to help keep ecosystems in balance. They remind us that we often intervene in the natural order, for example, by clear-cutting forests, by carefully spraying toxic chemicals and defoliants, and—perhaps most popular in the public consciousness—by burning circumscribed areas. Hunters consider their practice to be of a piece with these other environmental manipulations. When used properly, they claim, hunting certain animals in certain seasons makes a better ecosystem for all concerned, including those species whose members are hunted.

There is reason to believe that these artificial intrusions do not enhance the ecosystem. It is claimed, for example, that annual burning in a southern pine forest will stimulate the growth of the low vegetation that provides food and cover for bobwhite quail, mice, rabbits, bobcats, and many species of songbirds. But this is disingenuous. Quail, rabbits, and bobcats are game animals. Expanding their numbers makes for more hunting opportunities and so more deaths. Moreover, the hunters' concern for mice and songbirds is self-serving. As food for the game animals, they will help produce the highest yield of game animals that the altered environment will allow.

It may be suggested that I am being unfair in tarring all hunters with the same brush. Some hunters may be motivated by increased killing opportunities, but not all need be. Indeed, whatever the motivation behind the burning, hunters insist that the selected annual burning provides a better balanced and more fertile ecosystem. Careful, limited burning will give us a healthier ecosystem in which flora and fauna can best survive.

This claim can be forcefully challenged. Some wildlife managers believe that, all things considered, burning is never good for the forested ecosystem. Burning can deplete soil quality, kill shrubbery, and destroy small fruit-producing trees. And let us not forget that many animals are killed in the fire. Red and gray squirrels are very territorial, as are chipmunks, and if the fire does not kill them immediately, the destruction of their local habitat may do so more slowly. Toads, salamanders, and other ground animals will be either killed or injured. Also, even low-level burning can destroy berry bushes, which are staples for some small birds and mammals. Those who claim that planned burning benefits the environment, and particularly the animals in the environment, are implicitly making value judgments about animal lives. The covert assumption is that quail and rabbits are worth more than salamanders and toads. But what makes them more valuable has everything to do with the fact that, unlike salamanders and toads, quail and rabbits can be hunted.

More speculatively, a case can be made that over the long run, hunting in a natural environment harms animals both behaviorally and biologically. Foxes, coyotes, and raccoons, thought to be diurnal a couple of centuries ago, are now nocturnal. Deer too now forage mainly at night, twilight, and predawn, probably in part because of hunting. Ordinarily a species changes its behavior over a lengthy period of time; hunting, however, greatly accelerates such changes.

Moreover, the very biology of a species is not immune to hunting pressures. Douglas Chadwick, a wildlife biologist and former hunter, contends that heavy hunting pressures on large, palm-antlered moose in Europe rapidly led to the appearance of deerlike antlers on males. He proceeds to note that for moose, just as for deer, hunting results in an increased reproduction rate and that since most of the older males are killed in hunting, younger males do the mating. The precise consequences are unknown, but as with most unnatural change affecting wildlife, these developments are more likely to harm the animal and its ecosystem than to help them. Alterations are always more likely to be harmful than beneficial.

One almost universally shared assumption deserves attention, namely, the presupposition that the basic locus for value—the part of nature that is of ultimate importance—is the ecosystem, or biotic community. An ecosystem may be thought of as everything that affects the ecology of a naturally bounded area. This includes not only the fauna and flora but also the air, water, and land on which the animals, trees, and plants survive. On this view, individual animals and plants have at best a secondary significance. The whole is what must be preserved. This way of looking at nature and the obligations we have to it owes its contemporary expression to Aldo Leopold. The following Leopoldian mantra captures this holistic view of our relationship to nature: a thing is right when it tends to preserve the integrity, stability, and beauty of the biotic community; it is wrong when it tends to do otherwise.[4]

All three of this account's criteria face problems. Reflect, first, on the notion of the beauty of a biotic community. Is a lush tropical rainforest in Brazil more or less beautiful than a barren Australian desert? Are the Grand Canyon's sedimentary rock formations more or less beautiful than the running waters at Niagara Falls? It seems clear that, at least in cases such as these, beauty is in the eye of the beholder. There is not one absolute standard of beauty against which different ecosystems can be measured.

One is tempted to say that all these biotic communities are beautiful in their own ways. This suggests that different standards of beauty apply in different context. According to this conception, we can compare the beauty of two waterfalls or two deserts. Perhaps we cannot compare the beauty of waterfalls to that of deserts, yet we can compare examples of the same sort of natural phenomenon. But this rampant relativism will not do. If we cannot compare the beauty of waterfalls to that of deserts, then how can we ascertain whether someone is doing right or wrong by changing a watery environment into a desert environment? Leopold's criterion of right and wrong action is impotent to guide us.

Stability, too, presents a problem. How much time must pass before we judge a biotic community to be stable? What is now a desert was once a body of water and may well return to that prior state at some later time. How, then, do we go about preserving its stability if the very idea of stability is undermined by the constant change ubiquitous in every ecosystem? And why should we? Why is the instability of a biotic community a bad thing for it?

This leads to the fundamental objection to Leopold's notion that the biotic community is the ultimate object of value and the item by which we measure right and wrong action. Unlike individual human and nonhuman animals, biotic communities lack welfares. There is no better or worse way for a biotic community to be, since a biotic community (the "land," as Leopold sometimes calls it) lacks the capacity to have experiences. An ecosystem feels no pleasure or pain, no exasperation or elation. A biotic community does not *care* about its condition, because it is not the type of entity that can care or be conscious about anything.

We can, if we like, place great value on a lush tropical forest because this type of environment yields us fruit and herbs. But these are contrived, anthropocentric values. Creatures with different needs or tastes can with equal warrant place no value at all on these green areas. Unlike humans and other animals, biotic communities truly do have only instrumental value. They are resources whose worth depends solely on the goods they can provide for those types of things that have inherent value. To think of the biotic community as the object that deserves our ultimate concern is a conceptual confusion.[5]

## The Hunter as Natural Predator

At times hunters try to turn the tables on those who repeatedly ask them to respect the way nature operates and to stop insinuating themselves in the

workings of an ecosystem. The argument is that humankind, and in particular hunters, are part of nature and so have their ecological niche just as do
the fauna and flora we typically associate most closely with ecosystems. By
denying the hunter a role in the complex relationships present in any environment, it is the antihunter contingent that is acting unnaturally and artificially. The opponents of hunting are those responsible for placing undue
stress on nature, with likely devastating results.

But humankind is *not* just another predator on an ecological par with a
wolf or coyote. Nonhuman animal predators hunt for food, whereas humans
frequently hunt merely for recreation. I have seen hunters kill squirrels in state
parks and then just toss them away, as if they were trash. Some hunt to demonstrate their skill in killing animals and, as proof, place heads of sheep and
bears on their walls. To be fair, I have spoken to many hunters who dissociate themselves from these latter groups and claim that they hunt only to put
food on the table. They point out that nonhunters who buy their hamburger,
chicken, or venison are effectively having others do their killing for them. Better that meat-eaters be honest with themselves and others and do themselves
what they need to do to survive. Moreover, they claim that hunting is better
than buying meat in a supermarket because more of the animal is used and
thus less is wasted.

There are two problems with this response. First, chickens and cows are
not game animals, so that hunters are often not substituting a hunted animal for a factory farm animal but rather simply adding to the carnage. The
strongest way of making their argument would be to kill only deer (and eat
only venison) while forgoing all other meats that they would have eaten had
they not hunted. But this really brings us back to the major point: we do not
require *any* meat to live and to live well. The moral position of the carnivorous hunter who eats only hunted venison may be no worse than that of
one who buys cow, chicken, and hog from the supermarket, but neither is
it better. But this invites questioning why we should cause any gratuitous
pain and suffering at all. The venison-eating hunter is still violating the PGS.

This point often elicits a discussion as to whether humans are naturally
meat eaters, whether meat eating is part of our biological heritage acquired
over millions of years of evolution. This is a contentious anthropological
issue, but *even if* our ancient ancestors were meat eaters, this in no way justifies present-day meat eating in general and hunting in particular.

Some anthropologists think that our early ancestors were vegetarians and
changed to a partial flesh diet only when climatic changes substantially reduced plant life in the northern latitudes.[6] Human development occurred in
warm climates where fruits and vegetables would have been abundant. Humans differ from carnivores in a great many physiological respects. Carni-

vores have claws; perspire though their tongues; bear sharp, pointed front teeth; secrete acidic saliva; lack flat back molars; digest food with powerful hydrochloric stomach acid; and have short intestinal tracts to ease meat waste from their systems. Humans differ in all these respects. Intestinal tract length is especially significant: the ratio of intestinal length to body mass in humans is twelve to one, triple the ratio for carnivores. This is presumably evolution's way of telling us not to eat meat because its waste will be difficult to relieve. In addition, human canine teeth are more rounded than those of predators, making them sufficient to rip lettuce but hardly ideal for tearing meat.

For the sake of argument, though, assume that our bodies can digest meat and that our forebears were carnivorous. Still, we can *now* do well—indeed, better—on a vegetarian diet. We could spare the lives of billions of innocent, sentient animals if the 95 percent of Americans who eat flesh were to give up meat. It thus appears that we have no justification for maintaining our carnivorism, even granting the eminently doubtful claim that we are naturally carnivores, especially when we recognize that natural behavior entails neither its morality nor its inalterability.

## Hunting Alternatives: Testing the Sincerity of Hunters

I want to end this discussion by proposing two challenges to hunters. For the sake of discussion, grant that the hunters' major underlying assumption is correct; presume, that is, that hunted animals (especially deer, since the discussion usually centers on them) would be worse off if they were not hunted. Assume that more deer would die if they were left to fend for themselves during the cold winters than would die if herds were thinned. Accept that hunters are actually helping the species and even the ecosystem.

Even granted all this, hunters still face an important question: if they are concerned with the well-being of the deer population, and if they desire to cause the least amount of pain and suffering to the specific deer that they shoot, why not limit hunting to sharpshooters? We might utilize credentialed military personnel and civilians who have passed certain tests proving their expertise. This approach would lower the wound rate precipitously. There would be far fewer deer injured but not immediately killed and so far fewer deer who die the agonizing deaths that hunters always claim they do not want. We would be closer to satisfying the moral requirement of the PGS.

It will not work to respond that we have too few skilled hunters to thin the herds sufficiently, for we can let the sharpshooters keep at it until they kill however many deer it takes to reach the optimal population. Moreover, the number of civilians taking courses to improve their shooting skills would no doubt increase dramatically. Thus, the paucity of qualified shooters should not be especially problematic.

I wonder how many hunters would accept this solution to the putative deer overpopulation problem. Unless there are compelling environmental reasons to decline this suggestion, the natural inference is that hunters typically hunt for the pleasure of the kill, not merely for ecological reasons. Hunters may offer other justifications for their sport—that it builds camaraderie, teaches patience, fosters bonding between parent and child—but no longer is the environmental option open to them as a good rationale. Without a compelling opposing argument, the most common defense used by hunters would not be satisfactory, even granting all their ecological assumptions.

The other challenge may actually apply in the near future. Over the last decade immunocontraception has advanced to the point where it already has proven effective for some animals under certain conditions. There is good reason to believe that progress will continue to allow these techniques to be applied to any potential animal population problem. The porcine zona pellucida (PZP) is a noncellular membrane that can be "darted" into an animal. Because PZP is composed of glycoproteins, it avoids problems associated with steroidal contraceptives, which can allow steroids to accumulate in the tissues of an animal and be passed throughout the food chain. Unfortunately, PZP immunocontraception requires a booster injection for long-term infertility effects. That presents no problem with zoo animals, but wild animals living in unconfined areas are another story: it is difficult to dart the same deer twice. Still, even one-year pregnancy protection would reduce the deer population. Moreover, a three-year injection is in development. If perfected, this could reduce the deer population dramatically, precisely the result that hunters are claim to seek.[7]

Diethylstilbestrol (DES) is another immunocontraceptive that holds great promise. When administered as an ingestible pellet, this estrogen has been shown to humanely control rodent populations as well as lower the pregnancy rates of coyotes and prairie dogs. DES has one major advantage over PZP. As a pellet, it may be mixed with an animal's food. Wildlife departments sometimes distribute toxins and traps to control rabies by inhibiting population growth; surely they can lace deer feed with DES pellets to control deer population, too.

If these technologies were made available, we would reach the goal that environmental hunters seek in a far more humane manner. Are hunters willing to have parks and wildlife departments help in improving and using these methods of animal control? And if not, why not?

# CHAPTER FIVE

# ANIMAL EXPERIMENTATION

## The Scientific Case against Vivisection

### The Vivisectionist Manifesto

It might be thought that live animal experimentation, or vivisection, would prove to be the institution most immune to the charge of intentionally inflicting gratuitous suffering on innocent creatures. Animals undoubtedly suffer and die in experiments, and the infliction of pain, suffering, and death is clearly intentional, but apologists for animal experimentation balk at the idea that these unfortunate outcomes are gratuitous. Although many vivisectionists applaud the trend toward vegetarian diets, agreeing that this will likely help people live healthier and longer lives, and view hunting as at best a dispensable recreational activity, they portray the abolition of animal experimentation as biomedical suicide.

The science community has promulgated a certain picture of the relationship between biomedical research and the animals used as research subjects. Most important, we are informed that much biomedical research would be stymied without the use of nonhuman animals. Animals ranging from rats and mice to chimpanzees are absolutely necessary to scientific progress. Drugs, therapies, and other disease-management techniques cannot emerge unless the scientific community can use animals with virtually no restrictions. Scientists assure us that our great strides in curing and treating countless illnesses are due in large measure to the wise use of these animal resources by diligent, dedicated scientists. Furthermore, we are told that we have excellent reasons for believing that this success will continue and that our two biggest killers—cancer and heart disease—will eventually join the list of diseases that plague us only sporadically and infrequently. Of course, no responsible scientist will claim that the disappearance of these diseases is imminent, but public and private financial support and the freedom to use animals in a judicious manner justify optimism.

Scientists generally view antivivisectionists, be they animal activists or not, as well intentioned but ignorant. These people, lay citizens all, fail to grasp the methods of science in general and biomedical research in particular. When antivivisectionists suggest that scientists use cadavers, computer simulations, cell cultures, and the like as replacements for animals, they demonstrate their failure to understand that the study of live, intact animals is imperative. Only by using live animals can we trace the course of a disease, from the introduction of a virus or bacterium to its final effects. Viable management and treatment therapies are impossible without this longitudinal information. The tools suggested by vivisection's opponents may be useful adjuncts to research but, at this stage of our scientific development, that is all they can be.

Antivivisectionists are also pictured as having a distorted view of the scientists themselves. Animal experimenters care for the welfare of animals. They are not Cartesians, believing that animals are merely automatons without the capacity to feel pain and suffer. Nor are they Mengeles; they receive no perverted pleasure from the pain and suffering that must, at times, be inflicted on these animals. It is unfortunate that many nonhuman animals must be sacrificed, but at least at this point, we have no other way to achieve the advances that everyone wants. Scientists hope for the day when no animals are required for experimentation. In the meanwhile, researchers practice the "three Rs"—reduction, replacement, and refinement—so that they can use the minimal number of animals, lowest on the phylogenetic ladder, in the least painful manner possible.

## The Response to the Manifesto

For most of my life I accepted the manifesto. I was never naïve enough to believe that no scientists overstepped their bounds. Surely some experiments were so trivial that they should never have been conducted, and others consumed more animals than were absolutely necessary to gather the sought-after results. Still, any field includes practitioners who do not live up to the standards of their profession, and it is unfair to tar an entire institution because of a few of its members.

I am now far more dubious of the vivisectionist's claims in the manifesto. I am skeptical of the efficacy of animal experimentation. In fact, I now believe not only that animal experimentation is unnecessary to the development of drugs, therapies, and other disease-management techniques but also that it has retarded medical progress. We—to say nothing of the hundreds of millions of animals that have been subjected to indescribable suffering—would be better off had we used different modalities.

How can I justify claims so different from received opinion? My strategy is twofold. I first argue that the basic methodology underlying all animal testing is a sham. Part of the defense lies in logic, and part resides in reviewing how reliance on this fundamental methodological principle has caused enormous illness and death to the *human* population it is intended to help. I agree that there has indeed been great medical progress. In many important, quantifiable ways we are far better off than we have ever been before. Nevertheless, these improvements owe next to nothing to animal testing and in many cases have eventuated *despite* animal experimentation. Time-tested nonanimal modalities are the real cause of our better health, and they should be encouraged and financially supported. I need, finally, to explain why the notion that animal testing is scientifically necessary has reached the status of dogma and what we need to do to discard it and thus enhance the prospects for healthier lives for our progeny.

## Animal Experimentation: An Introduction

Animal experimentation is employed in three major areas: routine toxicity testing, education, and biomedical research. First, animals are used to test various household substances, from toothpaste and oven cleaners to mascara and hair dyes. Second, animals are teaching and research tools in educational settings. We dissect frogs to teach anatomy, deprive primates of their mothers to test the importance of familial bonding, and shoot goats on military bases to test the mettle of prospective doctors. Finally, animals are used in biomedical research. It is in this environment that scientists most fervently assure us of the necessity of animal experimentation. We are told that the intelligent use of animals has been crucial in virtually every major biomedical gain, and any hopes for curing cancer, heart disease, and other serious and pervasive ailments lie in the continued use of this approach.

Virtually all my efforts will address using animals in biomedical settings. I concentrate on this area because it seems to be the most defensible of the three areas where animals are used. It is difficult to imagine why anyone would reject biomedical animal research as either morally wrong or scientifically suspect yet accept animal testing for new cosmetics or educational purposes. The converse is more intelligible, however, since the prospective gains from biomedical research are so much greater, making (it is argued) the inflicted suffering less gratuitous. Therefore, if I can show that the biomedical use of animals is morally wrong or scientifically problematic, that should suffice to rule out using animals to test cosmetics and teach students.

Nevertheless, I begin with a phenomenon from the first area, routine product testing, for it dramatically introduces the major problem infecting biomedical research.

## A Case Study in Gratuitous Suffering

Unless you are a scientist or an animal activist, you probably do not know of the LD-50 test. The initials stand for "lethal dose." The LD-50 test determines the amount of a toxic substance needed to kill 50 percent of the animals to whom it is administered. The LD-50 is commonly used to test cosmetics. It is also used to test household and industrial products, such as cleaning agents. Its sole purpose is to set safe toxicity limits for human consumers of these products. Mice, rats, rabbits, birds, and fish are the usual victims, although dogs, cats, and monkeys have also been used.[1] Often the poison is poured through a tube inserted down the animal's throat, but the toxin may be applied by injection, forced inhalation, or topical application to the animal's skin. Assuming that some animals survive the ordeal, the test continues for two weeks, after which any living animals are killed and studied for the poison's effect on their organs. The animals suffer immensely, a fact that the experimenters themselves will usually acknowledge. When animals convulse, bleed, have diarrhea, and scream, it takes little imagination to acknowledge that they are in intense pain and distress.

Bracketing the cruelty for a moment, we might at least hope that these tests adequately indicate toxicity levels in humans and suggest ways that the poison should be treated. Our hopes are dashed when we realize that test results differ widely both between species and even within strains of a single species. The LD-50 for digitoxin in rats is almost 700 times that in cats,[2] and for the antifungal drug antimycin A, the LD-50 for rats can be up to 80 times greater than that in pigeons and mallards.[3] Perhaps more telling, the LD-50 of certain drugs can differ by a factor of 450 in different strains of rat.[4]

This is just the beginning. The LD-50 uses a single dose of toxin and thus may yield results completely irrelevant to humans who are subjected to more than one dose. Even more worrisome, the results of the test differ widely not merely between species or within strains of species but also in regard to sex, age, temperature, humidity, means of dosage, time of dosage, and density of animals in a given space. For example, studies in Germany have shown that when the ostensible LD-50 was administered in the evening, almost all the rats died; when it was given in the morning, however, all the rats survived. Survival rates in the winter were twice those in the summer. When mice were densely packed, nearly all died; when they were not, all survived.[5]

It is therefore hardly surprising that scientists familiar with the test reject it: "For the recognition of the symptomatology of acute poisoning in man, and for the determination of the human lethal dose, the LD-50 in animals is of very little value."[6] Or more emphatically, "As an index of acute toxicity, this is valueless."[7]

Fearing litigation, some companies persist in using the LD-50 and similar tests. In my fifteen years of speaking to physicians of all kinds, I have never heard of a single case where some determination of antidote was based on an LD-50 result.

## The Problem of Extrapolation

The salient scientific problem infecting the LD-50 test is determining which, if any, animals react to the toxins as humans do. For the LD-50 or any other animal experiment to have value, there must be some reliable means of extrapolating the results to human beings. As I will illustrate, this problem always has been and remains insurmountable. This fact alone should justify immediately discontinuing animal testing. As definitive as the problem of interspecies extrapolation is, however, it is likely to obscure an unjustified assumption. When we speak of extrapolating results of animal testing to humans, we presuppose that we humans form a homogeneous group. For example, to use the LD-50 is to implicitly assume that all humans will react similarly to a given substance. In fact, this supposition is false for many drugs therapies. Although I will not discuss the problem of intraspecies extrapolation extensively, it underscores the difficulties of interspecies extrapolation. If we frequently have problems extrapolating across segments of our own population, imagine how the difficulty is exponentially magnified when we deal with species other than our own.

Prestidigitating like a Las Vegas magician, vivisectionists turn this vice into a virtue. Since an indefinite number of parameters can enter into a testing situation, it is almost certain that some result *obtained by nonanimal modalities* can be replicated by using some animal under some condition. Effectively, the pervasive problem of extrapolation allows vivisectionists to "confirm" or "disconfirm" any theory whatsoever. I submit just a small list exemplifying this point.

—We can show that humans should avoid lemon juice, since it is toxic to cats.

—We can show that morphine puts rats to sleep, so it must do the same to people; unfortunately, the same substance drives cats into a frenzy, which should mean that we, too, will be made frenzied by it (in this respect we are more like the rat than like the cat, a fact many may find counterintuitive).

—We can show that prussic acid is an excellent aperitif by generalizing the results from toads, sheep, and hedgehogs (even though its fumes can in fact kill humans).

—We can show that we should drop parsley from our diet by pointing out that it kills parrots quite quickly.

—We can show penicillin to be toxic, since it kills guinea pigs within a couple of days.

—We can show that the addition of methyl alcohol to alcoholic drinks is not dangerous to humans, because it has virtually no damaging effect on the eyes of most laboratory animals (in fact, the combination causes blindness in many humans).

—We can show that arsenic is not poisonous to us by pointing out that sheep can digest it in large quantities without ill effects.

—We can show that vitamin C is useless because when we deny it to dogs, rats, mice, hamsters, and so on (i.e., the usual laboratory animals), their own bodies produce sufficient amounts; simultaneously, we can demonstrate the vitamin's necessity by withholding it from guinea pigs and primates, which will develop scurvy as a result.

—We can show that chloroform should not be used on humans, because it is poisonous to dogs.

—Finally, we can show that we never should have introduced some of our most beneficial medications: insulin (the prime drug in treating diabetes) causes malnutrition in chickens, rabbits, and mice, and digitalis raises blood pressure in experimental animals (in fact, we now know digitalis can prove very useful to humans *with* high blood pressure).

Toxicity tests, including the LD-50, are almost always performed on healthy animals. Scientists make healthy animals sick. (Vivisectionists, apparently, have a rather restricted reading of the major tenet of the Hippocratic Oath, which putatively binds physicians first to do no harm.) This is the basic method for assessing the toxicity of drugs to help humans who are already sick. But illness itself affects the way drugs are metabolized. Fevers exacerbate toxicity, liver diseases diminish the liver's capacity to neutralize toxins, and many kidney diseases retard the elimination of foreign substances, such as medicines and the products of their degradation. Immunotherapies depress reactions to allergens, congenital dysmetabolism can render a harmless substance toxic, and so on. Healthy experimental animals do not typically suffer from these conditions, and even if they did, the conditions would involve different aspects with different consequences.[8]

Most human diseases are naturally endemic to humans. To test on animals we need to give them the disease being studied. Sometimes, as in the case with the human immunodeficiency virus (HIV), this typically easy procedure is next to impossible.[9] Even when we manage to give an animal a human disease, however, problems of generalization remain. Different species can differ widely in their reactions to a given infection. For example, most monkeys, considered good test subjects because their DNA closely matches our own, are habitual carriers of the simian B virus. This virus typically does little more than produce irritation of their mucous membranes. The same virus in humans (introduced, say, by contamination) can cause death. Only humans are known to be affected by smallpox and yellow fever viruses. Most fungi infections do not yield spontaneous disease in virtually any laboratory animals. To make infections appear, inoculations must be made in sensitive organs, such as the peritoneum, or in the central nervous system. Under these conditions, it makes little sense to extrapolate from animal to human reactions.[10]

It might be thought that we could largely circumscribe plausible candidates for extrapolation by comparing and calibrating weights for the average human with those of the animal. Unfortunately, life is not so simple. Some of the aforementioned cases demonstrate that calibration will not do. Scopolamine offers a pertinent example. A 10-pound cat can ingest 100 milligrams of scopolamine with no ill effects. An average-size man—say, about 180 pounds—should thus be able to tolerate about 1,800 milligrams. Yet a mere 5 milligrams can kill a man.[11] Scientists implicitly concede that we cannot limit experimentation to only certain animals. After all, if they could, then why do they not? Presumably vivisectionists are not sadistic and so would do everything in their power not to injure, pain, and kill animals that have absolutely no value in their experiments.

Ironically, vivisectionists frequently pride themselves for their use of the scientific method yet violate perhaps its most important doctrine. If they are to have value, experiments must be predictive. We can allow some leeway, perhaps, and not require that extrapolations from animal responses to human ones be 100 percent certain (although this would not minimize the barbarism of vivisection), but animal experimentation does not even come close to offering certainty. In fact, interspecies extrapolation yields results no better than chance. It would be comical to propose a therapy that amounted to saying, "Heads, inject the vaccine; tails, withhold it," were it not for the fact that the lives of millions of animals are consumed in the process.

The problem of extrapolation is not some innocuous misstep. The consequences for the experimental animal are obvious, but the effect on progress for human health should not be minimized. This comes into high relief when we concentrate on our most serious health problems.

Consider, for example, the problem of human obesity. Researchers can produce obesity in rats and mice by giving them monosodium glutamate during their first week of life, feeding them a diet of 60 percent lard, and injecting them with gold. One might reasonably ask what possible connection this could have to the problem of human obesity, especially when we hear what is entirely expected, that different animals reacted differently to the same diet. The researchers themselves, after emphasizing the obvious point that divergent results occur with different models, clinch the case when they admit that "none of the models used are appropriate to the human condition."[12]

Arthritis afflicts tens of millions of people. A cure, and not just a medication that may relieve symptoms, would be worth millions of dollars to its producer. In 1980 Eli Lilly claimed to have found such a cure and intensely promoted its drug, Opren, to both the lay public and physicians. The drug did work—on laboratory mice. It failed miserably on humans. It was responsible for sixty-one deaths in Britain alone and was retracted from the market twenty-two months after its introduction.

The case of Opren shows not merely that extrapolation from animals to humans can be misleading and lethal but also that the energy going into production and marketing can be better spent on human clinical trials. Even giant drug corporations have finite financial resources, and so from a monetary perspective, we have a zero-sum process. Money spent in one area means money not spent in another.[13]

Atherosclerosis is similarly frightening. This common condition occurs when too much fatty substance (i.e., cholesterol) sticks to the inside walls of blood vessels. This is a prime cause of myocardial infarction, a kind of heart attack. Rabbits are the favored animals for experimentation on this disorder, not because they best mimic what happens in humans, but because they are docile and easy to handle. They do form arterial lesions after being fed a diet unnaturally high in cholesterol, but the lesions are different both in content and distribution from those found in humans. We should not find this surprising. Diseases artificially produced in animals will quite likely differ from the "same" disease that takes years to form in a human. Even in primates, however, the "evidence" is misleading. While the two "bad" forms of cholesterol—very low density lipoproteins (VLDL) and low density lipoproteins (LDL)—are most indicative of artherosclerosis in humans, the "good" cholesterol (high density lipoproteins, or HDL) indicates vessel disease in most primates. Primate "models" would thus give us results opposite to what we have since found to be accurate. We must also be quite careful about our anticholesterol medication. Clofobrate reduces cholesterol by some 20 percent in many animals and seems harmless. Nevertheless, although it also slightly reduces cholesterol in humans, it also increases the rate of heart attacks, liver damage, and gall bladder and gall duct problems, sometimes with fatal results. Even the most advanced anticholesterol drugs (e.g., the statin Lipitor) must be continually checked for damaging livers in humans.

Contrary to popular opinion, mortality rates for virtually every form of cancer have either remained steady or increased over the last thirty or more years. The fact that we have made so little progress on cancer can be attributed in large measure to the obsession with animal research. Consider the 1981 words of Dr. Irwin Bross, director of biostatistics at the Roswell Park Memorial Institute for Cancer Research: "Indeed, while conflicting animal tests have often delayed and hampered advances in the war on cancer, they have *never produced a single substantial advance* either in the prevention or treatment of human cancer."[14] Moreover, in 1982 the *British Medical Journal* issued a cautionary note that data from research on animals could not be used to develop a treatment for human tumors. Speaking at a 1978 conference in Naples, Professor Albert Sabin commented that "laboratory cancers have nothing in common with naturally occurring cancers in man. Human tumor cells are integral to the organism which gives rise to them. Human cancer differs profoundly from artificially produced tumors in laboratory experiments." This idea virtually replicates Professor Iain Purchase's 1978 claim that cancers produced in animals by means of implants or injections should in no way be compared with those in humans, in terms of either cause or effect.

A few examples will suffice to show why these scientists consider animal tests to be largely worthless in developing methods to treat or prevent cancer. In some mouse strains (mice are the most commonly tested animal) urethane yields tumors of the rectum and lungs; on other strains, t-cell lymphomas result. In humans, however, urethane has proven to be a helpful treatment for some leukemias. Carbon tetrachloride causes liver cancer in mice but cirrhosis in rats. Chloroform produces liver cancer in female mice of certain strains but not in males. In some murine strains all or nearly all the mice spontaneously develop cancer after their second year. Although leukemia can occur at any age in humans, no leukemias occur naturally in any other known species. Metastasis, the principal means by which cancers kill, is perhaps even more telling: whereas this phenomenon occurs in humans, it cannot be produced chemically or physically (let alone naturally) in monkeys, our closest animal kin except for apes.

Tests for recognizing carcinogenic agents fare poorly. The astounding results from one test showed that only 46 percent of drugs carcinogenic to the rat are carcinogenic to the mouse, too.[15] If data from tests for carcinogens done with rats cannot be reliably transposed to the mouse, should we expect any more reliability when transposing from rats or mice to humans? In fact, one study of mice and rats has shown that slightly fewer than half the substances that cause cancer in these rodents affect humans in similar ways and rates.[16] In a way, this is the worst result possible, for it indicates that we have approximately a 50 percent chance of either becoming or not becoming cancerous by taking a substance that proves carcinogenic to rats or mice. The coin-flipping figure is appropriate here. If the results had showed that 95 percent of the mice and rat carcinogens do not cause cancer in humans, at least those who put some stock in these tests could say with some confidence that these substances do not cause cancer in humans.

No two animals are precisely alike. Vivisectionists realize this and also realize that this inherent difference may affect their conclusions significantly. The solution to this problem is to make identical copies of a given animal. The hyperbole regarding cloning may suggest that at least this problem has a theoretical solution, although skepticism persists. A more low-tech solution has already been pursued, however. Generations of selective breeding have produced strains of virtually identical mice. Curiously, the two strains used in the United States spontaneously develop liver and breast cancer, but the two strains in Australia almost never suffer these effects. Why? The difference appears to relate to the cedar sawdust used as litter in the cages here, whereas the Australians use black pine sawdust. It seems that even the smallest, seemingly insignificant differences may prove important. This portends an almost insoluble problem in determining which circumstances are relevant to the experimental results and which are not.

Do clones share the precise microflora that contains the same microorganisms? And even if they do, will they continue to do so? Probably not. Since microflora can affect metabolism rates, moreover, it appears as if we never conduct tests on precisely identical animals, let alone precisely identical animals in identical environmental conditions.

## How Should We Proceed?

Extrapolation from animal tests fails miserably. Animals make poor models for human disease for a host of reasons. A disease introduced artificially progresses far differently than does one contracted naturally; anatomical structures, including fundamental blood vessels, differ significantly among species;

and different animals operate at wildly different metabolic rates. Neither mice, rats, fish, guinea pigs, hamsters, ferrets, cats, nor dogs are humans writ small.

The great variation in animal reactions to drugs and treatments allows scientists to "confirm" their hypotheses. Although they use modalities that do have predictive value, scientists can and do support claims by pointing to certain tests on certain animals that yield some result known prior to the testing. They can thus "prove" anything, which is to say that they prove nothing at all.

Dr. J. P. Whisnant, a consulting neurologist at the Mayo Clinic, makes the point emphatically: "For the most part these studies (referring specifically to a series of stroke studies performed in 1958) have tended to lag behind clinical and pathologic-anatomic investigation and too frequently have served as confirmatory work *after* clinical impressions have been virtually accepted. It is obvious at the outset that investigations with laboratory animals cannot be directed related to human disease."[17]

Dr. Charles Mayo, of the Mayo Clinic for Cancer Research, forgoes euphemisms when he says that he knows "of no achievement through vivisection, no scientific discovery, that could not have been obtained without such barbarism and cruelty. The whole thing is evil."[18] What would truly be useful, although perhaps not less barbaric, and what scientists cannot do, is select an animal before conducting tests and be certain that the results from this testing will translate into progress for the human condition.

I have alluded to the notion of time-tested modalities that have predictive value and that do all the real scientific work. It is now time to specify these modalities and demonstrate that our most successful tools for fighting our most ominous health enemies—cancer and heart disease—resulted from insightful scientists employing these means of gathering information and testing drugs and therapies.

Clinical observation is perhaps the most fruitful method of obtaining valid data about disease. This centuries-old modality, which involves observing patients who manifest symptoms of a disease, should be more heartily encouraged and appropriately financed. For example, clinical pharmacology often uses healthy human volunteers who, after giving their fully informed consent, are subjected to small doses of test drugs. These human subjects are closely monitored for innumerable physiological and psychological reactions. This latter point should not be glossed over. Although pharmacological studies are routinely performed on (nonvoluntary) animals, that introduces not only the problem of extrapolation but also the insuperable difficulty of being unable to interrogate the subjects.

Observant World War I physicians helped commence the successful treatment of cancer. These doctors noticed that soldiers who had inhaled mustard gas had unusually low white blood cell counts. Since white blood cells are overabundantly produced in leukemias and lymphomas, it seemed plausible to think that what had a horrible effect in the battlefield might have a salutary effect for some cancer victims.[19] As it turned out, mustard gas derivatives were effective therapeutics.

Advances in the treatment of breast cancer, too, derived from clinical studies. Tamoxifen was developed as a breast cancer preventative following examinations of human subjects receiving it as an adjuvant (something that helps or catalyzes a drug) in trials of another substance. Clinical research also showed that the larynx need not be removed in laryngeal cancer cases. Clinical trials in esophageal, lung, and colon cancers have resulted in improved management techniques.[20]

Two especially interesting cases confirm the dangers of relying on animal testing. Experiments on animals suggested that increased amounts of folic acid would deter cancer growth. Unfortunately, increased dosages exacerbated the disease in humans. Fortunately, scientists then thought to administer methotrexate, a folic-acid inhibitor. The results have proven beneficial to cancer patients. The second case deals with the administration of steroids. On some tested animals, steroids hinder the therapeutic effect of certain cancer drugs. Clinical observations in the study of Cushing's disease, however, have shown that steroids destroy human tissue. Although tissue destruction is not normally a desirable outcome, steroids have been profitably used to destroy cancer tissue.[21]

It is fitting to end this partial list by recalling that every major cancer was first observed and described clinically. Commenting on this point as it specifically relates to leukemia, Dr. A. Haddow tells us that the "characteristic effects in leukemia were detected solely as a result of clinical observation. The various leukemias in the mouse and rat were relatively refractory to the influence of urethane, and the remarkable effect in the human might have eluded discovery if attention had been directed to the animal alone. This illustrates the hazards of such work."[22]

Clinical observation has played a no less impressive role in cardiovascular disease. Recall that the idea that blood circulates throughout the body was a revolutionary result of William Harvey's observations of humans in the early seventeenth century. Although it was no secret that excessive eating and drinking are frequently associated with chest pain, William Heberden described this observed phenomenon to the Western world in the eighteenth century. More specifically, myocardial infarction—a painful heart attack caused by an insufficient supply of oxygen to the heart—was accurately described in 1934 by Sir Thomas Lewis, who wrote that clinical observation proved this condition to be caused by occlusion of the vessels that bring blood—and therefore oxygen—to the heart.[23]

While experiencing angina (chest pain) in 1867, Sir Lauder Brunton serendipitously helped himself to some nitroglycerin and was visited by quick relief.[24] This is still a common treatment for angina; I remember that my father often placed a small nitroglycerin pill beneath his tongue, waiting for—and almost inevitably receiving—major relief.

Perhaps the most amazing case of clinical observation was when a German surgical resident, Werner Forssmann, inserted a catheter in his own arm and threaded it to his heart, effectively developing a means to pump medications directly into the heart. This "pulmonary artery catheter" also allows physicians to measure heart pressure and the volume of blood being pumped at a particular time. Forssmann deserves much credit for founding the field of cardiology as we now know it, with angioplasties, stents, and pacemaker insertions being almost mundane. Slightly more than seventy years after Forssmann's brave endeavor, many hospitals routinely perform some forty angiograms and angioplasties daily, reducing the need for much more invasive and dangerous bypass surgeries.

Incidentally, Forssmann had tried to catherize rabbits before his self-experimentation. The tests failed, killing the rabbits from dysrhythmia as soon as the catheter touched the heart. And, as is the common modus operandi, Forssmann's results were not accepted until they were later replicated on animals. This disingenuous technique (I will soon provide more examples of it) falsely suggests that animal testing is the driving, if not essential, force of medical progress.

Epidemiology constitutes a second profitable nonanimal technique for gathering important medical data. Epidemiological research investigates certain segmented populations for disease quality and quantity. As one might expect, these studies are extremely helpful in discovering the effect that lifestyles have on the incidence and severity of disease. What may not be so obvious is that these studies have been used as jumping-off points for hypothesizing about the role that certain genes play in either the production of or immunity from disease. The advent of the computer has made the data collection, storage, and manipulation dramatically less cumbersome, thus improving a method that already has delivered enormous dividends.

Epidemiological studies are the bane of the tobacco industry. They have convinced virtually all scientists that cigarette smoking causes lung and other cancers and that pipe smoking causes lip cancer. These revelations have cost the tobacco industry billions of dollars and should result in plummeting rates of lung cancer. As I mentioned earlier, there is also a causal relationship between a high fat diet (especially saturated fat) and cancers of the colon and prostate, something else gleaned from epidemiology. Indeed, the World Cancer Research Fund recommends that we should avoid all red meat.[25] (Nevertheless, we should not be deluded into thinking that replacing red meat with chicken will solve our dietary problem. Although red meat tends to have higher concentrations of saturated fat, both meats have approximately the same amount of cholesterol, about 70 mg per ounce.)

In addition, epidemiology has led to earlier detection of cancers and therefore more fruitful treatments. Breast and prostate examinations resulted from epidemiological work with human populations. Detection techniques have dramatically improved for both these common cancers. We now have a scanning machine that sends electric currents through the breast; the resistance differential between cancerous and noncancerous tissues provides a diagnostic tool, making some biopsies unnecessary.[26] Prostate cancer screening via a prostate-specific antigen (PSA) test is far more accurate than any manual exam and requires only a simple blood test. Since prostate cancer often is asymptomatic, especially in its early stages, this antigen test should save lives and mitigate misery.

Advances in the prevention and treatment of heart disease are largely a result of epidemiological research. Shortly after World War II Ancel Keys discovered that cholesterol rates were substantially lower in poorly fed Europeans than in well-fed Americans. This marked the beginning of the idea that diet and coronary heart disease are closely linked.[27] The groundbreaking Framingham study initiated in 1948 clarified, confirmed, and added to Keys's initial findings. In virtue of this study, there is now little doubt that high blood pressure, smoking, and ingestion of high fats, especially saturated fats, greatly increase the chances of incurring coronary artery disease. This means that many heart attacks can be prevented by relatively simple changes in lifestyle. The study also led to the now widely known distinction between high and low density lipids. The more recent "Grand Prix" study confirmed the Framingham results by investigating the diets in populations of more than sixty countries: high-fat diets increase the probability of heart disease.[28]

Epidemiology played a crucial role in identifying the causes of stroke. Since strokes occur when arteries to the brain rupture or clog, it is unsurprising that we find the usual culprits. Hypertension, high levels of cholesterol, and smoking are three of the leading causes, all of which can be modified by lifestyle changes. Animal studies hindered progress, since most animals have cerebral blood reserves missing from humans. Although this fact had been known for years, it did not stymie horrendous experiments. From 1978 to 1987 twenty-five drugs were shown to help treat strokes in dogs. None worked in humans.[29] The uselessness of animal testing for helping human stroke victims is captured in an understated way by David Wiebers and others of the Mayo Clinic when they write that although the use of animal models "has provided much information about the methods of producing and potentially treating cerebral ischemia and infarction in specific animal species and experimental circumstances, the relevance of most of these data to human conditions remains dubious."[30]

In vitro research (experiments done "in test tubes"—that is, outside the body)—has proven productive in both cancer and heart disease research. The basic idea is to isolate particular cell cultures in a controlled environment and observe how they are affected by the introduction of various chemicals. Chemicals that cause cells to mutate or kill quickly dividing cells are poor candidates for helping human cancer victims. Chemicals that either block a disease-causing agent or kill diseased cells directly are good candidates in the war against cancer. The ability to create complex cultures now let scientists more easily study how certain chemicals will affect various tissues.[31] Researchers can now use in vitro methods to culture a patient's tumor and then subject it to various chemical assaults. This allows for treatments specific to the individual and not merely to the human species, a development quite removed from the extrapolation problem that infects all animal testing. In addition to showing certain agents, such as benzene, arsenic, and chromium, to be carcinogenic, in vitro tests led to the development of the Pap smear, the most widely used diagnostic tool for discovering cervical cancer.[32]

Probably the most important result for coronary artery disease to have come from in vitro methods is the development of the cholesterol- and triglyceride-lowering drugs that currently enjoy enormous popularity. Drugs in the "statin" family inhibit the enzyme that encourages the production of cholesterol. Some luck was involved. While searching for an antifungal agent, scientists recognized that statins had this cholesterol-lowering power. In vitro tests confirmed this fortuitous discovery, and as a result we now have a rather large class of statins, including lovastatin, pravastatin, and simvastatin.

The introduction of these lifesaving drugs circumvented animal testing. As we subsequently discovered, lovastatin produced large increases in the cholesterol and triglycerides of hamsters. Simvastatin caused optic nerve degeneration in dogs and cataracts in dogs and cats. Studies with rats produced more counterindications for human use, a particularly significant result since

rats were thought to process low density lipids as humans do.[33] It is no wonder that experts maintained that "any *in vitro* method using human tissue
gives a degree of reassurance not provided . . . by animal experiments."[34]

Scores of other episodes in medical history illustrate not only the significance of clinical research, epidemiological studies, and in vitro experiments
but also the essential use of autopsies, genetics, and other technological advances.[35] This fact cannot be overemphasized. Moreover, the inadequacy of
animal testing is not merely a neutral adjunct to scientific discovery. Not
only does it often lead us in the wrong direction; in addition, it exhausts
valuable resources that could otherwise be used to better effect. If all the
money—from governmental agencies as well as private contributions—and
all the brain power presently employed in animal experimentation went into
the other, proven modalities, the rate of progress would grow exponentially.

## Vivisectionist Disingenuousness

Few of us have the time or expertise to verify the expansive claims the vivisectionist community frequently makes. If we see a story in a newspaper or
magazine heralding the role that animal research played in an important discovery, we tend to accept it. The scientific studies that form the basis of these
popular articles would bedazzle and mystify all but a few experts, and so we
have little choice but to place our confidence in the authors of such pieces.
Unfortunately, our entirely understandable attitude produces an extremely
misleading picture of the role that animal experimentation has played in
some of the most significant medical discoveries.

Prior to the mid-nineteenth century, scientists believed that organ function was determined solely by events in our nervous systems. Discovery of
the endocrine system showed this picture to be simplistic. We now know
that hormones have important effects on the behavior of our organs. The
adrenal glands, an important segment of our endocrine system lying on top
of our kidneys, secrete adrenaline and various steroids. In 1855 Thomas Addison found—via clinical observations—that tuberculosis renders the adrenal glands nonfunctional. Vivisectionists removed the adrenal glands of
some animals trying to duplicate the results that Addison had observed.
They failed. This failure to duplicate in animals results that reputable scientists have observed in human beings unfortunately represents a common
sequence of events. The belief that only successful replication in nonhuman
animals suffices to prove a disease's etiology retards research, often at the
cost of great human pain, suffering, and death. In fact, it was only some
thirty years later that Addison's disease—as the adrenal gland disorder ap-

propriately became known—was recognized as a problem requiring treatment.

Revisionism entered the picture in 1893, when a physician named George Oliver tested adrenal secretions on his own son and showed that they increase blood pressure. (These secretions cause the familiar "rush" we get when we are extremely frightened.) Oliver then went to a physiologist's laboratory, where these findings were "verified" on dogs. What is scandalous is that many vivisectionists point to this story as confirming the significance, even necessity, of animal testing. The animal tests did not add anything to our stock of knowledge, yet if the animal experimenters are to be believed, this case shows why animal experimentation is more important than clinical observation.[36] It is also important to realize the serendipity involved in choosing dogs as test subjects; perhaps some other species of animal with adrenal glands would not suffer the atrophy that affects both human and canine adrenals.

Vivisectionists often attribute the development of angioplasty to animal testing. In angioplasties, balloons or stents are placed in arteries that are occluded by fats. This procedure has saved lives both directly, by keeping arteries open that would otherwise close and thus shut off the blood and oxygen supply to the heart, and indirectly, by making the far more invasive bypass operation more an option than a necessity. Good fortune entered the invention of this procedure when a physician who was attempting to insert a catheter into his aorta mistakenly placed it into an occluded iliac artery. Improved on cadavers and living humans, it was later tested on dogs and pigs.[37] Thus in an extended sense animal testing "played a role" in the development of the procedure. But this sense is quite attenuated, since the animal experimentation added nothing to our stock of knowledge.[38]

By the 1950s human epidemiological studies had demonstrated that arsenic is carcinogenic. Chimney sweeps exposed to far higher levels of tar than the average citizen displayed an extremely higher incidence of scrotal cancer. To "confirm" this relationship, vivisectionists applied tar to the ears of both mice and rabbits. The rabbits got cancer, and the mice did not. Is this to be hailed as a victory for the vivisectionist camp? What does it show? That chimney sweeps are (in this regard) more like rabbits than mice? The lunacy is magnified when we discover that the carcinogenic effects of arsenic were suspected as early as 1801 and that cancer from arsenic was described in the literature in 1887, whereas in 1977 scientists stated that "little evidence in animals" supported the conclusion that arsenic was carcinogenic."[39] This view was maintained until three years later, when the result was produced in lab animals.

## The Future of Medical Science

A detailed study of humans with certain diseases is the best way to achieve medical progress. The backward-looking quality of animal experiments is not only scientifically unnecessary, not only fraudulent, but frequently a hindrance to scientific progress. It is likely that testing the selected animal will yield poor and perhaps dangerous results, and such testing drains the money, time, and brain power of the people investigating disease. Moreover, the ex post facto "confirmation" of certain scientific hypotheses is apt to lead to a false sense of security.

We should continue using and refining the already quite successful clinical-pathological model for studying disease. Advances in in vitro technology allow us to keep human cells and tissues taken during therapeutic operations or after death so that researchers can test drugs and carefully trace the courses of certain diseases. These results can then be measured against clinical and epidemiological data—again, from human beings—to provide us with the best clues about the treatment and, more important, prevention of human disease.[40] I have noted some recent dividends that this methodology pays. Especially in the fields of embryology, cell physiology, and pathological apoptosis (self-limitation of tissue growth), the payoffs promise to increase exponentially.[41]

Epidemiological studies suggest viable courses of research. What differences may account for the great disparity in the prostate cancer rates of Sweden and Japan? Devising more sophisticated testing than we now have will probably circumscribe the relevant factors. Cancer of the liver occurs in far greater frequency in African blacks than American blacks. This gestures toward environmental factors as playing a pivotal role. Yet testicular cancer rates for blacks in general are lower than those for whites. Perhaps ethnicity plays a role here. Cancer of the penis tends to be lower in Jews. This suggests that circumcision may play a significant role. The litany can continue indefinitely.[42]

## The Moral Case against Vivisection

Whatever the merits of the scientific case against vivisection, it is likely to leave a misleading impression. It may suggest to some that *were* the science good, vivisection would be vindicated. Surely bad science conjoined with the intentional infliction of pain and suffering is immoral, but this does not mean that good science, performed as vivisectionists routinely practice it, *is* moral.[43]

The moral approach to the issue of vivisection begins in questioning whether these invasive animal tests are necessary for medical progress. And here the answer is simply and obviously no. Vivisectionists will undoubtedly disagree. They will repeat their claim that cell cultures studies, computer simulations, and cadaver research, though valuable in their limited sectors, cannot replace surveying how an intact organism manages (or fails to manage) some disease or poison. But this misses the point of the claim that animal testing is superfluous. Nonhuman animal experimentation is unnecessary in that many of the same tests that are routinely carried out on nonhuman animals could be performed on *human* animals. The medical benefits would prove enormous. No more concerns about similarity of physiologies or psychologies and no more worries about disparate introductions of germs, viruses, and toxins. Most beneficial, the problem of extrapolation is minimized. We now have the perfect model for human disease—disease in a human being.

## A Challenge to Vivisectionists

I assume that it is unethical to experiment *routinely* on humans. I leave it open whether, in extreme situations, human experimentation may be morally permissible. Some may accept human experimentation if it will definitely save an enormous number of people from immense pain and perhaps death. Some may even argue that invasive experimentation is morally obligated in such extreme circumstances. Others may allow that fully informed free consent suffices to make experimentation permissible.[44] My assumption is only the moderate one, that as a matter of routine institutional practice, human experimentation performed either against the subject's will or without the subject's fully informed free consent is morally out of bounds.

This modest assumption grounds a formidable challenge for vivisectionists. How can they adopt the commonsense assumption that it is morally *impermissible* to routinely experiment on humans who have withheld or cannot give permission while advocating that a similar set of experiments are *permissible* on nonhuman animals? Those who lack such a justification morally ought not continue with their experiments and should do what they can, as members of both the scientific and moral communities, to abolish further invasive experimentation on nonhumans. This is a fair requirement. If you torture, maim, and kill hundreds of thousands of innocent creatures, you bear an onus to justify your behavior.

## Clarifying the Challenge

What would constitute a satisfactory answer to the challenge? For vivisectionists to justify their experiments, they would need to articulate a morally relevant property (or set of properties) that all humans have and that all animals on whom they experiment lack. Recall that vivisectionists presumably advocate the common assumption that it is wrong (except perhaps in the most radical circumstances) to experiment on humans who do not or cannot consent. To warrant the experiments—experiments that they admit impose great harm, injury, and suffering on an animal—they must distinguish humans from animals. But not just any difference will do. The distinction must be a *morally relevant* difference. Additionally, it must be weighty enough to justify the enormously disparate ways in which vivisectionists conceive of and treat human and nonhuman animals. The vivisectionists must point to a morally relevant difference that obtains between all humans and all nonhuman animals, so that it is morally permissible to experiment invasively on members of the latter group but not on members of the former.

### The Unanswerability of the Challenge

The challenge posed to the vivisectionists is tantamount to the challenge that I previously presented to inherentists, who believe that all and only human beings possess a special sort of value that justifies a superior moral position. In fact, vivisectionists can be viewed as a type of inherentist. Although vivisectionists are free to argue for any property that morally justifies their different conceptions and treatments of human and nonhuman animals, most vivisectionists seem to be speciesists. By and large vivisectionists believe that an individual enjoys moral privilege solely in virtue of membership in the human species. And, they would need to add, this privilege is significant enough to warrant their different attitudes regarding the experimentation on human and nonhuman animals.

I have already cast doubt on the prospects of finding any distinguishing property that has this incredible power. Using the argument from marginal cases as the main weapon in the battle against the inherentist, I showed that the favored candidates of rationality and language ability are doomed to fail and that speciesism, if not arbitrary or even irrational, is at best ad hoc. The vivisectionists may continue their search for other candidates—autonomy and moral agency are two other relatively popular ones—but until and unless they can provide one that passes the criteria set forth for acceptance, immediate abolition of their practice is called for. I have spared readers the ghoulish details of what laboratory animals experience—documentation of life on a factory farm is probably as much horror as one book can expose without losing its audience—but let there be no doubt of the psychological and physical toll that these experimental "models" are forced to endure.[45]

In the end, we have dubious science and indubitable immoralism—scarcely a recommendation for maintaining any practice or institution, let alone one that creates so much pain, suffering, and death to innocent creatures. It is not without reason that Gandhi, speaking at the inauguration of the Medical Academy of New Delhi shortly before his death in 1948, described vivisection as the "blackest of black crimes that Man commits against God and Creation." Vivisection is a moral blight on our contemporary landscape and should immediately be eradicated, regardless of the medical benefits it is alleged to provide.[46]

# CHAPTER SIX

# The Law and Animals

A significant segment of the population believes that our legal system protects animals from egregious violations of the PGS. Most people believe that our laws govern the ways in which we may skin, experiment on, raise, transport, and slaughter animals. The significance we give to our companion animals is presumed to inform the laws that deal with animals generally. Undoubtedly these laws, like any others, are occasionally violated, but surely (it is thought) animals are by and large treated humanely throughout their lives.

These pervasive perceptions are grossly mistaken. Our present legal system offers virtually no protection of animal welfare. The remedy to this lacuna is neither to create more stringent laws nor to make greater efforts at enforcing the present laws. Although these tactics would provide some relief, the central cause of the legal system's impotence would remain. The basic premise prompting the legal treatment of animals is virtually Cartesian; although animals are (usually) acknowledged to have feelings and emotions, their affective lives lack legal significance. Animals are individuals with solely instrumental value. This attitude must be altered for real progress to occur.

## Legal Sham and Moral Shame

To vindicate my harsh assessment of the legal system's treatment of animals, it is necessary to investigate some actual cases. All these cases confirm the general notion that the law considers animals to be mere property, commodities with only instrumental value.

Immanuel Kant's rationale for not destroying a dog that no longer can serve us epitomizes the instrumentalist conception of animals. Kant argued that we have no direct moral obligations to a dog per se; rather, we have indirect obligations to it because we have direct obligations to humanity. We have, for example, the duties not to harm humans and to treat them kindly. If we were to kill a decrepit dog, we would be more inclined to treat our fellow humans poorly. Since we have an obligation to our species not to act this way, we ought not kill the dog and thereby invite disaster. Kant's legacy survives in the law.

The ruling in the 1887 Mississippi case *Stephens v. State* explicitly invokes Kant's rationale.[1] In the 1904 Colorado case of *Bland v. People,* moreover, the court ruled docking a horse's tail to be illegal because the sight of "disfigured and mutilated animals tends to corrupt public morals."[2] In the 1931 Massachusetts case of *Commonwealth v. Higgins* the court noted that the rationale against trapping animals is based on the fact that such a practice would "have a tendency to dull humanitarian feelings and to corrupt the morals of those who observe or have knowledge of those acts."[3] For a case of more recent vintage, consider Utah's *Peck v. Dunn* (1978), where, in discussing the legality of cockfighting, the court held that cruelty legislation is justified on the basis that it regulates morals and promotes the general good of society.[4]

Although these decisions yield results that please the proanimal community, they implicitly endorse the Kantian view that we lack any direct obligations to nonhuman animals. These courts did not say that docking, trapping, or cockfighting should be prohibited because they inflict gratuitous suffering on the animals; rather, they rationalized their decisions in terms of the benefits that will accrue to our species if these practices are abandoned. The welfare of the animal figures nowhere in the legal reasoning.

In a 1967 New Jersey case a local humane society sued the state's board of education.[5] New Jersey had an anticruelty regulation that classified the infliction of unnecessary pain or the needless mutilation or killing of an animal as a misdemeanor. It exempted "properly conducted" scientific experiments from the statute's purview. The humane society brought suit because a high school student was permitted to induce cancer in live chickens by infecting them with a virus.

Interestingly, no one argued that the experiment was medically necessary. The court admitted that many previous experiments had made it clear that the virus would cause cancer in chickens. Nevertheless, the court ruled in favor of the school board, noting that scientific experts supported using living animals in high school biology, because it "helps students have sympathy for living things."

If helping high school students gain sympathy for life falls under the rubric of "properly conducted" experiment, then there are several things to notice. First, this understanding confuses the moral acceptability of the goal of an experiment and that of the means for carrying it out. Clearly an experiment can have a worthwhile goal yet be impermissible because it uses wicked means to reach that goal. The court's position would allow scientists to give humans cancer to investigate the course of the disease. Second, it seems paradoxical to try to create sympathy by requiring that the student do something cruel. All agree that the chicken is inevitably going to suffer and die. The point here is that the school is using inappropriate means to accomplish a laudable end. The students are likely to learn not sympathy for living things but indifference to cruel treatment in the course of worthwhile experimentation. Last, but most important for my purposes, to accept this rationale would be to accept virtually any infliction of pain and suffering. If this pain is not unnecessary, if this is not paradigmatic of needless killing, then it is difficult to imagine any classroom experiment that will ever meet these criteria. One can always concoct some excuse to exempt an experiment from the statute, making a sham of the criteria of "unnecessary pain" and "needless killing." Thus, they are not really criteria for prohibiting experiments, because no experiment will ever rise to the level of violation. These legal proceedings would be comical, a punchline for a bad joke, were it not for the disturbing consequence that such decisions promote the suffering, mutilation, and deaths of thousands of innocent animals.

The 1993 California penal code makes it unlawful to maliciously or intentionally maim, torture, mutilate, wound, or kill "any dumb creature."[6] The penalty is a maximum of $20,000, one year in prison, or both. The statute also prohibits torturing, cruelly beating and killing, and overworking animals, even if the agent does so without malice or intent. Furthermore, it defines torture and cruelty as including any act or omission "whereby unnecessary or unjustifiable physical pain and suffering is caused or permitted."

Naturally enough, the rub comes in the way the terms *unnecessary* and *unjustifiable* are used. In fact, they are intimately connected. Effectively, an action is justifiable if it is necessary. In legal settings necessity and justification are normative notions. Normative notions receive their meaning, either implicitly or explicitly, from the assumption of certain norms or standards. To say that an act is (legally) necessary or justified is thus to say that it is necessary or justified according to certain standards. Practically speaking, animals receive no viable protection from these statutes because the standards are always and exclusively norms adopted by a particular institution. A necessary act, then, amounts to an act that is required to accomplish some task embedded in an already accepted human practice. A justified act is any act that is performed in an accepted practice or institution. Unfortunately for the animals involved, an acceptable practice is one that provides benefit for human society. In sum, animals can be exploited by virtually any means, as long as it occurs within a practice or context that meets the incredibly vague and minimal condition of providing *some* benefit to human beings. This is why virtually anything goes in a slaughterhouse or laboratory. Since slaughtering animals (allegedly) brings about benefits to humans, anything that aids in bringing about these benefits is justified. Some especially heinous modes of killing cows, chickens, and pigs are justified because other methods would diminish an industry's profits and thereby (putatively) have a deleterious effect on the general population. Analogous reasoning applies to the exploitation of laboratory animals. The practice is justified by the benefits it is alleged to bring to humans, so that virtually any actions within this practice are justified. Behaviors in the abattoir or the laboratory are unjustified only if other means could be used to increase the benefits to the human population.

A 1989 Alaskan statute makes any behavior that conforms to accepted veterinary or scientific practices or is "necessarily incident to lawful hunting and trapping activities" immune from anticruelty prosecution.[7] Under this statute, it would be next to impossible to prosecute trappers who neglect their traps for several days (see the discussion of trapping in chapter 4).

In the British case of *Bowyer v. Morgan* (1906), the court ruled that branding a lamb's *face* was legal and did not violate any anticruelty statute because it was "reasonably necessary" for identification purposes.[8] Face branding of cattle in the United States has only recently been replaced with branding on the hide. Since this procedure is never accompanied by anesthetic, it is still extremely painful.

The case of *People ex rel. Freel v. Downs* (1911) dealt with the cruelty of transporting turtles.[9] Trappers in Cuba pierced the fins of some sixty-five turtles so that they could tie them together. The turtles were then placed on their backs and shipped to New York. The other defendant subsequently untied the turtles, placed them upside down atop one another, and shipped them to a warehouse. The court acknowledged that this caused the animals discomfort but ruled that since it was "temporary," "unavoidable," and "necessary to protect the property involved," the latter defendant could not be prosecuted. (The court allowed for the prosecution of the defendant who perforated the turtles' fins.)

A section in the 1988 California Penal Code says that destroying certain birds or venomous reptiles, killing animals for food, and using animals in an academic setting are not prosecutable under the state's anticruelty laws.[10] A 1992 Kentucky statute promised enlightenment when it prohibited the "killing of any animal,"[11] but its exemptions quickly dashed any hope. Exemptions for hunting, trapping, fishing, processing, dog training, killing for humane purposes, and killing for any authorized purpose eviscerate the statute.

All these statutes and innumerably more are hoaxes. To characterize a practice as "acceptable," "necessary," "unavoidable," or "humane" or a purpose as "authorized" is merely to recognize what is currently fashionable in our society. There are no legal means to question the moral legitimacy of the practice itself. As I have documented in some detail, the entire institution of raising animals for food is fraught with intolerable horrors, but this carries no weight from a legal perspective. The institution is in place. The customary is used as the criterion of the acceptable. The commonplace sets the standard for determining when a behavior within an institution or practice constitutes cruelty. We should find this utterly offensive to our moral sensibilities. Slavery has been a common practice throughout much of humankind's history. The horrific treatment of Jews, Catholics, and Gypsies in Nazi Germany was an ordinary occurrence in the late 1930s and early 1940s. Certainly no one would suggest that an act is legitimate as long as it is an instance of a common practice.

Any residual doubt about the impotence of the anticruelty statutes should disappear when confronted with the next two cases. In *Commonwealth v. Anspach* (1936) the defendant placed a chicken in a bottle to advertise a special chicken feed.[12] The defense argued that most chickens endured practices more inhumane than was the treatment of the bottled chicken, and since these were permissible, the defendant should be found not guilty. The court agreed. Somewhat similar is the more recent case of *Commonwealth v. Barnes* (1993).[13] Although the defendants admitted neglecting their horses, they claimed that such neglect was common with horses destined for slaughter, and since they intended to slaughter their horses, they should be exempt from any cruelty statutes. The court ruled against the defendant, but only because they had failed to prove that they had intended to have the horses slaughtered for dog food. Had the defendants been able to prove their contention, their behavior would have fallen under "normal agricultural operations," and their case would have been made.

## Animals as Property

In highlighting my "animals are legal property" thesis, I ask you to consider two of the most startling court decisions. In *Deiro v. American Airlines*[14] the plaintiff boarded nine greyhounds on a flight from Oregon to Massachusetts. The airline allowed the dogs' kennels to be exposed to staggering heat when the flight stopped at the Dallas–Fort Worth airport. It also failed to

provide the greyhounds with adequate ventilation and water and even prohibited the dogs' owner from tending to the dogs. As a result, seven of the
dogs had died and the other two were seriously ill when the plane arrived
in Massachusetts. The plaintiff sued for $900,000 to recoup damages for
the dead animals and the veterinary care that the two ill dogs required. An
appellate court decided that the plaintiff should be awarded only $750, rul-
ing that the plaintiff's plane ticket set this limit to the airline's liability for
damaged or lost luggage.

The court clearly equated the dogs with luggage. In other words, it conceived of these animals purely as property. In terms of value, allowing seven
dogs to die and two others to suffer to the point of needing medical care is
apparently equivalent to mishandling a few pieces of Samsonite luggage.

In *Fredeen v. Stride*,[15] a surreal case from 1974, the plaintiff brought her
sick dog to be "put down" (destroyed). Two kind veterinarians were able to
nurse the dog back to health and find it a good home in the neighborhood.
Several months later, after discovering the fate of her dog, Fredeen sued for
mental anguish, claiming that she feared that her sons might locate the dog
and attempt to reunite with him. The plaintiff was awarded $4,000 for men-
tal anguish and $700 in punitive damages because the veterinarians saved her
dog's life.

Punitive damages are set to punish a wrongdoer and to deter others who
may be contemplating similar acts. Bracketing the plaintiff's depraved attitude in even bringing this suit and the chutzpah one would need to start such
legal proceedings, consider only what the decision tells us: we ought not try
to save an animal's life, even if we can find it a good home, if its owner orders
us to destroy it. It is difficult to imagine a case where the law more transpar-
ently disregards any inherent value an animal has. The life of the dog meant
nothing to this court. All that mattered was that the plaintiff *owned* the animal. Thus, since the animal was mere property, its welfare had no bearing on
the legal deliberations.

## Animals and Slavery

About a decade ago I lectured on animal rights to a large group of high
school students. During the lecture I explored the fruitfulness of comparing
the contemporary plight of animals in our country to that of slaves prior to
the Emancipation Proclamation of 1863. I was greeted by jeers and flying
objects. Some of the students thought that I was implicitly identifying blacks
and other minorities with nonhuman animals. They obviously viewed me
as bigoted and insensitive. This is diametrically opposite to the point of the

analogy, which was never intended to disparage any human. My hope is rather that reflection on some of the similarities between our treatment of slaves and our current relationship with animals will modify how we act toward animals. It is in this vein that I want to briefly discuss the dismissiveness with which our legal system treated slaves and treats animals.

Before 1863 U.S. law permitted the sale of human beings as if they were commodities, which is precisely how the law currently treats nonhuman animals. Black men, women, and children could be mortgaged and used as barter to settle personal debts. If someone other than his master injured a slave, the attacker was liable to legal recourse for damaging the owner's property. Slaves could not enter into contracts, have their interests contractually represented, own property, or sue.

A brief look at two nineteenth-century legal cases is chilling. In *Commonwealth v. Turner* (1827) a court in Virginia claimed it had no jurisdiction in the severe beating of a slave.[16] The court ruled that since the slave had not died from the attack, it lacked jurisdiction in the matter, even if, as seemed apparent, the beating was "willful, malicious, violent, cruel, immoderate, and excessive." A private beating, it created no threat to society, and the court deemed it improper to insinuate itself in the personal affairs of a citizen. Indeed, the court explicitly commented that privately beating a slave was legally equivalent to beating a horse.

An 1823 North Carolina case, *State v. Hale,* also makes explicit the analogy, even identity, of slaves and animals in terms of legal status.[17] The court noted that public cruelty toward animals mirrors the wanton beatings of slaves. It conceded that public cruelty toward animals and wanton beatings of slaves were and should be prohibited, but its rationale had nothing to do with the inherent value of either the animal or slave. The court reasoned that wanton beatings should be prohibited because such prohibitions most effectively guarantee the slaveowner's right to use property as he or she deems fit. A slave open to the abuses of strangers would be less capable of serving his or her master. In other words, a stranger should be prevented from beating a slave not because it causes severe pain and suffering but because the crippling fear of wanton beatings would make slaves less effective workers.

Another striking similarity between the legal assessments of slaves and animals is their disingenuousness. There were some laws on the books in the eighteenth and nineteenth centuries that, on their faces, seem to conceive of slaves as persons. A late eighteenth-century law provided that anyone maliciously killing a slave receive the same punishment as someone who killed a free person. A reasonable parsing of this would construe slaves as unfree persons. One's suspicions may be aroused, however, by reading further and finding the exceptions to this equal punishment. The law did not apply to "an outlawed slave, nor to a slave in the act of resistance to its lawful owner, nor to a slave dying under moderate correction." These exemptions eviscerate the law. The owner only need claim that the slave "resisted"; moreover, any slave that escaped his or her owner's plantation became an "outlawed slave." The law was toothless.

It now seems obvious that Americans acted immorally toward a large class of humans. Both the immorality and the obviousness is explained by the PGS; we act immorally when we inflict gratuitous harm on those who do not deserve it. Our immorality extends further. Slaves are autonomous; they have desires and aims whose fulfillment gives meaning and satisfaction to their lives. By frustrating their autonomy without warrant, we wrongly eliminated the possibility of slaves leading good lives.

We need to realize that our current institutional practices concerning animals parallel our predecessors' immoral conduct toward slaves. Like slaves, animals are sentient beings with goals and desires. The fact that they are of different species does not alter this basic truth. Reflection on this analogy between slaves and animals should—and one hopes will—spur dramatic changes to the horrid ways we treat animals.

## The Federal Animal Welfare Act

The Federal Animal Welfare Act (FAWA), first passed in 1966 and amended several times since, is supposed to be the primary vehicle for protecting nonhuman animals used in biomedical experiments. In reality the value of FAWA is negligible. The root problem is identical to the one that plagues anticruelty statutes generally. They all accept without question the dogma that animals are our resources or property and that we can thus do virtually anything we desire to them. Historically the legislative branch has viewed its laissez-faire attitude as constitutionally mandated, as being of a piece with the general liberal idea that a government that governs less governs best. Just as the government has no right to tell us how to decorate our homes, Congress has deemed it unconstitutional to interfere with the affairs of the biomedical establishment.

Not only does FAWA simply assume the propriety of using animals in experiments; it also condones any experiment deemed appropriate by the medical community. The act intercedes—minimally—when there are questions about the treatment of animals in a proposed experiment. In practical terms, the research community is regulated only to the extent that only certain means of transport are permitted and that the animals must be given enough food,

water, and air to survive. These "restrictions" simply confirm the general thesis that FAWA, like the other anticruelty statutes, conceives of animals as property without any rights of their own. The regulations to provide minimum
subsistence conditions in transport, food, and water are intended primarily
to keep the animal alive and sufficiently healthy so that a reliable experiment
can be performed. In effect, it is virtually impossible to conduct an inhumane
experiment in the biomedical establishment. That the animal ought not to suffer through the experiment or, *mirabile dictu,* has the right not to be subjugated to this horror in the first place does not enter into the formation or enforcement of the regulations.

## Reasons for Hope

Despite the long history of legal neglect regarding nonhuman animals, there
are some encouraging signs. Certain prestigious law schools have taken steps
that encourage optimism. In 1990 Gary Francione established the Rutgers
Animal Rights Law Center, where law students earn credits for learning how
to use the law to further animal causes. In 1999 the law schools at both Harvard and Georgetown introduced courses in animal law. The imprimatur of
such prestigious universities confers added respectability on the discipline of
animal law. It now becomes more difficult to scoff at the idea of nonhuman
animals having legal rights and to dismiss the entire notion as the warped
idea of some wacky fringe elements of our society.[18]

There is now a law journal dedicated to legal issues regarding animals.
Since 1994 the Northwestern School of Law at Lewis and Clark University
has published *Animal Law.* It is more than coincidental that some thirty years
ago this same university began publishing the first environmental law journal. What now appears as quirky and trendy may in retrospect be viewed as
the start of a long-overdue movement. In fact, this is virtually definitional of
any great revolution, be it scientific or moral. Einstein faced incredulity, skepticism, and ridicule when advancing his theory of relativity. The reactions
against King and Gandhi were more life threatening. Attempts to advance
the interests of others, of those who are not already included in established
privileged circles, will always be met with bewilderment and hostility. When
our dearest interests and beliefs are threatened, it is the rare person who can
dispassionately canvass reasons for allowing others to share what has been
solely the property of those in that person's community.

In a landmark case that as of this writing is still proceeding, the U.S. Court
of Appeals for the Washington, D.C., Circuit granted a zoo visitor the right
to sue on the behalf of a chimpanzee. Citing a 1985 amendment to FAWA

that requires primates' housing to ensure their psychological well-being, the court granted a human the legal standing to sue for companionship for the chimpanzee. Although the crucial jurisdictional notion of standing has a tortured history and is still far from transparent, it is required before a court will even listen to a case. The courts have recognized standing for people regarding wild or unowned animals (since these animals are not the property of any particular individual), but to the best of my knowledge, this is the first time a person has been granted standing regarding a nonferal and owned animal. Thus the decision goes some way in reconfiguring the legal orthodoxy that animals are no more than property.

One would hope at least that the concerns for the psychological well-being of the animal stem from concern for the animal herself and not because a psychologically healthy zoo animal makes for better viewing. This at least indicates that the legal system may finally be receptive to thinking of animals as having inherent value. If the appellate court verdict is maintained, the tradition of conceiving of animals as property may be questioned enough that some real legal progress can be made for animal causes. Perhaps some caring, innovative lawyers can finally put FAWA to some productive work.

## A Personal Note

Some years ago, two friends and I chained ourselves to a gated entranceway to a "pigeon shoot." Pigeons were crowded into boxes and shipped from other states to San Antonio, Texas, where they were to be released as live targets for shooters. Birds used in such events are deprived of food, water, and mobility for days before the killing to minimize their chances of escape. The shooters are mere yards away from the terrorized birds, most of which are killed soon after they are released, since they are so weakened and disoriented that normal flight is impossible. A great many birds are wounded rather than immediately killed. Young boys gather injured birds and either break their necks or repeatedly thrash them against barrels into which dead pigeons are collected. At times the birds are simply left to bleed to death or suffocate as a result of being weighed down by other birds tossed on them in the barrels. Wounded birds who land outside the shooting area are simply left to die agonizing deaths.

We were charged and convicted of criminal trespass, a class B misdemeanor, after a two-day jury trial. For idiosyncratic reasons the three of us received different penalties. (In fact, one of my fellow "criminals," a young woman who was pregnant at the time, was let go without penalty.) I spent a couple of days in jail after posting a $400 fine.

I mention this with neither pride nor remorse. The case demonstrates the legal system's inanity when dealing with animals. There could be no clearer case of gratuitous violence and killing, yet three people who tried merely to stop this murder were the ones subjected to punishment. The killers were within their legal rights; apparently we were not. Virtually everyone aware of this situation believed that the moral proprieties are the opposite of the legal ones.

There is hope. After years of futile attempts to abolish the largest pigeon shoot in the country, at Hegins, Pennsylvania, pigeons can now rest somewhat easier on Labor Day. This sixty-five-year-old tradition has been terminated because of the efforts of a group of lawyers specializing in animal law. This victory not only ensures the end of the senseless suffering and death of thousands of pigeons at Hegins but also promises to lead other pigeon shoots throughout the country to reconsider. It may also signal a plasticity in the law that compassionate persons can exploit to garner better treatment for animals. And perhaps most important, this ruling may encourage reflection both by the general public and the legal community that our legal relationships with animals need to be more closely aligned with our personal relationships with them.

The states themselves have made at least minor moves recognizing the gravity of animal cruelty. In 1994 only six states saw violations of cruelty statutes as possible felonies. As of 1999 the number had increased to twenty-seven. Whereas only a handful of years ago the maximum penalties for violations of anticruelty statutes were minor fines and jail time (neither of which happened with any regularity), now, at least in principle, one can be fined up to $100,000 and be sent to prison for up to ten years. Although legal history suggests that such penalties will rarely be meted out, having the increased penalties on the books sets an important precedent.

There is even a glimmer of hope that the routine torture and murder of farm animals may finally come under scrutiny. In the first felony animal cruelty indictment ever handed down in North Carolina, several defendants face up to fifteen months of jail time if convicted of beating and skinning live hogs. This indictment may hold out the greatest promise for an improved life for many animals, for, as I have detailed, the institution of factory farming surpasses all other of our societal practices in the pain and suffering we inflict on animals.

# CHAPTER SEVEN

# WOMEN AND ANIMALS

It is an inarguable historical truth that both women and animals have been systematically and institutionally oppressed. It may not be too speculative to explain the disproportionate number of women involved in animal rights and animal protection organizations—some estimates have women constituting 70 percent of this population—by supposing that their history of exploitation provides many women a feeling of kinship with animals. Indeed, some feminist thinkers cite just this supposition in claiming that women can address animal oppression with a novel and distinctive voice. A second reason for thinking that women may bring a unique perspective to the debate is not so much historically based as it is biologically and culturally founded. Women are birth-givers, and be it for biological or social reasons, they have been and continue to be the primary caregivers in our society. Women generally are and must be more emotionally sensitive to the needs and concerns of others than men are. Perhaps this has a genetic component. Were women less attached to their children, the species would be at far greater risk of extinction. Whatever the explanation, the differing attitudes that characterize the ways in which men and women tackle interpersonal problems and disputes are real rather than imagined.

I second the idea that women have tools to approach our moral relationships with animals in distinctive ways. In fact, I hope to show that female resources can be used in ways that comparatively few feminists have realized. Nevertheless, contrary to the assertions of some feminists, we ought not replace all longstanding traits of "masculinist" moral theories with feminist ones. Although some reconfiguration is unavoidable, there are ways of melding the significant moral insights of both masculinist and feminist accounts to produce a powerful theoretical basis for changing our attitudes, institutions, and personal behaviors toward animalkind.

## Women and Animals: The Lower Rungs of the Ladder

One persuasive way of showing the intertwining ways in which our society derogates women and animals is to examine portions of our language. Women are described as bitches, cows, vixens, shrews, dumb bunnies, and old crows. These characterizations are not flattering. Literally a bitch is a female dog with the capacity to bear offspring. Dog breeders typically view these animals as having no purpose beyond reproduction, as nothing more than reproductive machines whose product can earn them a living. Bitches are resources whose worth is a function of their procreational capacities in a given market environment. When their reproductive abilities falter or demand for their product falls, the bitch becomes a liability. The food, shelter, and health care that she may have previously received become a waste of time, money, and effort. She is "used up" and thus must be discarded. To compare women with bitches is to depersonalize them, to make them into mere things without any value in their own right.

Cows, too, are valued only for what they produce. They are viewed as fat, dull, and unassertive. In the mechanical, institutionalized environment in which virtually all cows presently live, profits are maximized by keeping the cow perpetually pregnant or lactating. This, in turn, causes a swollen belly that gives the impression of continuing corpulence. Cows are kept still when they are milked, giving the impression of dull wittedness and vacuity. To be called a cow is to be labeled a lazy dullard.

Comparisons with chickens are longitudinally pejorative. When young, a woman is a chick; when married, she is all cooped up, relieving the humdrum of her everyday, insignificant existence by cackling to her friends over the telephone. She begins her brood on giving birth, henpecks her husband for more attention and money, and finally, on the inevitable encroachment of old age, becomes a useless old biddy. The lesson is that only young, reproductively able women have any value. This value is wholly instrumental; females are worth keeping only as long as they do their master's (husband's, boyfriend's) bidding. Chickens' confinement in their productive periods and their unceremonious slaughter when they can no longer supply their product (eggs) provides the factual basis for the analogy with women.

Many of the comparisons with animals suggest that women are nothing more than sexual objects, mindless creatures whose only value derives from their useful bodies. But even those epithets lacking this suggestion are hardly flattering. To call a woman a social butterfly is to say that she has no goals or ends worth serious consideration. These women just flitter about to absorb the insignificant and ephemeral pleasures that social affairs and parties occasionally deliver. There is no weight, no seriousness, to their gender. And as always, this misconstrues and mischaracterizes the analogized animal and its activities. Butterflies hardly execute their rapid starts and stops for their own amusement; their very survival depends on this innate ability.[1]

## Hierarchies

For all his greatness, much of the blame for the historically poor treatment of women and animals must be placed at the feet of Aristotle. This most influential of philosophers advanced a hierarchical view of nature where the lesser exist only to serve the needs of the greater. As this hierarchy is "in the nature of things" and so not a human contrivance, women cannot alter their naturally dictated position or appeal their case to some moral court. There is no person or institution on which one can lay blame or from which one can demand a hearing. Finding oneself in either an advantaged or disadvantaged position is simply a function of the type of thing one is, be it dirt, woman, animal, barbarian, or member of a Greek city-state. This system, far from being merely one of class—where through hard work and luck one may eventually progress—is one of an iron-clad caste, completely insensitive to any efforts at self-improvement. Aristotle's criterion for position at the top of the natural hierarchy was rationality, the ability to reason. He deemed women "incomplete" and "imperfect" in reasoning ability and so eternally doomed to a second-class status.

It is difficult to exaggerate the influence of Aristotle's thought. Throughout the Middle Ages, for example, arguments were frequently settled by referring to one of his passages. The determination that Aristotle had adopted a particular position often precluded further discussion, much as citations of biblical passages did and still do today. For some two thousand years after his death, Aristotle was basically left unchallenged as a source of infallible wisdom. The work of the medieval Christian theologian St. Thomas Aquinas essentially reaffirms the major ideas of Aristotle and integrates them in a religious worldview. It is difficult not to perceive a diminution of women, if not pure misogyny, when Aquinas tells us that female ensoulment occurs forty days later than the male counterpart. Similarly, it is impossible not to be startled by Aquinas's pronouncements that, because no nonhuman animal is significantly rational, actions performed for their sake are not only silly and misplaced but border on blasphemous.

Hierarchical dualisms initiated by Aristotle some 2,400 years ago still dominate our intellectual and practical landscapes. In virtue of this heritage, we unthinkingly use the binary categories rational/irrational, human (cultural)/nonhuman (natural), human/animal, mind/body, reason/emotion, and even male/female to characterize the world. Equally spontaneous is our assessment that the first attribute of each pair is better than the second. The contemporary feminist movement challenges both the hierarchical nature of these dualisms as well as, more radically, the legitimacy of the dualisms themselves. Denying the hierarchies, or at least drastically redrawing their boundaries, evaporates the putative warrant from nature or God that confers legitimacy to a particular group's oppression. In denying the appropriateness of the dualisms per se, feminists suggest that they are ersatz constructions reflecting nothing more than rationalizations to immunize the people in power from criticism or revolution. The distinctions are neither naturally nor divinely inspired but simply politically prudent.

## A Feminist Critique of Masculinist Morality: Part 1

It is in our social nature to justify behavior. We expect others to have valid reasons for their behavior, and we normally feel ourselves obligated to have valid reasons for our own. If somebody does something we dislike or with which we disagree, we want to know why he or she did it. This practice of justification becomes most salient when a group of individuals oppresses another individual or group. Someone who beats a dog or a woman owes us an explanation or a reason that justifies this apparently untoward behavior.[2] Perhaps some believe that such behavior can never find justification. But even brief reflection will show that all but the most extreme pacifists will view this as far too strong a position. Cases of self-defense provide the clearest cases where some assaults are warranted. If a mad woman attacks a man on the street, he surely has the right to defend himself. While it may reasonably be thought—as the law asserts—that we are not entitled to use more force than is necessary to thwart an attack, vigorous physical assault is sometimes the only manner to protect oneself from serious injury or death.

One always unacceptable type of justification appeals to force or power. We cannot justify beating our wives or dogs simply because we are stronger and more powerful than they are. While our superior strength may well *explain* why we attempted and even succeeded in these beatings, it cannot *justify* them. Few accept the dictum "might makes right." Feminist ethicists believe that most moral theories (i.e., "masculinist" moral theories) make just this mistake. Feminists charge that, at root, what counts as right and wrong has been a matter of who has the power to make the rules. Although few of us are likely to accept "I am stronger than you" as an acceptable justification for our actions, feminists claim that masculinist ethics effectively does just that.

A prime target for this sort of criticism is the moral theory of Thomas Hobbes, the seventeenth-century British political philosopher who speculated about the origins and scope of morality.[3] To discover the source of morality, Hobbes asks us to imagine a presocietal, pregovernmental time when humans lived in a "state of nature." Those living in such a state know neither ethical rules nor state protections. It is easy to see why Hobbes thought that life for these inhabitants would be "solitary, poor, nasty, brutish, and short." Without any legal or moral rules, everyone would be constantly guarding against prospective evildoers. Eventually all will realize that they can improve their lives if they abdicate some of their freedom. It would be best for all if everyone were to enter into a contract, an agreement, that binds each to certain restrictions. No longer need Jack worry about his grain being stolen or his house damaged (at least he need not worry as much as before), since all the others have agreed to abandon these activities. In return, Jack will no longer steal tomatoes from others' gardens. Everyone gives up a little to gain a lot. According to Hobbes, the rules of morality are what emerge from these contractual deliberations.

Reciprocity is the governing idea of this contractualist morality. Jack has no reason not to steal from others unless these others, either individually or collectively, pose a threat to him. Jack pursues his self-interest rationally, avoiding conflict with more powerful parties. The contractors—those who formulate the rules for permissible behavior and who are bound by them—are those with power. The powerless—women, children, the infirm, and animals—are simply ineligible to participate in the bargaining process. Having no power, they have nothing to offer for the security and safety that they would receive, and so there is no reason to include them as members of the club. The powerless are morally disfranchised from the outset. They have no input into the negotiations, nor are they counted as morally important after the negotiations end and the moral rules are established. With no way to affect the security of the powerful, the interests and well-being of the weak are not a matter of concern. Rational self-interest gives us no reason to help those who cannot hurt us.

The rules that emerge from the deliberations will have a universal or general form. The social contract will yield prescriptions such as "everyone ought not to steal," "everyone ought not to cheat," and "everyone ought to be honest," since only they will satisfy the demands of rational self-interest. After all, if Jack wants to protect his tomatoes from theft, the law must apply to any person who might try to steal his vegetables—and what goes for Jack goes for everyone involved in the deliberations.

The requirement that moral rules be general corresponds to one of our most cherished pretheoretical beliefs. If it is wrong for us to perform some action in a given situation, then it is wrong for anyone in the same situation to perform that action. If beating your wife is wrong in a particular context, then it is wrong for anyone in similar circumstances to beat his wife. No one can claim special dispensation. Of course, none of this runs counter to my previous point that there may be circumstances in which beating your wife is not wrong. In these cases—such as self-defense—such violence may be permissible, but the point regarding the generalized or universalized quality of the rules remains intact. If it is morally permissible for a specific man in a specific situation to beat his wife, then it is permissible for any man in the same situation to beat his wife. Justice requires rules of a generalized nature.

Along with demanding generalized rules that apply to everybody in similar circumstances, Hobbesian moral theory requires a generalized punishment of wrongdoers. If Jack is punished by two years in prison for stealing my tomatoes, than Phil should be, too. If either steals the same quantity of your tomatoes, each will receive the same penalty. Persons are to be treated similarly in similar circumstances.

With this background of a paradigmatic masculinist ethic, we can begin to understand the general feminist critique. I will start with the feminists' qualms about the exceptionless, universal forms of rules and punishment that evolve from Hobbes's theory.[4] The most basic objection is that evaluating actions as right and wrong only insofar as they abide by or violate (general) rules entails omitting the specifics of the case under consideration. Feminist moralists insist that these particulars may prove crucial in making moral evaluations.

Suppose, for example, that John steals from Jane. Since this violates the general rule "no one ought to steal," John's action is counted as wrong. But feminists argue that such moral accounting is far too simplistic. Did Jane first steal from John? Did John just have a terrible day at work, where Jane was the cause of his frustration? Did John lose his job an hour earlier? The feminists' point is not that these considerations necessarily excuse John but that a full moral assessment demands more information than just a yes-or-no answer to the question of whether John stole. Indeed, even this central question may have an indeterminate answer. Does John steal if he takes a dollar from his friend Jane's wallet but leaves a note telling her that he took it and will return it tomorrow? Perhaps the fundamental masculinist moral categories of right and wrong need revamping or revision. Some feminists suggest that basic moral evaluation should say whether the act is *understandable* in the situation. Feminists complain that moral assessment in terms of rules impoverishes our knowledge of and sensitivity to the concrete situation in which actions are performed.

A related feminist concern with Hobbes's contractualist account is that instead of thinking of people in real flesh-and-blood terms, in terms of their particular histories and personalities, it construes people as characterless participants in a moral game. Hobbes's morality depersonalizes people, considering them as abstract objects, with their only relevant characteristic being their self-interested rationality.

An analogy may help explain this concern. The shape, color, and constitution of chess pieces matter not at all to the game. We have all seen bishops, rooks, and pawns of varying shapes, colors, and material. All that matters is each piece's function—so that, for instance, a red bishop is permitted to move only on a red diagonal. This is what *makes* a piece a red bishop. Whether the bishop itself is white or blue or is made of wood or copper is totally irrelevant. Shape, color, and constitution are merely accidental properties of the bishop and can be "abstracted away" without stripping the bishop of its identity. Feminist moralists view Hobbes's moral theory as treating persons in this abstract way, which they see as a vice, not a virtue. According to feminist philosophy, the personal details of a person's life are essential to the way he or she should be treated in our moral community. That a woman has been raised in a single-parent household, that a man was molested by his uncle at an early age, that a woman was surrounded by few friends in her formative years—all such factors should be included in a moral assessment of a person's actions. To think of these particulars as mere accoutrements to the person's "real" identity—an identity constituted solely by one's rational self-interest—is to grossly misunderstand persons and their moral relationships.

John Rawls, a contemporary political theorist who advances a view strikingly similar to Hobbes, epitomizes the abstract approach to moral theory.[5] To ensure fairness in these contractual deliberations, Rawls asks us to suppose that the participants are completely ignorant of their particularities. The contractors do not know their physical strength, intellectual prowess, social skills, or even what they find important in life (i.e., their "conceptions of the good"). Acting under this "veil of ignorance," a self-interested rational deliberator will not accept any rules that may prove detrimental to his or her own cause. Since, for example, no one knows one's color, race, or creed, no one will agree with proposals that would discriminate against any of these factors. If you don't know how intelligent you are, you won't agree with favoring the more intelligent; if you don't know how much money you have, you won't agree with favoring the rich.

A more characterless person would be hard to envision. Rawls's theory asks us to think of the contractors as beings without individuality. Completely separated from the specific talents or interests of any concrete individual, the rules that would emerge from their deliberations will be highly abstract. These rules would be fully impersonal in the sense that no particular person's strengths or weaknesses, likes or dislikes, would play any role in their constitution. We have a dual abstraction, then, an abstraction of both persons and the rules that result from their deliberations. Beginning with depersonalized (i.e., abstract) people, we develop general (i.e., abstract) rules. Feminists suggest that these abstractions yield a false picture of morality by omitting the personalized particular situations in which moral questions occur.

Feminists also accuse Hobbes, and masculinist theorists generally, of overemphasizing the role reason plays in our moral lives. Hobbes's moral account makes reason the sine qua non of morality. First, one must reason to understand the contractual deliberations in the first place. Thus, animals, infants, and marginalized human beings cannot deliberate the contract. Second, the contractors are then to use only their self-interested reason in forming the prescriptions that become the society's moral rules. Unfortunately, feminists claim, focusing on reason leads to discounting the moral significance of emotions and personal relationships.

Stealing tomatoes from John is not the same as stealing from Phil if John is your father. Feminist moralists understand Hobbes's masculinist ethics as minimizing morally significant differences among similar actions occurring within, say, friendship and family units. In support of this feminist idea, consider our different attitudes when informed that someone stole from his own father rather than from a stranger. We are often incredulous about the news, commenting simultaneously with surprise and disgust, "He stole from his *own* father"? This reaction demonstrates that moral assessments require specific information about the parties involved, whereas masculinist accounts omit just this sort of information in the belief that only by such omission can impartiality be ensured. Feminists take pains to point out that impartial reason is not sufficient for viable moral evaluations. Emotions such as love, for example, play a pivotal role in assessing both an act's rightness or wrongness and the appropriate quality and quantity of any applicable punishment. To wrong your own mother or father is not akin to breaking a contract, promise, or bargain. It is a breach of love and respect and not a violation of a rule.

Rawlsians insist that their moral view can account for rules that offer protections to their children, marginalized loved ones, and companion animals, who themselves cannot be party to deliberations of the social contract. They suggest that since those in the original bargaining position do not know whether they will have children, marginalized family members, or companion animals, some of the rules they adopt will offer these nonparticipating individuals protection. This suggestion is also supposed to show that the feminists unfairly characterize masculinist ethics as having no place for emotion, sentiment, or feeling. The affective life does play a role, albeit an auxiliary one, in the contractual discussions.

Feminists remain skeptical. The significant fact remains that these nonparticipants become morally enfranchised only because their membership in the moral community serves the self-interest of the contractors. This indirect way of enfranchising our children, disabled conspecifics, and companion animals into the moral realm does not reflect the way in which we think of these individuals. Our children deserve to be treated morally not because we have sentimental attachments to them but rather because they are the type of creatures who warrant moral enfranchisement in their own right. They are moral patients and have inherent value. We surely think it wrong to inflict gratuitous injury on any child, cherished or not. It is not as though orphaned children left without anyone to care about their interests now become moral "free game." We certainly do not believe that others can treat them in any way they please without being rebuked and punished.

Although feminists justifiably view the contractualist moral theory of Hobbes, Rawls, and others as the paradigm of masculinist ethics, many of their criticisms apply to other moral accounts as well. Consider utilitarianism, which found its modern formulation in the works of the British philosophers and political theorists Jeremy Bentham and J. S. Mill. Classical utilitarianism characterizes the right action as the one that produces the greatest total pleasure.[6] The theory is completely egalitarian in the sense that no particular person's pleasure is to count more than anyone else's. The net pleasure subsequent to an act totally determines its ethical status (i.e., whether it is right or wrong). Basically, we add up all the pleasure that accrues to all the people affected by an action and subtract all the pain that accrues to all the people affected by an action, repeating this simple arithmetic for all possible alternative actions. The right act is the one with the greatest balance of pleasure over pain.

On such a theory, we have no special obligation, for example, to help a family member before helping a stranger. Particular emotional and familial relationships may be sources of pleasure or pain but bear no weight beyond that. Impartiality is the essential formal quality of this masculinist account of morality. As with other theories, morality is given by rules (in this case, just the one) that are universal and exceptionless, although *self*-interest is not a prime motivation for the adoption of this altogether egalitarian theory. Feminists argue that familial and other personal relationships *should* matter, and so we should not be completely impartial. Thus, to feminists, utilitarianism is a flawed account of right and wrong.

## A Feminist Critique of Masculinist Morality: Part 2

Contemporary feminist morality began in earnest with the publication of Carol Gilligan's book *In a Different Voice*. Although Gilligan herself (unlike many subsequent feminists) sees her contributions as a helpful adjunct to the traditional, masculinist theories rather than a repudiation of them, the onset of feminist ethics was more than just a change in emphasis. In fact, the last two decades have seen a moral revolution challenging the long-standing traditional conception. Gilligan's work offers a markedly different notion of the origins of ethics and the considerations relevant to our moral decision making. We can profitably recognize the radical shift from masculinist to feminist ethics by first focusing on the basic notion of a person.

John Locke, a seventeenth-century British political philosopher, was the first to formulate the modern idea of personhood.[7] According to Locke, persons are both rational and self-conscious. Self-consciousness extends beyond mere consciousness, or sentience. It includes such potential awareness of the world—the capacity for visual, auditory, tactile, gustatory, and olfactory sensations—but requires something more: the capability of distinguishing the perceiver from that which is perceived. Self-consciousness demands that we have the concept of "I," the concept of a self or mind that endures through time.

One can see why this conception of a person plays such a pivotal role in the contractualist ethics that most feminists take as their foil. Without recognizing oneself as persisting through time, there is no way to understand how agreements could be made or employed. To make a promise, you must identify yourself now with the person who will later be obligated to keep the promise. More basically, the deliberative process itself will be unintelligible unless the contractors themselves implicitly recognize that they are the persons who are listening, debating, and finally agreeing to the ultimate terms. Mere momentary awareness, however keen one's perceptual apparatus, is insufficient for either grounding or implementing the rational, self-interested deliberations that contractualists forward as the source of morality.

In addition to requiring rationality and self-consciousness, masculinist ethics views persons as autonomous. Persons are independent, free decision makers. Persons are formed individuals, complete with preferences, temperaments, and personalities, before they enter into their social or moral worlds. Life may be solitary, poor, nasty, brutish, and short in a Hobbesian state of nature, but it is still personal. Rawls, too, thinks of persons in this way, although his heuristic device of the "veil of ignorance" entails that persons be abstractly conceived.

Opposing this conception of personhood, feminist ethics suggests a relational, socialized notion. Feminists do not deny the significance of rationality and self-consciousness for a viable morality, but typically they either deny these qualities the central role masculinist accounts give them or suggest that, far from existing in individuals abstracted from a social structure, they obtain only within social settings. As an example, consider how the notion of self-consciousness may be generated from recognizing one's own hierarchical position within a tribe of monkeys. It does not take too long for a younger monkey to realize that he has no business antagonizing an "elder statesman." His role—as mandated by the group in which he finds himself—may be to groom some of the elders as well as to play with his peers. Much the same transpires in human families. We learn to know who we are—we gain the conception of our selves—by carrying out our familial roles. Mundane activities such as eating, playing, and communicating with our family make us who we are. This account of self-consciousness offers a congenial setting to the relational and social components emphasized by feminist morality. In opposition to masculinist ethics, whose picture of self-consciousness is essentially independent of the place one inherits in society, feminist morality understands the person as a social work in progress.

This relational, social conception of a person should produce accounts of morality that are rooted more in actual situations than in the abstract and idealized circumstances that dominate masculinist moral accounts. Where masculinist theories of right and wrong have concentrated on the notions of impartiality, fairness, rights, and rules, feminist ethics as epitomized by Gilligan present a more flexible (and so less rule-governed), particularistic, situational account that speaks more of the responsibilities that people share with one another. Masculinist morality diminishes the significance of the historical context of behavior. It is as if personal history is extraneous to serious moral deliberations and could—and should—be neglected when someone is deciding what to do. The emotions are similarly slighted, for masculinist ethics tends to view them as annoyances or even hindrances to moral thinking. In masculinist ethics the crux of the matter is to describe the act in neutral terms and then investigate whether it is subsumed under a moral rule that either demands, permits, or prohibits it. Male morality, in virtually all its guises, wants to make morality a branch of science, where right and wrong can be determined by a more-or-less mechanical procedure.

Working within the template of a relational, social self instead of a discrete, individualistic self also influences how one thinks of the role that reason plays in morality. Traditionally the study of reasoning or logic has been embodied by a code of rules of right reasoning or rules of inference. Suppose, for instance, that John buys tofu whenever he goes to the store and that John is going to the store; we are permitted (i.e., good reasoning allows us or it is rational) to infer that John will buy tofu. Good reasoning, exemplified by following certain rules, does not require interpersonal interaction. In masculinist ethics, rationality, like self-consciousness, is not a social phenomenon but a purely intellectual one that can be carried out in the privacy of one's study.

Feminist morality, however, while not denigrating the value of deductive reasoning in mathematics or the sciences, sees it as largely peripheral to moral decision making. Feminists suggest that imaginative discourse should prevail instead. Here, there are no set rules, no rigorous canons of regulations intended to guide our thought dispassionately. In a freer, more conversational, less systematic manner, morality requires that we first and foremost get as full an understanding as we can about the motives, mindsets, and particulars of the persons involved in the situation. Far from using timeless logical truths to guide our thought, we need to know—often in great detail—the particular context of an action, along with its historical antecedents, before we can come to any conclusions about the course of action we should follow. Rather than abstract away the alleged irrelevancies of ethnicity, gender, nationality, and upbringing, we should count these as extremely important factors in our moral deliberations. It is only by attending to persons in their irreducible concrete particularity that we treat them with the fairness and respect that moral dealings require.

There is some irony here. Immanuel Kant, the seminal eighteenth-century Prussian moralist, grounded his moral theory on the notion of respect for others. In suggesting a modified version of the Golden Rule—one ought not to act toward others in ways that one would not want reciprocated—Kant made his criterion of right action contingent on an abstract, general, formal rule.[8] Feminists, however, remind us that the constitution and dispensation of respect is relative to a person's life history. Any stories that the participants of an action want to tell us are not to be dismissed as tangential to the "real" work that morality requires. Indeed, just the opposite is true. A sympathetic, attentive ear to these narratives will help us better understand what it was like for those participants at the time they acted, and quality moral counsel demands this empathetic response.

Feminist morality suggests a different group dynamic to the resolution of ethical conflict. There are no parties privy to all the moral truths who need only be supplied the unvarnished facts before they can, by sheer intellectual power, produce the correct and final verdict. This illusory ideal observer or godlike perspective, which is fostered by an allegiance to unyielding rules, should be superseded by a conversation among, if not equals, at least those without intellectual or ethical pretensions. There is no longer The Truth, which only an intellectually elite few can know and articulate. There are many truths, all relative to the concrete situations and histories of the participants. These truths can be revealed only through honest give-and-take discussions.

The sine qua non of rationality is consistency. Reasoning fraught with inconsistency or contradiction effectively evacuates debate of any sense. Feminists, however, tend to model morality on discussion rather than argument. So, while inconsistency may be the bane of masculinist ethics, it need not sound the death knell of a feminine ethics that privileges conversation. You might begin your discussions, narratives, and stories by talking about the hate that you feel toward another and end by talking about the love you feel. People commonly describe others as well as themselves in inconsistent ways. Rather than signal the speaker's unintelligibility—the epithet that the traditional male ethicist would hurl—these incompatible descriptions may provide important clues to the participants' states of mind. Perhaps Jennifer is simply ambivalent about John; perhaps she is deeply confused. In either case the genealogy of these emotions may provide us with important insights that will help resolve a moral issue.

Masculinist ethics, as exemplified by Hobbes, Locke, and Kant, have emphasized the significance of grounding ethics on a solid foundation. Essential to the work of all these political and moral theorists is the idea that absent convincing reasons to act morally, people would not. Moral prescriptions tend to act against self-interest; indeed, if they did not, why would we need morality at all? If self-interest generally coincided with morality, if what best serves us matched what we ought to do, the need for a moral code would evaporate. It is only because we often want to do what is incongruent with what we ought to do that ethical questions come to the fore. As I have shown, masculinist ethics tends to ground morality in enlightened self-interest, claiming that moral behavior ultimately benefits the individual. Although ethical behavior and self-interest may appear typically to operate at cross-purposes, the benefits from living in a moral society, a society wherein you can generally count on the moral behavior of others, outweigh any short-term benefits you may derive from immoral behavior. In effect, masculinist accounts base morality on prudence.

Once this moral community comes into existence, we can speak of moral rights and ethical entitlements. So, with the inauguration of a moral community, people now have the (negative) right not to be gratuitously harmed and the (positive) right to do anything that does not infringe on the rights of others. When moral rights emerge, however, so does the need for sanctions. This mirrors what happens in the legal sphere, where legal punishments ineluctably arise with the creation of legal rights.

Drawing on the ethics of close interpersonal relationships, feminists reject the masculinist emphasis on moral rights and their corresponding grounding as overly narrow and misplaced. In short, ethics encompasses more than just rights. Children do not have a right to be loved, and friends do not have a right to be liked; conversely, we have no duty to love our children or our friends. It should strike our ears as strange to speak in terms of rights and duties when we describe our relationships with the people closest to us. To speak in terms of rights and duties misses the point; such relationships do not operate on these terms. Better, say the feminists, that we understand them in terms of the affective and emotional parts of our lives—tempered by reason, of course—and not as relationships that arise from contractual or quasi-legal obligations. Furthermore, genealogical considerations indicate that this more affective approach warrants extension far beyond the close-knit relationships that form its core. For example, the Scottish philosopher David Hume bases morality on the innate sympathy almost all of us possess.[9] Morality gets off the ground in virtue of our natural feelings of compassion. According to the Humean ideal, we act morally not because it satisfies our enlightened self-interest but because we are born with a natural tendency to help others who are in need.

Feminists believe this Humean alternative has great appeal. We help a stranger who has just been hit by a car not because we see this as being in our long-term self-interest but because we spontaneously want to help another. Undoubtedly, many cultural influences can dull this natural impulse. We constantly hear of strangers manipulating and harming people who tried to help them: motorists who feign car trouble so that they can steal from unwary good samaritans or hitchhikers who murder those who were kind enough to offer them a ride. We are told at a tender age to "mind our own business" and to "never trust a stranger." But these stories and warnings confirm the idea that we do have some innate inclination to help and do good, for we would have little need of this cautionary advice were we moral blank slates at birth. Feminists are not oblivious to the conditions we face in the real world. They are suggesting only that our natural inclinations to do good—and not the self-centeredness favored by masculinist ethics—form the basis of moral relationships.

The most intimate relationship of all, and the one that serves as a paradigm for most feminist moralists, is that of mother and child. The mother carries the fetus within her for nine months, and this experience gives women a relationship to their children that fathers can never duplicate. Generally, mothers take the predominant nurturing role following the child's birth. These considerations are not antimale, as some have claimed; the father-child relationship can be even closer than that of mother and child. The point is that pregnancy typically establishes certain feelings that are biologically closed to prospective fathers.

This deep relationship is quite one-sided. Unborn children and young infants are completely dependent on their parents. The mother is responsible for the health and welfare of her baby, especially during pregnancy. The child is not only fully vulnerable to every decision the mother makes but also incapable of intentional reciprocity. This latter fact is crucial, for contractualist ethics makes it difficult to incorporate anything incapable of intentional reciprocity—such as children—directly into the moral sphere. With fetuses, infants, and young children, there is no tit for tat. We can help them, but they cannot return the favor. The favored traditional tactic—allowing them into our moral domain because our self-interest is enhanced—seems bizarre, if not perverse. Indeed, we treat them not only as robust members of our moral sphere but as exemplars of persons that morally deserve our most devout attention. There are few moral rebukes worse than the label of uncaring, irresponsible parent. The censure is serious for two reasons; the child is a member of your family, and the child is totally vulnerable.

I can now expand on my earlier comments. Appropriate behavior for family members is not a function of duties, obligations, and other quasi-legal notions. To act responsibly toward one's child, for example, because one has a duty to do so is to mischaracterize, misunderstand, and caricature the nature of the relationship. This becomes transparent when we consider how utterly out of place it would be to save your son from drowning from a sense of duty or from an obligation incurred from raising the child. We hope that the motivation would be your love and concern for him. Moreover, since these sorts of affective attitudes are thought to manifest themselves in all normal households, such explanations of behavior become in a way redundant. If asked why you saved your son, the proper answer is simply that he is your son. Nothing more need be said. That an individual is a family member—at least a close family member—is all the reason a person ever needs to help. In fact, reference to notions such as obligations and duties make us rightly suspicious that all is not well within the family unit. These are tools that families employ only when there is a failure in the normal caring and loving relationships that bind families.

The fact that fetuses and the very young are vulnerable suggests that morality was not originally intended to guide behavior among equals. Recall that Rawls's heuristic "veil of ignorance" is meant to establish an equal or fair point of departure for the subsequent contractual deliberations that culminate in a code of morality. The implication is that morality can originate only by conceiving its rules and regulations as prescribing behavior among those who think of themselves as having no distinct advantages over others. Feminist ethics, holding familial relationships as paradigmatic, views morality as an outgrowth of our natural proclivity to help and protect those who are most vulnerable to life's challenges. Once again, this has great appeal. On the one hand, consider the admiration many feel toward someone who helps the less fortunate or more vulnerable with no expectation of receiving anything in return. Most of us think of such a person in the highest of moral terms, as being someone who is truly kind, caring, sensitive, and magnanimous. This is the person who stars in our narratives to our youth, the one who is put forth as a model of these and other virtues and whose life is worth emulating. Gandhi and Martin Luther King Jr. are prime examples of great moral visionaries at least in part because they selflessly battled for the downtrodden and powerless. On the other hand, the calculating man whose motivation to help others derives from the hope that he will be subsequently compensated is surely not thought of as highly. Such a person need not be evil or malevolent, but most of us think of his motivations as somewhat base and less than ideal.

## How Feminists Can and Should Deal with Animals

I have described both the positions generally held by important feminist moralists and their interpretation and critique of traditional masculinist theories. Still, particular feminist theorists working within this broad framework differ one from another in important ways. The following sections flesh out the differences among the major thinkers in this group and suggest how nonhuman animals naturally occupy a place of importance in their ethics. I hasten to note that none of these writers says a great deal about how her particular theory applies to animals. Thus my comments are not intended to describe how these authors portray animals in their work. With rare exceptions, then, my aim is to fill a large lacuna in the scope of feminist ethics. It is to the credit of this novel view of ethics that it accommodates so well the notion of nonhuman animals as constituting a central segment of our moral population.

## Ethics of Care: Part 1

Carol Gilligan and Nel Noddings have proposed the two most important ethics of care. Gilligan believes that the differences between male and female views of morality derive from the different ways in which boys and girls are raised in our society. Males strive for independence from the family and have great need to express their autonomy outside the family structure. This disposition for independence and separation may have a psychosexual explanation, but regardless of the etiology, it explains why masculinist ethics has been dominated by talk of justice, rights, and rules. These moral tools may not be necessary consequences of the male view of persons as being independent, autonomous agents, but they are at least natural accompaniments. The institutions that maintain justice and rights enjoy pride of place in a competitive world with limited resources.

Women, however, are more involved with family concerns. The priority of rules and rights gives way to notions of relationships and responsibilities. Not tied to the model of independent, autonomous selves seeking the best possible outcome, women ground moral values on the idea of cooperation rather than competition. This conception, epitomized in family relationships, suggests that we be far more concerned with the desires, aims, and aspirations of others not solely for the good of others or solely for the good of ourselves but for the good of both. Family happiness and family success is not a zero-sum game in which the betterment of one person necessitates the detriment of another.

Gilligan sees *caring* as the glue of family relationships. She asks us to consider care's centrality to mother-fetus, mother-infant, and mother-child relationships. Caring is also manifested in the father-child and the older sibling–younger sibling relationships. For Gilligan, caring consists of a desire to closely relate to others, which can be accomplished only when there is an openness of hopes, fears, dreams, vulnerabilities, and desires.

The most significant point for extending this idea to our moral obligations regarding animals is that caring entails an unbalanced or hierarchical relationship. In fact, hierarchical relationships form the fabric of our society. Consider as representative the parent-child, doctor-patient, teacher-student, government-citizen, and caregiver-caretaker relationships. The members of these pairs are inherently unequal, but this inequality does not mean that some members ought to be dismissed from our moral community. Gilligan takes these relationships as the foundation of morality and extracts caring as their ethical heart.

In any particular instance in which a caring relationship exists, there is a caregiver and a caretaker. The person who provides the care must, at least in a limited respect and for a limited time, have a privileged position vis-à-vis the caretaker. Although speech often facilitates caring, it need not be present. Caretakers need only be able to communicate their needs to the caregivers. In this respect, an animal is often in at least as good a position as that of an infant or marginal human and in a better position than that of a fetus. Animals are generally capable of signaling when they are hungry, need affection, or are in pain. Infants and many marginal humans do this less well, and fetuses, not at all.

If not antithetical to the ethical notions of rights, rules, and justice, an ethics of care diminishes their importance. It is not as if the mother treats her fetus or infant well because the baby deserves or has a right to such treatment or because certain rules or regulations prescribe this motherly solicitude. As I claimed earlier, if parents rationalize their behaviors toward their young on these grounds, we tend to view them as abnormal. I am not suggesting that talk of parental *responsibility* is inappropriate. Since presumably most parents freely and intentionally went about creating another creature, they assume the large burden and responsibility of rearing him or her. Responsibility is certainly an intelligible rationale for care, but—and this is the main point—the more natural and appropriate "reason" for caring for your baby is simply that you love your child.

The contractualist model looks just as silly when applied to our relationships with our older children. Few would praise parents who care for their children so that their children will take care of them in old age. This does not imply that children should not care for their aged parents or even that grown sons and daughters do not have some sort of obligation to act reciprocally to loving and caring parents. It simply points out that this contractualist model is strained—to put it mildly—when used to explain why parents tend to their offspring in caring and loving ways.

These latter points apply naturally to the treatment of companion animals. We should treat them well not because they provide us pleasure and serenity (though they undoubtedly do) but because we love them. They are family members, and caring for them and showing concern for their welfare requires no further reason or explanation. Of course, one could propose some account to the effect that human providers are obligated to care for animals they adopted from a shelter; indeed, this might well be relevant for adoptive owners thinking of abandoning an animal. We might do well to mention obligations to pet owners who want to give up their dog because he clashes with their home furnishings. Normally, however, these sorts of considerations are out of place.

Caring occurs in degrees. We care more for our own children than for a friend's and more for a friend's than for a stranger's. We care more for our children than we do for our cousin's and more for a close cousin's than for a distant one's. But this is not to say that we do not, let alone should not, care for a strange person in a strange land. Our natural sympathy has a virtually unlimited scope, a fact that can induce both great satisfaction and great consternation. We are all familiar with pleas to help the starving peoples of lands so foreign that most of us cannot even locate them on maps. Their language and customs are a mystery. Despite these facets of distance, most of us sympathize and empathize with them. We wish that their plights were far less drastic, and we are often moved by these feelings to give money, time, and effort to bring some small benefit to them.

Again, the point transfers easily to animals. Our own companion animals receive the great bulk of our attention, but we also feel for the plight of those strangers of whom we somehow learn. Many of us try to improve their unfortunate situations. We send money to animal protection groups, we volunteer at shelters, and we adopt as many unwanted animals as we can. Once again, it is not as though references to rights, rules, and obligations cannot theoretically account for the different intensities of concern. Contractualists might claim that we care more for our own children than other children because our own children are far more likely to help us in times of need. This suggests that we do not and should not care for those who cannot provide aid. We do care more for family and believe this attitude to be legitimate. Nevertheless, we generally think it inappropriate to curtail our natural inclinations to care for others that are so foreign and remote that they cannot possibly return the favor. Caring cannot be reduced to reciprocity.

## Ethics of Care: Part 2

Not all care-centered ethicists would condone extending their ideas to our relationships with nonhuman animals. Nel Noddings, a feminist ethicist who argues against a reason-based, rule-based ethics in favor of one that emphasizes receptivity, relatedness, and responsiveness, agrees with much of what Gilligan offers but suggests some addenda. First, she is somewhat more radical than her predecessor, asserting that an ethics of care is better than an ethics of justice and not merely—as Gilligan sometimes claims—a helpful, even invaluable ally to masculinist theories. Second, and more important, Nodding's interpretation of caring is self-interested and not altruistic. According to Noddings, when we act ethically (i.e., engage in ethical caring), we act to fulfill our "fundamental and natural desire to be and remain related."[10] We try to meet the needs of others not because we have a natural impulse to act for the sake of others but because doing so meets our own needs—that is, because it is prudent.

Noddings's picture of personhood opposes that presupposed by masculinist ethicists. As I have shown, contractualism paints a picture of isolated, rational souls cleverly bargaining over what they see as being in their long-term best interests. Persons who enter into these bargaining sessions are already well formed prior to any society of which they will eventually become a part. Noddings, however, understands persons as essentially relational, rendering the picture of isolated, autonomous, presocietal persons not only fictitious but also useless and misleading. In her typical straightforward manner, Noddings tells us that she is "really defined by the set of relations into which my physical self has been thrown."[11] We should never forget that the importance of the caring relationship lies not only with the recipient. The essential relational aspect of the attitude means that the caregiver's interests must be considered just as seriously. This implies that the recipient, however abject, must consider how the exchange will affect the caregiver. This places some traditionally difficult social and moral issues in a different light. Abortion and euthanasia, for example, no longer should be debated in terms of the "rights of the fetus" or "the rights of the prospectively euthanized." Using this language already assumes both autonomy's centrality and the outdated masculinist ontology of a world occupied by independent, separate, reasoning beings. The debate needs to consider that the senile, such as those with advanced Alzheimer's disease, as well as early term fetuses, cannot respond to our caring in ways that are characteristically human.

In this we have the beginning of the rub. Since entities that cannot respond to us in characteristically human ways, such as marginal human beings, are unable to satisfy this demand for reciprocity, it is no wonder that Noddings has a cavalier attitude toward our moral relationships with animals. If having an early term abortion is conceived in terms of ending a responsive relationship before it begins—and so of no great moment—killing animals will generally be a relatively insignificant decision as well, since many animals cannot consider the caregiver's needs. Something can be part of the moral world only if "it calls forth our desire to care and can respond to our demonstration of care."[12] Maybe dogs, chimpanzees, and cats can squirm their way onto Noddings moral map, but it is highly unlikely that mice, hamsters, and fish stand much of a chance.

Nor does it help to think that fetuses enjoy at least the potential to form responsive relationships, whereas few if any nonhuman animals enjoy this possibility. Noddings's attempt to square her account with common sense faces problems from two sides. On the one hand, we *can* eventually form responsive relationships with many nonhuman animals. Those who have dogs and cats as companion animals can attest to this. We know when they are happy, sad, tired, hungry, and playful, and these moods—and ours—are mutually affected. On the other hand, one may question the necessity of such responsiveness in the first place. When Noddings tells us that we can kill a rat at our door with moral impunity (as long as we do not torture it) because there is no possibility of forming a responsive relationship with it, one may ask whether we can do the same to a newborn who suffers from brain damage that rules out such a relationship with it.[13] Responsive, reciprocal relationships should not form an indispensable part of ethical relationships, as Noddings would have us believe they do. Nor need we talk of marginal humans to make this point. Many of us in the West will never form responsive relationships with sub-Saharan Africans. Are we then to say, as Noddings concedes, that we have no moral obligations to make their plights more bearable? I demur, and I suspect you do, too.

It is unsurprising that Noddings sees no ethical obligation to become vegetarian. She tells us not only that we lack responsive relationships with cows, chickens, pigs, and goats but also that it is the fate of every living thing to be eaten. This is intended to remind us of the similarity between the natural processes of death, decay, and erosion with the slaughtering of animals in abattoirs. If the point is meant to demonstrate that we need not have moral qualms about carnivorism, it fails miserably. One might as well argue that we are all fated to die, so there is nothing wrong about killing an adult human. There is nothing natural to a cow's existence that incorporates the activities in a slaughterhouse.

To be fair, Noddings allows *some* animals into the moral sphere. She admits that we have some moral obligations toward animals with whom we have formed personal and affectionate relationships. Moreover, she is apparently willing to extend some sense of obligation even to stray cats that we happen on because they are "formally related" to our pets.[14] Still, she cautions that the scope and intensity of these obligations pale next to those we have for our fellow human beings, since cats and dogs lack the capacity for intellectual and spiritual growth that characterizes infants and presumably fetuses.

Once again, this cannot be a correct account of our moral lives. Humans who lack the capacity for any intellectual and spiritual growth still merit our moral concern. In fact, there are strong reasons for believing that our ethical obligations are even greater to these unfortunate humans. These are the most *vulnerable* of creatures, creatures whose very existence is contingent on the acts of others. One might expect that an ethics of caring, one rooted in the fact that many of our most profound moral relationships consist in the more able aiding the less able, would see our moral obligations toward the less fortunate as quite stringent.

It is also bizarre to be told that unknown cats (and, I suppose, unknown humans) deserve our moral concern merely because they resemble our (human and nonhuman) family members. Surely there is something *inherent* in these others that makes them worthy of moral concern. It is not as if a lack of family members would make our moral obligations toward these strangers disappear. Perhaps we have stronger moral obligations to those with whom we share close, personal relationships, but we ought not infer that all moral obligations are derived from their similarities to this significant source of moral obligation.

Insofar as Noddings's ethics of care differs from Gilligan's, it is less adequate. It yields a less satisfying explanation of moral relationships among humans. That it also results in a diminished moral status for animals is not surprising. These are not reasons to discount the contributions that an ethics of care makes to our understanding of morality. They are reasons to further appreciate Gilligan's seminal work.

### Ethics of Empathy

Best viewed as an extension of the caring/relationship ethics of Gilligan and Nodding, "empathy ethics" sees attempts to meet others on their terms as the model for a system of morality. Most forcefully advocated by Diana Meyers, empathy ethics emphasizes the great differences among persons and claims that honest attempts to understand these differences are essential to any successful moral account.[15] Because it bases moral decisions on abstract rules, masculinist ethics discounts such attempts to understand the ethical situation from the participants' particular perspectives. The impartial reasoning esteemed in masculinist moral accounts actually hinders understanding and appreciating differences among persons. We must understand factors of race, religion, health, peer and familial group dynamics, and education levels, to mention but a few, before we can develop the "correct moral response" to an ethical dilemma.

Meyers offers a case to show how a strict application of the universalizability criterion for right action—a favorite moral tool for masculinist ethics—can engender an ethical blindness and insensitivity. Consider the case of a university professor who, as an undergraduate, was the target of unrelenting "nerd" jokes. He consequently adopts the attitude that students should be coarsened to the slings and arrows of the real world that await them after graduation. To do this, he frequently uses sexist remarks in his classroom in an honest attempt to help his female students cope with the corporate environment. His (genuinely universalizable) precept is that university professors should act in ways that will toughen their students.[16] As Meyers suggests, although there is no logical incoherence in adopting this guide of action, the professor's behavior devalues the differences between men and women in our society. Empathy ethics, on the other hand, "celebrates" difference and diversity. These are legitimate values because acknowledging them tends to enlarge our view of the world and enables us to recognize the talents and skills of persons whom we may otherwise dismiss. Provincialism is poor policy both for those whose lives get discounted and for those who are doing the discounting.

The key notion of empathy should not be identified with appreciation. Not a merely cognitive or deliberative process, empathy is rather a willingness to act in ways that allow others to thrive. Empathy is a matter more of attitude and action than of intellectual comprehension. Nor should empathy be equated with sympathy, where the latter is understood as feeling sorry for another who suffers misfortune. This purely psychological response is far too thin to account for empathy. To empathize we need to imagine ourselves in the other's shoes, to try to experience what it is like to be in that particular situation. We need to feel and think what the other feels and thinks. Only in this way we can really grasp what the other is going through. Only in this way is it possible to resolve moral problems.

When real empathy occurs, we adopt the other's perspective. We are then freer to transcend our own prejudices and biases and view the situation not from an impersonal perspective, as masculinist ethics would have it, but from particular personal perspectives. Empathy increases the possibilities open to us, and each is particular, individual, and significant. There is no overarching regulation or rule that we can use to abstract away the differences in these newly disclosed possibilities of thinking about the moral circumstance. General rules distort the richly complex and real situations in which the participants find themselves. In the end, we are left with perhaps nothing more than honest, open, knowledgeable discourse on which to base a resolution. In recognizing that this is the best we can do, we allow ourselves to do our very best. Masculinist ethics (e.g., utilitarianism) provides us with a neat, determinative calculating device to resolve disputes, but we gain this precision only by reshaping and trivializing the dispute we are hoping to settle.

The intractable problem of abortion provides a good test case for empathy ethics. Masculinist ethics focuses the debate either on rights and obligations or on abortion's effect on society. The first approach, common in contractualism, inevitably generates talk of the "obligations of the mother" and the "right of the fetus." The issue is posed in terms of competing rights or obligations, and the ensuing discussion examines which rights or obligations triumph. The second, utilitarian approach asks us to consider what our society might look like were abortion permitted. Would we then start murdering infants with certain diseases or those with undesirable traits, such as, say, blond hair? Conceived this way, abortion looks like a eugenics program gone wild, an invitation to an Aryan master race that insults all who have a conscience.

The empathy advocate encourages us to rid ourselves of these abstract and general considerations and focus on the particular circumstances of each case. In each case of abortion, then, we must listen attentively to the woman, seeking to understand her particular, concrete history and to appreciate both cognitively and affectively why she wants (or does not want) the abortion. An atheistic, white, affluent, generally well treated woman may have to put herself in the place of a deeply religious, black, poor, poorly treated woman twenty years her junior. She will need to feel the younger woman's anxieties, fears, doubts, and concerns, even though, at the outset of the discussion, they may be utterly antithetical to her own mindset. She must embrace the younger woman's "radical particularity," her valuable individuality. She (and her interlocutor) may have a "eureka" experience: "Wow, I never thought (or felt) of the problem in *that* way." With any luck, a rich debate will occur. Maybe— albeit not inevitably—the two women will reach a satisfying resolution, but at least they will both gain the satisfaction of knowing that they have straightforwardly approached the moral dilemma and have done their best.

How might adopting the major tenets of an ethics of empathy shape our moral relationships with animals? Obviously, much depends on the viability of engaging in an empathetic relationship with a nonhuman animal. In turn, this question largely rests on the plausibility of the idea that animals have minds in much the same way that humans have them.

Nowadays virtually everyone believes that at least some nonhuman animals have minds that mirror our own. At a bare minimum, most people concede that mammals feel pain and pleasure and have some of the other affective and emotional states that humans typically have. We have moved beyond the Cartesian attempt to characterize animals as mere automatons. We need no longer give credence to the seventeenth-century Dutch philosopher Baruch Spinoza's remark that attributing thought and feeling to nonhuman animals is "womanish superstition."

The loving keepers of animals unashamedly empathize with their animals' suffering. It is no overstatement to say that a dog owner knows what is in the mind of a dog who steps on a sharp nail and yelps. The dog feels pain, undoubtedly of the same general sort that we feel when we step on sharp objects. We empathetically feel the fear that the veterinarian's office can elicit in an animal who has had unpleasant experiences there. We see the cowering and sudden stop of tail-wagging as sure indications of being afraid. We can place ourselves in the animal's position—just as we can with our fellow humans. Significantly, this empathetic response happens spontaneously, without any cognitive effort. That we automatically know what it is like for our dog at these particular moments indicates that empathy is not only easily learned but also part of our natural inheritance. Those unfortunates who lack the capacity for empathy—be it through an impoverished upbringing or artificially austere surroundings—lack a cherished part of the normal human psyche.

In fact, feminist empathy ethics suggests that we owe many nonhuman animals more than we owe human fetuses. It is far more speculative to imagine oneself to be a two-month-old fetus than it is to empathize with an orangutan, a dog, or a cat. Part of the difficulty is physiognomical; a two-month-old fetus does not look much like a normal human. Primates and mammals have recognizable faces and limbs, making empathetic relationships with them much easier. Part of the difficulty is behavioral. We do not normally perceive the movements of a fetus and so have no behavioral data to use in forming judgments about any possible cognitive or emotional states the fetus might occupy. In fact, we do not know whether a very young fetus can occupy any affective states at all. The facts of biology preclude a mental life for anything that lacks a fairly well developed nervous system.

Note that both feminist conceptions of ethics, the empathy-based one as well as the caring-based one, dispense with the idea of reciprocity that lies at the heart of much masculinist ethics. One can care for another without being cared for in return. Indeed, the most vulnerable of us—the very young, the senile, and the most marginal of humans—are incapable of returning the helping acts of others. But so much the better, I suggest, for the feminist conception, for to position reciprocity at the core of ethics transforms morality into an exercise in self-interest. And whatever morality amounts to, it is not a deliberative attempt to manipulate situations so that they will satisfy self-interest in the long term. We do—and should—think of ethics as something finer and nobler. Requiring that right actions eventually pay off misses the point of moral action. Regardless of whether animals can return care and empathy to those who give it, there is no reason to exclude them from the moral sphere. As with the most vulnerable humans, they should be not only part of the moral domain but a primary beneficiary of our morally guided behavior.

## Ethics of Trust

As it has evolved, feminist ethics has moved away from caring and empathy to the related but importantly different idea of trust. While agreeing with her fellow feminists that contractual relationships constitute an improper paradigm for moral relationships, Annette Baier advocates trust as the key element in understanding morality. To trust is to allow yourself to be open and vulnerable to the harms that others may inflict on you, to leave yourself at least partially defenseless against the potential onslaughts of another, believing that the relationship formed up to this point will not lead to embarrassment, humiliation, deception, and mental and physical pain. In trust one essentially relies on the goodwill of another but cannot be certain of it. Such relationships, regardless of their familiarity and genuineness, always carry some degree of risk for the trusting person.

In its most primitive and natural embodiment, trust is manifested in the infant-parent relationship, where infants thoroughly depend on the love and goodwill of their parents. As this relationship demonstrates, trusting relationships need not be cognitively based. It is not as though infants realize their dependency on their parents and conclude that they should or even must trust. On the contrary, this trusting precedes any thoughts about trusting. Rationalization for the trust comes, if it comes at all, far later in a child's life. In fact, although robust trusting relationships based on cold self-interested calculations may be possible, this process of formation seems to be an exception. Rather, most trusting relationships occur in virtue of closeness and familiarity with others. For example, you may come to trust someone who has kept one of your secrets for many years and despite many temptations to reveal it.

It is easy to overlook the pervasive roles that trust plays in our society. Our very survival requires that we trust not only other people but also our institutions. Consider the havoc that a general distrust in our medical and legal professions would wreak. The institutions of judge, jury, and trials cannot work without a general trust that the legal system is effective and just. Even the most cynical of us probably believe that court decisions are usually fair and correct. Like those between individuals, moreover, trusting relationships involving institutions often include unequals. In trusting a doctor or lawyer, for example, you typically trust someone to have knowledge of some field beyond your own. Trusting the legal system as an institution involves this sort of power differential as well. The system can harm you enormously— for example, by imposing fines or jail time—while you can do relatively little to injure the institution. Consider, finally, the education system. Without our implicit trust in our teachers, professors, and textbooks, we could learn but little. We could learn only what we perceived, which would drastically parochialize our knowledge.

What consequences does this feminist theory have for our moral relationships with animals? In almost every way, the very survival of animals, especially our companion animals, depends on our meeting their trust in us. They need and trust us for their food, shelter, and health care. The analogy with our human fetuses, infants, the senile, and the otherwise marginal holds well. These humans cannot live unless we meet their trust in us. As do animals, they count on us. If we fail to live up to their trust, we normally believe that we have done something morally wrong. Of course, there can be circumstances where this trust is justifiably flouted. We cannot tend to grandma today because the baby suddenly needs to see the pediatrician; we cannot feed Knish lunch because Margot needs to visit the veterinarian. We try to sustain their trust by making other arrangements. We do the best we can.

As is the case with all feminist moral conceptions, the significance of reciprocity is downplayed. Many of our trusting relationships are asymmetrical. We do not trust, nor need we trust, our infant daughters—let alone fetuses or the senile—to do something in return for satisfying their trust in us. As in the prior feminist conceptions, a trusting ethics owes its genealogy to familial situations, especially in parent-child relationships. But we should not forget that nonhuman animals are, and throughout much of history have been, frequently considered members of the family. We share our homes, food, attention, and love with them. An ethics of trust rightfully reminds us of the kinship that binds humans and animals.

# CONCLUSION

This essay began with an examination of a principle that accords well with our prereflective moral beliefs. It surely strikes us as wrong to intentionally inflict gratuitous pain and suffering on innocent creatures. Since common sense tends to signal the beginning and not the end of investigation, the principle was articulated and defended. Adherence to this precept conjoined with knowledge of the abusive treatment animals receive from many of our institutions morally requires huge changes in our present lifestyles.

Once again, this is not to imply that the premature *painless* death of a nonhuman animal is not also wrong. Indeed, just the opposite is true. Although terminating the life of an animal (human or not) is obviously worse when accompanied by suffering on the part of the animal, ending a sentient life, even painlessly, makes it impossible for the creature to experience pleasure, amusement, and happiness. Bracketing extreme situations (e.g., euthanasia), this is something we ought not do.

Interpretations of religious scripture have served as the major imprimatur for the way our society interacts with animals. The unbridgeable schism between the value attributed to animals—instrumental value—and the value attributed to humans—inherent value—makes us unreflectively comfortable with our standard relationship with animals. We have seen, however, that Judeo-Christian texts provide resources to ground a far more respectful treatment of animals, even to the point of incorporating them as robust members of our moral community. Nor do those with a more secular bent have any reason to think that humans and animals are creatures with essentially different kinds of worth. Both theists and atheists, therefore, have no refuge from the changes that morality requires. Nor, I hope, after becoming acquainted with factory farming, hunting, and vivisection, would they want one.

The legal system provides animals no relief. It and the institutions that directly involve animals need a complete overhaul. Far more important, our attitudes regarding nonhuman sentient creation requires drastic revision. Recent feminist theory may provide an intellectual entry to the required revamping, but as is the case in all moral revolutions, a change in our hearts will have more significance than a change in our heads.

# NOTES

## CHAPTER 1: THE PRINCIPLE OF GRATUITOUS SUFFERING

1. See my article "Explaining Evil," *Religious Studies* 34 (1998): 151–63, where I counter some recent attacks on the idea that the existence of evil is consistent with the existence of God.

2. See Peter Singer, "Famine, Affluence, and Morality," *Philosophy and Public Affairs* 1 (1972): 229–43; and *Practical Ethics* (Cambridge: Cambridge University Press, 1993), 218–46. Many of the criticisms and responses that I entertain are discussed in the latter text.

3. Singer, *Practical Ethics*, 230–31.

4. Philosophers disagree as to whether this "deprivation" account of the badness of death is correct. Suffice it to say that virtually all nonphilosophers think of death in this way and that we would need strong considerations to abandon this view. The painless termination of an animal's life is almost always wrong. Legitimate euthanasia—killing an animal as painlessly as possible for the animal's sake—is justified, however, whether the animal is human or not. This is one of the few areas where loving and caring people treat their companion animals better than they treat their human loved ones.

5. The classic contemporary article on this principle is Phillipa Foot, "The Problem of Abortion and the Doctrine of Double Effect," *Oxford Review* 5 (1967): 5–15.

6. See René Descartes, *Discourse on the Method,* chapter 5, in *The Essential Descartes,* ed. Margaret Wilson (New York: New American Library, 1969), 137–39.

7. See my book *On Moral Considerability: An Essay on Who Morally Matters* (New York: Oxford University Press, 1998) for a detailed discussion on the necessary and sufficient conditions for being a moral patient.

## CHAPTER 2: THE VALUE OF HUMANS AND THE VALUE OF ANIMALS

1. For the most detailed discussions of the marginal case argument in the literature, see Evelyn Pluhar, *Beyond Prejudice: The Moral Significance of Human and*

*Nonhuman Animals* (Durham, N.C.: Duke University Press, 1995); Daniel Dombrowski, *Babies and Beasts: The Argument from Marginal Cases* (Urbana: University of Illinois Press, 1997).

2. See Bernard Williams, *Ethics and the Limits of Philosophy* (Cambridge, Mass.: Harvard University Press, 1985), 118–19.

3. Reprinted in Elijah Judah Schochet, *Animal Life in Jewish Tradition: Attitudes and Relationships* (New York: KTAV, 1984), 3.

4. See "Summa Contra Gentiles," in *Basic Writings of St. Thomas Aquinas,* ed. Anton Pegis (New York: Random House, 1945), 220–24.

5. See Thomas Aquinas, *The Summa Theologica of St. Thomas Aquinas,* trans. the Fathers of the English Dominican Province (New York: Benzinger Bros., 1918), pt. 1, question 65.3.

6. St. Augustine, *The Catholic and Manichean Ways of Life* (Boston: Catholic University Press, 1966), 102.

7. John Calvin, *On the Christian Faith* (New York: Bobbs-Merrill, 1957), 131–32.

8. Joseph Rickaby, *Moral Philosophy,* vol. 2 (London: Longman, 1901), 248ff.

9. This point has been made by many, including the famed Kabbalist Moses Cordero.

10. See the selection on Butler in *Animals and Christianity,* ed. Tom Regan and Andrew Linzey (London: Peter Smith, 1992).

11. Here, as in other segments of the biblical case for the stewardship interpretation of dominion, the "marginal case argument" is relevant.

12. Kabbalism is the mystical Jewish sect from which the extremely pious Hasidism was born.

13. Cited in Roberta Kalechofsky, ed., *Judaism and Animal Rights: Classical and Contemporary Responses* (Marblehead, Mass.: Micah, 1992), 183.

14. Regan and Linzey, *Animals and Christianity,* 14.

15. For a detailed look at this forward-thinking rabbi, see the collection of his writings *Abraham Isaac Kook,* trans. and intro. Ben Zion Bokser (New York: Paulist, 1978).

16. Qtd. in Jon Wynne-Tyson, comp., *The Extended Circle: A Commonplace Book of Animal Rights* (New York: Paragon House, 1989), 65.

17. Chapter 3 details these conditions.

18. Personal correspondence, Gordis to R. Schwartz, qtd. in Kalechofsky, *Judaism and Animal Rights,* 229.

19. An interpretation (unique, as far as I know) is given by J. W. Rogerson, who claims that "for some priests at least, the system of animal sacrifice symbolized the failure of humanity as represented by Israel to live in the world as God intended" (in *Animals on the Agenda,* ed. Andrew Linzey and Dorothy Yamamoto [Urbana: University of Illinois Press, 1998], 17). Apparently Rogerson's idea is that God intended us to live in a violence-free world and we failed him. By sacrificing animals and thereby creating violence, we symbolize our inability to live in the sort of nonviolent world that God prefers.

20. J. H. Hertz, trans. and ed., *The Pentateuch and Haftorahs: Hebrew Text, English Translation, and Commentary*, 2d ed. (London: Soncino, 1960), 558–59.

21. See John Robbins, *Diet for a New America: How Your Food Choices Affect Your Health, Happiness, and the Future of Life on Earth* (Tiburon, Calif.: H. J. Kramer, 1987), for many other examples of the beneficial effects of a vegetarian diet for both the environment and the poor.

## Chapter 3: The Holocaust of Factory Farming

1. I do not discuss the plight of fish in this manuscript. The omission is pragmatically based; given our zeitgeist, generating sympathy for fish is far more difficult than generating sympathy for land animals. Current science indicates that fish have the capacity to feel pain and suffer, and so these animals would clearly be subsumed under the PGS. (The case for shrimp, scallops, and oysters is far less clear.) Fishing—be it commercial or avocational—is therefore just underwater hunting. Although numbers are hard to come by, undoubtedly billions of fish are killed annually.

2. The best book I know that speaks to the conditions in slaughterhouses is Gail Eisnitz, *Slaughterhouse: The Shocking Story of Greed, Neglect, and Inhumane Treatment inside the U.S. Meat Industry* (Amherst, N.Y.: Prometheus, 1997). I borrow heavily from it when I speak about slaughterhouse conditions. Eisnitz's book is far more than an exposé. It is a gripping story of a brave woman facing obstacles throughout her investigation of slaughterhouse conditions. It also discusses how these poorly run plants have detrimental consequences for human health. Eisnitz deals quite sympathetically with the workers at the various slaughtering plants. Although I have somewhat less sympathy for the workers who do the slaughtering, she and I agree that the entire system needs revamping. I believe, and probably Eisnitz would concur, that abolition is what is needed.

3. This remark came in response to complaints filed under the Whistleblower Protection Act by a former plant worker named Timothy Walker. The episode is recounted in Eisnitz, *Slaughterhouse*, 226–30; quotation on 228–29.

4. Most of these reports come in the form of verbal statements by former plant employees, many of whom worked for several plants over many years. That many of these reports are quite similar adds to their credibility. Also, the workers had nothing to gain by lying; it is not self-aggrandizing to admit that you've rectally raped a hog or bludgeoned one to death with a steel pipe. Eisnitz spoke to many of these workers and heard their remembrances. Reports of these encounters are peppered throughout her book.

5. Before researching material specifically for this book, I thought that I knew virtually all the horrors that both layer and broiler chickens endure on factory farms. I had read quite a bit of material and had many conversations with people more knowledgeable than I was about the conditions to which they are subjected. I was wrong. The lives of chickens (and turkeys) are much worse than I had believed. For much of what follows, I owe a debt to Karen Davis. Her book *Prisoned Chickens,*

*Poisoned Eggs: An Inside Look at the Modern Poultry Industry* (Summerton, Tenn.: Book Publishing, 1996) is the most thorough critique of the chicken industry of which I know. It is extensively documented and written by someone who has visited many of these factory farms, and I cannot recommend it highly enough for those who desire more details than I supply.

6. See Davis, *Prisoned Chickens,* 46–49.

7. See Peter Roberts, "Egg Production," *Compassion in World Farming Fact Sheet* (Petersfield, Hamphire, U.K.: 1987): 2; Danny Hooge, "Laying Hen Nutrition at High Production Stocking Densities," *Poultry Digest* (Aug. 1994): 16, 20; C. E. Ostrander and R. J. Young, "Effects of Density on Caged Layers," *New York Food and Life Sciences* (July–Sept. 1970): 5–6.

8. See Michael Baxter, "The Welfare Problems of Laying Hens in Battery Cages," *Veterinary Record* 134 (June 11, 1994): 617; Klaus Vestergaard, "Aspects of the Normal Behavior of the Fowl," *Tierhaltung* 12 (1981): 150–51.

9. See R. Brown, "Egg Producers Concerned about the Loss of Spent Fowl Slaughter Market," *Feedstuffs* 65, no. 2 (Dec. 20, 1993): 1; Richard Wall, "Caged Layer Fatigue," *Poultry Digest* (Jan. 1976).

10. *Merck Veterinary Manual,* 7th ed. (Rahway, N.J.: Merck, 1991): 1619; M. S. Hofstad et al., *Diseases of Poultry,* 9th ed. (Ames: Iowa State University Press), 669–73.

11. John Avens, "Overview: Salmonella—What's the Problem?" *Third Poultry Symposium Proceedings: Managing for Profit* (Fort Collins: Colorado State University, 1987): 122.

12. See Hofstad, *Diseases of Poultry,* 852; Fiona Carlile, "Ammonia in Poultry Houses; A Literature Review," *World's Poultry Science Journal* 40 (1984): 99–113.

13. Wieber van der Sluis, "Will We Ever Get Rid of the Disease?" *World Poultry* (Aug. 1993): 16.

14. See Chris Sirgudson, "Perdue's 'Kinder, Gentler, Chicken' Moves into Real World Test," *Feedstuffs* 67, no. 3 (Jan. 16, 1995): 47–78; James V. Craig, *Animal Behavior: Causes and Implications for Animal Care and Management Domestic* (Englewood Cliffs, N.J.: Prentice-Hall, 1981), 208–12; Lesley Rogers, *The Development of Brain and Behavior in the Chicken* (Wallingford, Oxon, U.K.: CAB International, 1995), 96.

15. See Charles Wabeck, *Raising Your Home Chicken Flock,* Cooperative Extension Service, University of Maryland System, Institute for Agriculture and Natural Resources (rev. 1991-2), 10; *California Poultry Letter,* Department of Avian Science, University of California at Davis, March 1994, 7–8.

16. Ian Duncan, "The Science of Animal Well-Being," qtd. in Davis, *Prisoned Chickens,* 155.

17. See Mack North and Donald Bell, *Commercial Chicken Production Manual,* 4th ed. (New York: Van Nostrand Reinhold, 1990), 250.

18. See Klaus Vestergaard, "Alternative Farm Animal Housing: Ethological Considerations," *Scientists Center Newsletter* 9, no. 3 (1987): 10.

19. See Robert H. Brown, "Hot, Humid Weather Kills Millions of Poultry," *Feedstuffs* (July 24, 1995): 5.

20. See Allison Taylor and J. Frank Hurnik, "Conditions of Laying Hens," *Poultry Science* 73, no. 2 (Feb. 1994): 270; R. J. Buhr and D. L. Cunningham, "Evaluation of Molt Induction to Body Weight Loss of Fifteen, Twenty, or Twenty Five Percent by Feed Removal, Daily Limited, or Alternate-Day Feedings of a Molt Feed," *Poultry Science* 73, no. 10 (Oct. 1994): 1499–1510; North and Bell, *Commercial Chicken*, 433–52.

21. See Donald Bell, *The Poultry Tribune*, Sept. 1995, p. 16.

22. See Jim Mason and Peter Singer, *Animal Factories*, rev. ed. (New York: Harmony Books, 1990), 45; Michael Lilburn, "Skeletal Growth of Commercial Poultry Species," *Poultry Science* 73, no. 6 (1994): 897–903; S. C. Kestin et al., "Prevalence of Leg Weakness in Broiler Chickens and Its Relationship with Genotype," *Veterinary Record* 131, no. 9 (Aug. 29, 1992): 190–94.

23. See Ted Odum, "Ascites Syndrome: Overview and Update," *Poultry Digest* (Jan. 1993): 14–22.

24. Ibid., 20–21.

25. See R. J. Julian et al., "The Relationship of Right Ventricular Hypertrophy Failure and Ascites to Weight Gain in Broiler and Roasted Chickens," *Avian Diseases* 31 (1987): 130–35.

26. See Clare Druce, *Chicken and Egg: Who Pays the Price?* (London: Merlin, 1989), 18–19.

27. See R. T. White, "Aerial Pollutants and the Health of Poultry Farmers," *World's Poultry Science Journal* 49, no. 2 (July 1993): 139–56; Carlile, "Ammonia," 77.

28. *Poultry Digest* (May 1990): 44; qtd. in Davis, *Prisoned Chickens*, 100.

29. See A. W. Brant et al., *Guidelines for Establishing and Operating Broiler Processing Plants*, Agricultural Handbook 581 (Washington D.C.: Agriculture Research Service, U.S. Department of Agriculture, 1982): 23.

30. See Charles Perry, "Whither Spent Hens," *Poultry Digest* (Jan. 1994): 4.

31. See S. F. Bigili, "Electrical Stunning of Broilers—Basic Concepts and Carcass Quality Implications: A Review," *Journal of Applied Poultry Research* 1, no. 1 (Mar. 1992): 136.

32. See N. G. Gregory and S. B. Wotton, "Effect of Stunning on Spontaneous Physical Activity and Evoked Activity in the Brain," *British Poultry Science* 31 (1990): 215–20.

33. Wayne Austin, Simmons Engineering Company, letter to C. Druce, Feb. 1, 1994. For details of this letter, see Davis, *Prisoned Chickens*, 167 n. 64.

34. See *A Practical Guide to Neck Cutting in Poultry*, Meat Research Institute Memorandum no. 54 (Langford, Bristol, U.K.: Agricultural and Food Research Council, 1984), 5–24.

35. In the USDA fiscal year 1993 about 7 billion poultry were officially slaughtered. More than 3 million entered the scald tanks alive. Assuming that the same percentage applies to the greater number of birds now slaughtered yields the figure of about 4 million. This information, from "Poultry Slaughtered, Condemned, and Ca-

davers" (June 30, 1994), was obtained through the Freedom of Information Act 94–363 and is cited in Davis, *Prisoned Chickens,* 166. These numbers seem to be at odds with Eisnitz's figures, however (see Eisnitz, *Slaughterhouse,* 114, 166 n. 47).

## CHAPTER 4: HUNTING

1. Several books are worth consulting on natural population control: David Lack, *The Natural Regulation of Animal Numbers* (New York: Oxford, 1954); Ian McLaren, ed., *Natural Regulation of Animal Populations* (New York: Lieber-Atherton, 1971); Lawrence Slobobkin, *Growth and Regulation of Animal Populations* (New York: Dover Books, 1980).

2. Some philosophers would find this conclusion too quickly drawn. Derek Parfit, for example, seems to support the so-called replacement argument, which allows the painless death of one non-self-conscious creature by another if the former's death is required for the latter and the latter will live at least as good a life as the creature killed (see Parfit, *Reasons and Persons,* [Oxford: Oxford University Press, 1986], 366–71). My main theoretical objection to this argument is that it really proves too much, since I see no good reason to limit its compass to creatures that lack self-consciousness. Moreover, it is unabashedly consequentialist, and there are reasons to believe that violations of autonomy, for example, are not to be permitted even if better consequences result. This being said, a far more protracted argument is needed to discuss the merits of the replacement argument.

3. Several years ago a Texas Parks and Wildlife commissioner threatened to come to a board meeting with a trap around his arm to show those in the vocal antitrapper contingent that they were exaggerating the trapped animal's pain. He never followed up on this threat, but it would have proven little if he had. As I argued earlier in the text, the animal clearly feels pain. In addition, a trap holding a fox's leg differs markedly from a trap around the rather burly arm of a large man. The commissioner would have had to put the trap around his less fleshy fingers. Finally, I doubt that the tension on the trap on his arm would have been set as high as it is on the ones left in the wild to trap animals.

4. See Aldo Leopold, *A Sand County Almanac* (New York: Oxford, 1949). Although Leopold's views changed somewhat as he aged, he continued to believe that wildlife manipulation is the key to a healthy ecosystem. He also remained a hunter to the end. I have never understood why, on Leopold's holistic conception, there must be anything wrong with hunting *humans.* Are not the 1.2 billion people in mainland China destructive of the ecosystem in which they live? They would have far less pollution of air and water if, say, half their population was eradicated.

5. I address this in much greater detail in my book *On Moral Considerablity: An Essay on Who Morally Matters* (New York: Oxford, 1998). I argue extensively there not only that ecosystems have no intrinsic value but that the entire "deep ecology" movement, which attributes intrinsic value to insentient parts of nature, is fundamentally flawed.

6. Barbara Parham's *What's Wrong with Eating Meat* (Denver: Ananda Marga Publications, 1979) is a good source for reasons that humans are not naturally carnivores. Nor are they, probably, naturally omnivores. The ancestors of omnivores were probably carnivores, and so an omnivore with unadulterated lineage is difficult to find.

7. Jay Kirkpatrick is probably the world's leading authority on immunocontraception; see J. Kirkpatrick, I. K. M. Liu, and J. W. Turner, "Remotely Delivered Immunocontraception in Feral Horses," *Wildlife Society Bulletin* 18 (1990): 326–30.

## CHAPTER 5: ANIMAL EXPERIMENTATION

1. See G. E. Paget, ed., *Methods in Toxicology* (Oxford: Blackwell, 1970).

2. See L. E. Davis, *Journal of the American Veterinary Medical Association* 175 (1979): 1014–15; cited in Robert Sharpe, *The Cruel Deception* (Wellingborough, U.K.: Thornsons, 1988), 94.

3. See M. Dawson, *Cellular Pharmacology* (Springfield, Ill.: Charles C. Thomas, 1972); cited in Sharpe, *Cruel Deception,* 98.

4. See G. Zbinden and M. Flury-Roversi, *Archives of Toxicology* 47 (1981): 77–99; cited in Sharpe, *Cruel Deception,* 98.

5. These data were supplied by the surgeon Dr. Werner Hartinger of Waldshut-Tiengen. See Pietro Croce, M.D., *Vivisection or Science* (Rome: CIVI, 1991), 19.

6. Zbinden, cited in Sharpe, *Cruel Deception,* 119.

7. Dr. Sharratt, *New Scientist,* June 23, 1977; cited in Sharpe, *Cruel Deception,* 119.

8. Cited in Sharpe, *Cruel Deception,* 77.

9. In her foreword to C. Ray Greek and Jean Greek, *Sacred Cows and Golden Geese* (New York: Continuum, 2000), Jane Goodall notes that of the hundreds of chimpanzees that have been infected with the retrovirus causing AIDS in humans, *none* has developed typical human symptoms. Of the only two who apparently died of AIDS, the course of the disease was very different from that in humans. For a detailed account of the utter failure of animal experimentation in AIDS research, see Greek and Greek, *Sacred Cows,* ch. 10.

10. Ibid., 30–33.

11. See Croce, *Vivisection,* 21–24.

12. See M. Massoudi et al., "Thermogenic Drugs for the Treatment of Obesity: Screening Using Obese Rats and Mice," *Annals of Nutrition and Metabolism* 27 (1983): 26–37; cited in Sharpe, *Cruel Deception,* 74.

13. See "The Opren Scandel," *Panorama,* BBCI broadcast, Jan. 10, 1983; cited in Sharpe, *Cruel Deception,* 71.

14. Irwin Bross, "How We Lost the War against Cancer" (congressional testimony, 1981), reproduced in Brandon Reines, *Cancer Research on Animals* (Chicago: National Anti-Vivisection Society, 1986); cited in Sharpe, *Cruel Deception,* 77 (emphasis added).

15. See F. J. Di Carlo, "Carcinogenesis Bioassay Data: Correlation by Species and

Sex," *Drug Metabolism Reviews* 15 (1984): 409–13; cited in Sharpe, *Cruel Deception,* 134.

16. David Salzburg, "Lifetime Feeding Study in Mice and Rats: An Examination of Its Validity as a Bioassay for Human Carcinogens," *Fundamental and Applied Toxicology* 3 (1983): 63–67; cited in Sharpe, *Cruel Deception,* 105.

17. J. P. Whisnant, in *Cerebral Vascular Diseases,* ed. C. H. Millikan (New York: Grune and Stratton, 1958), 53–67 (emphasis added).

18. *New York Daily News,* Mar. 13, 1961.

19. Greek and Greek, *Sacred Cows,* 137; E. Boesen, *Cytotoxic Drugs in the Treatment of Cancer* (London: Edward Arnold, 1969).

20. Greek and Greek, *Sacred Cows,* 138.

21. Ibid., 139.

22. A. Haddow, *British Medical Journal* (Dec. 2, 1950): 1272; as cited in Greek and Greek, *Sacred Cows,* 234.

23. See Thomas Lewis, *Clinical Science* (Kent: Shaw and Sons, 1934), 120.

24. See L. K. Altman, *Who Goes First? The Story of Self-Experimentation* (New York: Random House, 1937), 95–96.

25. Cited in Greek and Greek, *Sacred Cows,* 141.

26. Cited in Greek and Greek, *Sacred Cows,* 142.

27. National Center for Chronic Disease Prevention and Health Promotion (CDC), "Decline in Deaths from Heart Disease and Stroke—United States, 1900–1999," *Journal of the American Medical Association* 282 (Aug. 25, 1999): 725.

28. *New York Times,* May 8, 1990.

29. Greek and Greek, *Sacred Cows,* 171.

30. In ibid., 172.

31. Ibid., 101–2.

32. Ibid., 140.

33. Ibid., 162.

34. *Alternatives to Laboratory Animals* 13 (1985): 38–47; qtd. in Greek and Greek, *Sacred Cows,* 162.

35. See Greek and Greek, *Sacred Cows,* 61–76; Sharpe, *The Cruel Deception;* Niall Shanks and Hugh LaFollette, *Brute Science: Dilemmas of Animal Experimentation* (London: Routledge, 1997).

36. Greek and Greek, *Sacred Cows,* 35–36. Exhaustive references to this event are provided on p. 228.

37. Ibid., 175.

38. Stephen Westaby, with Cecil Bosher, *Landmarks in Cardiac Surgery* (Oxford: ISIS Medical Media, 1998), 201.

39. M. Lee and Joseph Fraumeni, "Arsenic and Respiratory Cancer in Man: An Occupational Study," *Journal of the National Cancer Institute* 42 (1969): 1045–52.

40. See Sharpe, *Cruel Deception,* 71–143.

41. See Croce, *Science or Vivisection,* 165–215.

42. See ibid., 143–52, for a far more extensive list. As the title of his book sug-

gests, Croce claims that vivisection is not a science and that its raison d'être is primarily money. Vivisectionists, universities, and pharmaceutical companies all play a role in perpetuating this failed methodology.

43. George Bernard Shaw said very much the same thing. He tells us in the preface to *Doctor's Dilemma* that "you do not settle if an experiment is justified or not by merely showing that it is of some use. The distinction is not between useful and useless experiments, but between barbarous and civilized behavior. Vivisection is a social evil because if it advances human knowledge, it does so at the expence of human character" (qtd. in Jon Wynne-Tyson, comp., *The Extended Circle: A Commonplace Book of Animal Rights* [New York: Paragon House, 1989]). This section can be read as an extended argument vindicating Shaw.

44. This is ticklish business. Can the permission fully informed prisoners grant in exchange for shortened sentences legitimately be considered voluntary?

45. See Croce, *Animals;* Greek and Greek, *Sacred Cows;* Shanks and LaFollette, *Brute Science;* and Sharpe, *Cruel Deception.*

46. I give a positive account of the criteria (or set of properties) that *should* be used to determine moral priority in "Marginal Cases and Moral Relevance," *Journal of Social Philosophy* 33, no. 4 (Winter 2002): 523–39.

## CHAPTER 6: THE LAW AND ANIMALS

1. *Stephens v. State,* 3 So. 458, 458 (Miss. 1887) (123). For an explanation of the legal citations, see Gary Francione, *Animals, Property, and the Law* (Philadelphia: Temple University Press, 1995), 265–67 (the parenthetical numbers following the legal cases in the notes to this chapter refer to pages in Francione's book). I owe a great debt to Francione, who not only discusses these legal cases in far more detail than I do (as its title indicates, his entire book is devoted to this subject) but also enumerates and comments on scores of others. Our basic views are virtually identical, and although I disagree with some of his philosophical explications, I recommend this book heartily to anyone interested in pursuing this part of the animal movement.

2. *Bland v. People,* 76 P. 359, 361 (Colo., 1904) (123).

3. *Commonwealth v. Higgins,* 178 N.E. 536, 538 (Mass. 1931) (123).

4. *Peck v. Dunn,* 574 P.2d 367 (Utah), *cert. denied,* 436 U.S. 927 (1978) (124).

5. *New Jersey Society for the Prevention of Cruelty to Animals v. Board of Education* 219 A.2d 200 (N.J. Super. Ct. Law Div. 1966), *aff'd,* 277 A.2d 506 (N.J. 1967) (141).

6. Calif. Penal Code, §597b (West Supp. 1993) (121).

7. Alaska Stat., §11.61.140(b) (1–3) (1989) (139).

8. *Bowyer v. Morgan,* 95 L.T.R. 27 (K.B. 1906) (147).

9. *People ex rel Freel v. Downs,* 136 N.Y.S. 440 (City Magis. Ct., 1911) (149).

10. Calif. Penal Code, §599c (West 1988) (120).

11. Ky. Rev. Stat. Ann., §525.130(1)(c) (Michie. Supp. 1992) (139).

12. *Commonwealth v. Anspach,* 188 A. 98 (Pa. Super. Ct. 1936) (150).

13. *Commonwealth v. Barnes,* 629 A.2d 123 (Pa. Super. Ct. 1993) (150).

14. *Deiro v. American Airlines,* 816 F.2d 1360 (9th Cir. 1987) (53).

15. *Fredeen v. Stride,* 525 P.2d. 166 (Or. 1974) (61).

16. *Commonwealth v. Turner,* 26 Va. (5 Rand.) 678, 678 (1827) (153).

17. *State v. Hale,* 9 N.C. (2 Hawks.) 582, 585 (1823) (111).

18. See Steven Wise, *Rattling the Cage* (Cambridge, Mass.: Perseus Books, 2000), for a detailed case for according legal rights to primates.

## Chapter 7: Women and Animals

1. For a fuller discussion of animal names as epithets for women, see Joan Dunayer's "Sexist Words, Speciesist Roots," in *Animals and Women: Feminist Theoretical Explanations,* ed. Carol Adams and Josephine Donovan (Durham, N.C.: Duke University Press, 1995): 11–32.

2. With regard to battery, the examples of women and animals are not random. Most wife batterers have also beaten animals. For a discussion of the connection between abuse of animals and abuse of women, see Carol Adams, "Woman Battering and Harm to Animals," in Adams and Donovan, *Animals and Women,* 55–84.

3. Hobbes's classic work is *Leviathan,* in which all the claims I attribute to him can be located.

4. I will not even try to discuss every feminist ethicist. For the most part I restrict myself to four of the movement's most important figures, each having a somewhat unique view of feminist ethics. Still, many core issues pervade the works of all four, including the previously mentioned concern about the role of generalized prescriptions in ethical resolution. The following works will attract most of my attention: Carol Gilligan, *In a Different Voice* (Cambridge, Mass.: Harvard University Press, 1982); Nel Noddings, *Caring: A Feminist Approach to Ethics and Moral Education* (Berkeley: University of California Press, 1984); Diana Meyers, "Personal Autonomy and the Paradox of Feminine Socialization," *Journal of Philosophy* 84, no. 11 (1987); and Annette Baier, "Trust and Anti-Trust," *Ethics* 96 (Jan. 1986), and "Sustaining Trust," *Tanner Lectures on Human Values,* ed. G. B. Peterson (Salt Lake City: University of Utah Press 1992).

5. See John Rawls, *A Theory of Justice* (Cambridge, Mass: Harvard University Press, 1971).

6. Bentham's classic work is *Principles of Morals and Legislation.* Mill, who was Bentham's protégé, is deservedly most famous for his essay *Utilitarianism.*

7. See Locke's classic, *An Essay on Human Understanding,* ch. 27, sects. 9–29.

8. See Kant's *Metaphysics of Morals.* A more precise statement of his formal rule is as follows: act only on the maxim that, at that time, can be willed to be a universal law. Less formally, Kant saw the central idea constituting morality as the universalizability (generalizability) of the principles that motivate actions.

9. See Hume's classic work *A Treatise of Human Nature,* pt. 3, sect. 1.

10. Noddings, *Caring,* 83.

11. Ibid., 237.
12. Ibid., 151.
13. Ibid., 156–57.
14. Ibid.
15. See Meyers, "Personal Autonomy."
16. See Diana Meyers, *Subjection and Subjectivity: Psychoanalytic Feminism and Moral Philosophy* (New York: Routledge, 1994), 29–38.

# INDEX

Abarbanel, D. I., 75, 77; and sacrifice, 74; and scriptural language, 54
Abraham, 58; and Isaac 73; and ram, 74
Adam, 65, 77
Addison, T., 144, 145
Amalekites, 89
animal experimentation, 22, 44, 47, 60, 91, 189; in cancer research, 137–38; challenges to, 147–48; and clinical observation, 139–41; and disingenuousness, 145; and Doctrine of Double Effect, 32; and epidemiology, 142; and extrapolation problem, 133–36; as introduction to biomedical research, 131; and in vitro research, 143–44; and LD-50, 132; moral case against, 146–47; and obesity, 136; and painless death, 29; scientific case against, 129–44; skepticism about, 130
anthropocentrism, 86
argument from evil, 12; and gratuitousness, 13
Aristotle, 4; biological account of humanness of, 51; and domination, 56–57; and essentialism, 52; and hierarchies, 163; and rationality, 45–46
arthritis, 136
atherosclerosis, 136–37
Auschwitz, 93

Bacon, F., 57
Baier, A., 186–87
Balaam, 65, 80
battery hens. See chickens

Bentham, J., 169
Bergen-Belsen, 93
Bradford, J., 61
broiler chickens. See chickens
Bross, I., 137
Brunton, Sir Lauder, 141
Butler, J., 61; and animal souls, 62

Calvin, J., 57
cancer, 83, 129, 151, 152; and animal testing, 137–38; of the breast, 140–41; and epidemiological studies, 145–46; and tobacco, 142
cattle. See cows
Chadwick, D., 124
charity, 26, 83
chickens, 4, 11, 68, 81, 83, 92, 93, 95, 122, 134, 142, 151, 152, 154, 181; as battery hens, 104–10; compared to women, 162; and coyotes, 122; diseases of, 112; and Doctrine of Double Effect, 32; factory farming of, 103–15; and game animals, 126; genetic engineering of, 103; housing of, 113; slaughter of, 114–15
Churchill, W., 85, 86
clinical observation, 139; fruitfulness of, 140
Coggan, D. 90
communitarianism, 26; and Principle of Moral Importance, 27
contractualism, 170, 175; and abortion, 184; and children, 178–79; and Hobbes, 165–67; and persons, 180; and Rawls, 168
cows, 4, 11, 34, 68, 81, 115, 181; beef, 95;

MARK H. BERNSTEIN is a professor of philosophy at the University of Texas at San Antonio. He has published *Fatalism* (1992), *On Moral Considerability* (1988), and articles in the areas of metaphysics, animal ethics, and social philosophy. Prof. Bernstein is a past president of Action for Animals, an Austin-based animal rights organization, and has cohosted weekly television and radio programs regarding animal rights.

The University of Illinois Press
is a founding member of the
Association of American University Presses.

---

Composed in 10/13 Sabon
with Sabon display
by Type One, LLC
for the University of Illinois Press
Designed by Dennis Roberts
Manufactured by Maple-Vail Book Manufacturing Group

University of Illinois Press
1325 South Oak Street
Champaign, IL 61820-6903
www.press.uillinois.edu